DIABETIC
COOKING
FROM
AROUND
THE WORLD

DIABETIC COOKING
FROM
AROUND
THE WORLD

VILMA LIACOURAS CHANTILES

GRAMERCY BOOKS
New York • Avenel

This 1995 edition is published by Gramercy Books, distributed by Random House Value Publishing, Inc., 40 Engelhard Avenue, Avenel, New Jersey 07001.

Random House
New York • Toronto • London • Sydney • Auckland

Printed and bound in the United States of America

Library of Congress Cataloging-in-Publication Data
Chantiles, Vilma Liacouras.
    Diabetic cooking from around the world / Vilma Liacouras Chantiles.
        p. cm.
    Includes index.
    ISBN 0-517-12284-7
    1. Diabetes—Diet therapy—Recipes. 2. Cookery, International. I. Title.
[RC662.C46 1995]
641.5'6314—dc20   94-25252
                                                                    CIP

10 9 8 7 6 5 4 3 2 1

For Niko, with love

CONTENTS

Acknowledgments   ix
Foreword   xi
By Judith Wylie-Rosett, Ed.D., R.D.
Introduction   xiii

Seasonings, Condiments, and Sauces   1
Appetizers   35
Breakfast, Brunch, and Lunch Dishes   55
Soups and Stews   71
Salads and Dressings   101
Vegetables and Starchy Vegetables   125
Grains, Legumes, Nuts, and Seeds   165
Fish and Shellfish   193
Meats, Poultry, and Game   213
Casseroles, Stuffed, and Rolled Specialties   233
Breads   259
Desserts and Fruits   273
Beverages   303

Exchange Lists for Meal Planning   313
Resources   329
Index   331

ACKNOWLEDGMENTS

I thank the following international diabetes associations and individuals who contributed recipes: Asociación de Diabeticos del Uruguay (Montevideo, Uruguay), Angela Vera, nutritionist, and Dr. Juan José Fraschini, author of *Preparaciones Dietéticas para Diabéticos*, for recipes I adapted from this pamphlet; All India Institute of Medical Sciences (New Delhi, India) and Rekha Sharma, dietitian; Bangladesh Institute of Research and Rehabilitation in Diabetes, Endocrine, and Metabolic Disorders (Dhaka, Bangladesh) and Shane Ara Kabir, assistant director of diet and nutrition; Bermuda Diabetic Association (Devonshire, Bermuda) and Jill Kempe, who is the producer and distributor of *Bermuda's Best Recipes*; Cyprus Diabetic Association (Paphos, Cyprus), C. Theophanides, M.D., F.R.M.S., director, and Moira Beaton, dietitian and food journalist; Deutsche Diabetes-Gesellschaft (Munich, West Germany) and Professor P. Dieterle, M.D., author of *Diät bei Zuckerkrankheit*, a pamphlet with recipes for people with diabetes developed by Brigitte Zöllner; Diabetes Association of Malta (Valletta, Malta) and Marie-Louise Mifsud, secretary; Kenya Diabetic Association (Nairobi, Kenya) and Dr. E. N. Mngola, chairman; Liga Argentina de Proteccion al Diabético (Buenos Aires, Argentina) and Ana Maria Malerba, nutritionist-dietitian; Saiseikai Central Hospital (Tokyo, Japan) and Kempei Matsuoka, M.D., chief of endocrinology and metabolism; Schweizerische Diabetes-Gesellschaft (Association Suisse de Diabète) (Zurich, Switzerland) and Myrtha Frick, nutritionist and editor of *Swiss Diabetes-Journal* published by this diabetes association; University of Torino (Torino, Italy) and Prof. G. M. Molinatti, of the Clinica Medica 2, and to Dr. Franco Tomasi and Claudia Artioli, dietitian, for recipes from the pamphlet, *A Tavola con il Diabete* (Ferrara, Italy); diabetes experts of the Zentralinstitut für Diabetes "Gerhardt Katsch" (Karlsburg bei Greifswald, East Germany); Manuel Machado Sá Marques, director of assistance services, Associaçâo dos Diabéticos de Portugal.

I appreciate the valuable suggestions of many dietitians and nutritionists, particularly Judith Wylie-Rosett, Ed.D., R.D., Research and Training, Albert Einstein College of Medicine, Bronx, New York, and Faith Winter, R.D., Mount Sinai Hospital, New York. I was assisted by the following individuals: Lawrence A. Wheeler, M.D., Ph.D., and Madelyn L. Wheeler, M.S., R.D., C.D.E., who allowed me to use their unique Recipe Analysis Program (RAP) to compute the recipes in this book and whose assistance was valuable; nutritionist Dennis L. Drake, Nutrient Data Research Branch, USDA, Grain Section; Swaran Pasricha, assistant director, National Institute of Nutrition, Indian Council of Medical Research, Hyderabad, India; Mukta Buckley, M.S., R.D., consultant/nutritionist, New York; M. Manimen, head of the dietary department, Christian Medical College and Hospital, Vellore, India; Shigeko Kimura, who translated from the Japanese pamphlet, *Medical Treatment with Food for Diabetes* by Tadayoshi Takai and Kayoko Asami suggested by Kempei Matsuoka, Tokyo; Claudia Graham, neighbor and teacher; Adul Vinaiphat, Thai journalist in New York; Rasika and Nur Mezmi, Tunisian diplomats in New York; Anahi Palapini of Buenos Aires, of the Argentine Consulate General, New York; Julian Bach, who had confidence in me; and Patricia Brown, who was enthusiastic about the project and who made excellent suggestions.

FOREWORD

Looking through the recipes that Vilma Liacouras Chantiles has collected for *Diabetic Cooking from Around the World* is a pleasure. When an international culinary expert is interested in making the dietary management of diabetes easier, the result is a wonderful collection of spice and herb combinations, cultural food preparation tips in addition to recipes.

When she contacted me about writing this cookbook she expressed concern about how pleasure is taken out of eating for many people with diabetes. She sought the advice of individuals with diabetes and dietitians to find out what type of food preparation tips and recipes would allow anyone with diabetes to enjoy the exotic international dishes. After diligently studying the recommendations for the dietary intake in the management of diabetes, she contacted dietitians and diabetes associations on every continent as well as using her own cultural food expertise to develop a truly international focus on diabetic cooking.

The recipes come from all over the world. Experts in nutrition and diabetes who enjoy cooking and food preparation have shared expertise that represents culinary art and the science of diabetes management. However, one's thoughts are clearly on the pleasure of eating when turning through the recipes.

The recipes are low in fat and sodium, high in unrefined carbohydrate and fiber and can easily be incorporated into the meal plan of anyone with diabetes. Relevant nutrient information is provided to facilitate use of the recipes for people who are on modified fat or low-sodium diets or for health-conscious individuals who may be trying to control intake of calories, salt, and/or fat. The recipes are so delightful that any invited to share a meal prepared may only know that they have had a culinary treat and not think about "diabetic" cooking. With this cookbook there is no reason to even think about serving a separate meal for family members or guests who regard diabetic cooking as bland and boring.

Judith Wylie-Rosett, Ed.D., R.D.

INTRODUCTION

Variety's the very spice of life,
That gives it all its flavour.

COWPER

William Cowper's famous quotation about variety captures the essence of
this book. We all need variety—in our work, in neighbors and friends, in
our hobbies, and especially in the meals and snacks we eat.

How richly we can be rewarded daily by sprinkling this need into our
lives! Begin at home. Look into your own cuisine and cupboard. Revive
those childhood recipes you tasted at your mom's knees and in your grand-
ma's kitchen. Learn how your neighbor cooks the delicious samples she
offers you. Create new recipes as a hobby.

For those with diabetes or any restricted diet, it is certainly important
to consider the body's biological needs. Maintaining and managing blood-
glucose and blood-fat levels are crucial. Meals and snacks must include
the appropriate calories and carbohydrate, protein, and fat grams. The
grams, however, can be in suitable portions of dishes you prefer, new
foods you'd like to try, comforting foods essential to your well-being.

This book is based on the assumption that it is possible for everyone to
prepare many healthful international foods. Nutritionists agree that the
versatility of ethnic foods is stimulating for those who feel deprived when
given rigid, lusterless diets.

I've begun this fruitful activity for you, strewing the chapters of this
book with a fragrant collection of specialties from people living in distant
neighborhoods. You will feel warmly embraced by using their recipes.
When researching this book, for instance, I asked diabetes counselors and
physicians in diabetes clinics around the world for recipes that are not
only characteristic of their countries but also good for people with diabetes. I was overwhelmed by their responses and deluged with authentic

dishes from Uruguay to Bangladesh, Bermuda to New Zealand, Japan to Argentina, Malta to Kenya, Cyprus to Switzerland.

Other recipes are contributed by foreign-born chefs and excellent cooks of all ages who live in the United States. Still others are from outstanding cooks and homes in places I visited—including China, India, Israel, Greece, Mexico. It was the most delightful part of my work to contact and interview so many friendly professionals and just plain folks. Above all, people are usually very proud of their country's dishes and culture. As in its arts and history and in its flag, the cuisine mirrors the country's traditions, its legacy. We understand more about countries by learning how they use their ingredients and serve their dishes. Then, the recipes do not seem strange or the people so foreign. Individuals and organizations are mentioned in the acknowledgments or in recipe notes.

PRINCIPLES OF GOOD NUTRITION

Expand your culinary and nutritional horizons by introducing many cuisines and foods for variety beyond the basic ones. This book is planned for an extensive audience: 11 million people with diabetes mellitus in the United States, and those in other English-speaking countries, who like to cook exciting dishes for themselves and their families and friends; family members and friends who plan to entertain someone with diabetes; readers eager to find good international recipes that include nutritional calculations; and dietitians and nutritionists.

Recipes—ingredients and proportions—were tested and adapted to conform to principles of good nutrition and a sensible diet. Principles include the following suggestions of the U.S. Department of Agriculture (USDA) and the U.S. Department of Health, Education and Welfare:

- Eat less fat.
- Eat more carbohydrates (starches and breads), especially those high in fiber.
- Eat less sugar.
- Use less salt.
- Although it is best to avoid alcohol altogether, use alcohol only after consulting your dietitian or physician.

In keeping with the USDA suggestions, there are many high-fiber recipes using legumes, whole grains, vegetables, and fruits. In fact, sixty-four recipes contain 3 or more grams of fiber (considered high) per serving; many more have 2 or 2.5 grams. Among the fruits, you'll find a fascinating array of tropical and subtropical varieties, which are increasingly available seasonally.

Fats in recipes have been reduced and unsaturated fats recommended. Foods high in sugar have been avoided. Salt use has been minimized in recipes to compensate for the hidden sodium in foods or dishes with salty ingredients (cheese, olives, etc.) and in canned foods. If you use canned tomatoes instead of fresh, for example, you can expect the sodium content of the recipe to rise. The USDA estimates 236 milligrams (mg) per 100 grams (3.5 ounces) in every can of vegetables. Flavor of food is livelier when not overwhelmed by salt, anyway.

EXCHANGE LISTS FOR MEAL PLANNING AND VARIETY IN THE DIET

Another assumption of this book is that readers are familiar with the Exchange Lists for Meal Planning published by the American Diabetes Association and The American Dietetic Association and used extensively throughout the country in meal planning. The lists are divided into six different groups (starch/bread, meat, vegetable, fruit, milk, and fat) because foods vary in their nutrient values. To simplify choices, foods in each exchange list are alike—about the same amount of carbohydrate, protein, fat, and calories.

It is not a goal of this book to suggest the daily nutritional requirements for each reader. People with diabetes and special needs consult their own physician, nutritionist, and/or dietitian for direction in meal planning and diabetes management. With the meal plan in hand, readers can choose from the recipes to prepare a snack or dish for any time of day and see the estimated nutrients in each serving. For instance, if your meal plan allows 9 starch/bread, 4 lean meat, 5 vegetable, 4 fruit, 2 milk, and 3 fat exchanges daily, choose them in recipes you like and distribute them throughout the day as you have been advised. The Exchange Lists for Meal Planning are included with permission on pages 313 to 327 as a handy reference for you to use.

As you explore new recipes in the thirteen chapters of this book, begin with Seasonings, Condiments, and Sauces. Use the spice blends and vegetable seasonings, dipping and hot or mild sauces creatively. In Appetizers, you'll discover preprandial tidbits that can also double as great snacks when you are in the mood to graze. Breakfast, Brunch, and Lunch Dishes carry you to Monaco and Tunis, to Mexico and Italy, to Spain and Holland for easily prepared fare. As for Soups and Stews, you can feast on any one of them rather than cook an entire meal. (These are especially good to freeze in small portions to reheat on a rainy day.)

When meandering among the Salads and Dressings, you'll travel from Russia to Israel, from France to China or Uruguay for crisp or cooked, simple or mixed salads of superb variety. Vegetables and Starchy Vegetables are chock-full of curried, stuffed, baked, whipped, stir-fried, marinated, and steamed dishes, using all parts of the vegetables from the leaf, pod, or stem to bulbs, tubers, or rhizomes. Grains, Legumes, Nuts, and Seeds offer the rich diversity of the international scene, including popular rice, bean, lentil and dal dishes, fragrant with herbs and spices.

If Fish and Shellfish with broiled, poached, and steamed specialties take you to sea and stream, then Meats, Poultry, and Game bring you back to shore with savory rolled and braised, marinated and broiled, baked and stir-fried dishes.

The fabulous mixed dishes with Indonesian, South American, Hungarian, East German, Bermudian, North African, and Persian flavors are featured in Casseroles, Stuffed, and Rolled Specialties. Among Breads, you can find flat breads, oat scones, English grain bread, and cheese muffins from New Zealand. The focus of Desserts and Fruits is on climaxing meals with fresh and natural foods and an unmatched selection of tropical and subtropical fruits that are increasingly available. For maximum versatility in their use, the fruits are included with general instructions and nutritional content rather than with specific recipes. You can always vary the way you enjoy them according to your needs and daily menu. Comfort and refreshment are bywords of Beverages, with delicious shakes and drinks using herbs and spices.

The goal of this book, therefore, is to provide infinite selections from the world's diversity to enrich your meals and snacks.

ESTIMATED NUTRIENT CALCULATIONS

With each recipe, *estimated* calculations are given for exchanges, calories, and seven nutrients for one serving of the recipe. Nutrients are listed in the usual method of expressing value: carbohydrates, proteins, fats, and fiber (total dietary fiber) in grams (g); potassium, sodium, and cholesterol in milligrams (mg). Totals are rounded out to the nearest number: 2.1 to 2.4 as 2; 2.6 to 2.9 as 3. If, however, the amount falls midway between two numbers, it is indicated as .5 (2.5 or 25.5 or whatever). When the total amount is less than 1 gram, it is indicated "negligible." When there is no nutrient present, it is shown as 0. When an estimated nutrient is not known or not available, it is indicated as NA or "not available." Recipe nutrient values are calculated with the *first* ingredient, for example, *fresh* or canned tomatoes, or *margarine* or butter. Optional ingredients are not included in calculations, unless specified. Low-fat milk and low-fat yogurt are calculated with *2% fat*, unless specified 1% in the ingredients list.

Calculations for the recipes were computed on an IBM-AT computer using the Recipe Analysis Program (RAP), CAI/Video Concepts, Inc., developed by Lawrence A. Wheeler, M.D., Ph.D., of Indianapolis, Indiana. This is the same program used by Madelyn L. Wheeler, M.S., R.D., C.D.E., to compute the American Diabetes Association and The American Dietetic Association *Family Cookbook*, volumes I and II and the revised edition (1987). This program matches the approximate nutrients as closely as possible to the actual nutrients in the recipe, based on the USDA figures in the data base. The program also indicates exchange value equivalents that correspond to the nutrients. For foods not available in the RAP data base, I used the revised sections of *Composition of Foods, Agriculture Handbook No. 8*, published by USDA. Other references consulted are included in Resources (pages 328–29).

May you enjoy using these recipes and sharing the results with your friends. As people all over the world say in their own languages, *bon appétit* (good appetite) and *eis hygeian* (to your good health)!

V.L.C.

SEASONINGS, CONDIMENTS, AND SAUCES

Do not buy soy with money intended for vinegar.

CHINESE PROVERB

Garam Masala

A blend of ground spices to sprinkle into curried dishes—without adding calories. *Garam masala* is the Indian term for "hot spice" or curry powder. Cooks in India mix their own powder. To be truly yours, the spice combination must be your own. As a starter, here is mine. It is tangy in Masala Lassi (page 310) or any savory dish. For desserts, use less pepper and cumin but more cloves and cinnamon. Be sure to label your jar as a reminder.

For about 1 tablespoon

1 teaspoon coriander seed	Small piece stick cinnamon
1 scant teaspoon cumin seed	4 cloves
10 black peppercorns	¼–½ teaspoon cayenne pepper
8 cardamom pods, peeled	

1. Roast spices separately (a small muffin tin works well) at 250°F for 15 minutes. When the spices begin to smell fragrant, remove from oven and cool where they are.

2. To blend, use a mortar and pestle or blender. Caution: Before mixing, hold back on the spices with strong flavors. Add as you taste and blend. Grind together to achieve a flavorful, pleasing blend. Store, labeled, in a covered jar with the rest of your spices.

Nutrients for any amount.

No calories. Use freely.

Korean Sesame Salt

Here's a great salt substitute, tasty sprinkled on your vegetables and stews. You can omit the salt from this seasoning, and the sesame seed alone is delicious, too.

Makes ½ cup

½ cup white sesame seed   **¼ teaspoon salt**

1. In a heavy skillet or wok, gradually heat the sesame seed over low heat until golden and puffy. Shake the pan frequently to toast evenly.
2. When the sesame begins to turn light brown, and you can smell the delicious flavor of sesame, remove from heat.
3. Stir in the salt, if you are using it. Cool the mixture.
4. Grind in a blender or mortar. Store in a tightly covered jar.

Nutrients for 1 teaspoon.

Calories: 17
Exchange: ½ fat

g	mg
carbohydrate: negligible	potassium: 14
protein: negligible	sodium: 18
fat: 1.5	cholesterol: 0
fiber: negligible	

Toasted Almonds

Here's a golden and crunchy topping, a great garnish for Asian or any other dishes.

For about ½ cup

50 blanched almonds   **¼ teaspoon unsaturated vegetable oil**

1. Sliver the almonds as fine as you like them.
2. Heat a wok or skillet, and just coat the bottom with the oil. (Or, if you prefer, you can toast almonds without oil.) Drop in the almonds, and stir-fry or shake skillet continually over very low heat until the almonds turn golden brown. Cool thoroughly. Store in covered container in a dry place.

Nutrients for 1 teaspoon toasted with oil.

Calories: 16
Exchange: ½ fat

g	mg
carbohydrate: negligible	potassium: 21
protein: negligible	sodium: negligible
fat: 1	cholesterol: 0
fiber: negligible	

Fried Onion Flakes

This onion garnish from Indonesia is sprinkled on noodle, vegetable, and rice dishes. The flakes absorb very little oil.

For 10 tablespoons fried flakes

1 large onion (6 ounces)   **½ cup corn oil for frying**

1. Peel, and quarter the onion. Slice into paper-thin slices. Spread on a paper towel to absorb the moisture.
2. Heat the oil in a small saucepan or skillet. When the oil is very hot, fry the onions in small batches until crisp and golden brown, turning frequently. Watch closely, and remove before they burn, or they'll taste bitter. Remove with slotted spoon, and spread on paper towels. Continue frying, and keep changing the towel to remove all the oil. (You should use only about 2 teaspoons oil from the ½ cup. Cool oil and reuse.)
3. When cool, store in refrigerator, and use within a few days.

Nutrients for 1 tablespoon.

Calories: 15
Exchange: ½ vegetable

g	mg
carbohydrate: 1	potassium: 32
protein: negligible	sodium: 2
fat: 1	cholesterol: 0
fiber: negligible	

Mock Beurre Blanc

Here's a velvety sauce with a French wink, to enhance steamed fish and vegetables.

For about 1 cup

½ cup White Fish Stock
  (page 100)
½ cup dry white wine
1 teaspoon white wine vinegar
2 shallots, minced

2 tablespoons unsalted
  margarine
1 teaspoon light soy sauce
Freshly ground white pepper

1. In a saucepan, combine the stock, wine, vinegar, and shallots. Simmer for 10 minutes.

2. Stir in the margarine, cooking over low heat until blended.

3. Season with soy sauce and pepper. To serve, ladle sauce on warm plate. Place steamed fish over the sauce, and garnish with chive. Serve warm.

Nutrients for 1 tablespoon. Nutrients do not include those in the soy sauce. Check the label.

Calories: 38
Exchanges: ½ vegetable; ½ fat

g	mg
carbohydrate: negligible	potassium: 25
protein: negligible	sodium: 1
fat: 3	cholesterol: 0
fiber: negligible	

Ghee

Ghee—clarified buffalo or cow's butter—is a staple of every Indian kitchen. It is used in religious rituals by high-caste Hindus to purify what is cooked in it. In southern India, a few drops of ghee are stirred into hot rice before serving to enhance it with distinctive flavor. Ghee is also used to fry everything from the famed flat breads (pages 270–71) to curries, spices, and bananas. When cooking with ghee, you will be able to heat foods to much higher temperatures than with butter, since the milk solids have been removed. Therefore, ghee can be stored for several months in a bottle (without refrigeration). You'll find bright yellow ghee on grocery shelves in many Indian shops. Try making it at home.

For about ¾ cup

½ pound unsalted butter

1. In a heavy pan, slowly melt the butter but do not brown.
2. With a spoon, skim off, and discard the foam floating on the surface. Boil the ghee for a few minutes.
3. Strain by spooning the ghee through a piece of thin muslin or cheesecloth into a container. Discard milk solids at the bottom.
4. Pour ghee into a glass jar. Cover, and store in a handy place. Use and heat as needed.

Nutrients for 1 teaspoon.

Calories: 37
Exchange: 1 fat

g	mg
carbohydrate: 0	potassium: 1
protein: negligible	sodium: 41
fat: 4	cholesterol: 11
fiber: 0	

Sofrito

Caribbean stews flavored with sofrito acquire a lingering spiciness—not too hot, not too mild. Ajicitos, tiny peppers of beautiful pastel colors, are available in Caribbean and Hispanic markets as are the recau and coriander (cilantro). You may prefer to mix all the ingredients in a blender and freeze in small portions to cook when needed.

Makes about 1 cup

1 tablespoon vegetable oil
1 onion, or 2 green onions, or 6 shallots, minced
3 garlic cloves, minced
1 large handful (about ½ cup) ajicitos
1 small green bell pepper, finely chopped
1–2 hot green chilies, seeded and chopped (optional)
1 tablespoon recau (fresh herb), chopped
2 tablespoons fresh coriander, chopped
Freshly ground black pepper

1. In a small saucepan, heat the oil, and drop the onion, garlic, ajicitos, and green pepper into the pan. Cook over low heat, stirring frequently, until vegetables are soft, about 4 minutes. Stir in the remaining seasonings.

2. Cool sofrito, and freeze in tablespoon-size portions. Season stews, soups, beans, and pigeon peas with your sofrito.

Nutrients for 1 tablespoon.

Calories: 24
Exchange: ½ vegetable

g	mg
carbohydrate: 2	potassium: 45
protein: negligible	sodium: 1
fat: 2	cholesterol: 0
fiber: negligible	

Gremolata (Italian Seasoning)

Use these aromatics to flavor your stews. Gremolata *(gremolada)* is the principal seasoning in the famous veal dish from Milan, *ossobuco con gremolata alla milanese.*

For 1 pound meat

½ stalk celery, finely diced
2 tablespoons fresh parsley, finely chopped
1–2 garlic cloves, minced

2 teaspoons lemon rind, grated
2 sprigs marjoram, chopped, or ½ teaspoon dried

Mix together all the ingredients. Stir half into the stew as it cooks. Sprinkle the remaining on top just before serving.

Nutrients for entire recipe.

Calories: 13
Exchange: ½ vegetable

g	mg
carbohydrate: 3	potassium: 182
protein: negligible	sodium: 54
fat: 0	cholesterol: 0
fiber: 1	

French Mirepoix

French cuisine blessed us with many delicious cookery ideas. *Voila!* Mirepoix, a seasoning for sauces, gravies, seafood, and meat dishes, is one of the simplest creations—and fun to use. It originated during the early seventeenth century in the kitchens of the Duke of Mirepoix, a French marshal. Like Sofrito (page 8), mirepoix can be made in advance and stored in the refrigerator. Spoon 2 tablespoons per serving into braised or baked dishes. Nutrient calculations are given for each serving, with and without the bacon.

Makes about 2 cups

2 medium carrots, scraped and finely diced
1 medium onion, finely diced
2 tender stalks celery heart, finely diced
1 tablespoon bacon or ham, finely diced (optional)
1 sprig fresh parsley, finely chopped
2 tablespoons unsalted margarine or butter
Pinch ground thyme
Pinch bay leaf, crushed

1. Spread out a clean double cheesecloth or linen towel. Heap and mix the carrots, onion, celery, bacon, and parsley in the middle. Wrap tightly, and squeeze to extract all the liquid.

2. In a dry saucepan, cook the mixture over medium heat, stirring constantly, until vegetables appear drier. Transfer to a plate.

3. In the same saucepan, heat the margarine or butter, and add the vegetables. Cook over medium heat, stirring constantly. Season with the thyme and bay leaf. When cool, store in the refrigerator, covered, until ready to use.

Nutrients for 2 tablespoons with bacon.

Calories: 22
Exchange: ½ fat

g	mg
carbohydrate: 2	potassium: 47
protein: negligible	sodium: 18
fat: 2	cholesterol: 0
fiber: 1	

Nutrients for 2 tablespoons without bacon.

Calories: 19
Exchange: ½ fat

g	mg
carbohydrate: 2	potassium: 45
protein: negligible	sodium: 12
fat: 2	cholesterol: 0
fiber: 1	

Wine Marinade à la Maria Nicole

Thanks to my daughter Maria Nicole, who creates superb meals by marinating beef (such as London broil) or leg of lamb with her own spicy and quick marinade.

For 1½ pounds beef or lamb

1 lemon
¼ cup dry white wine
2 large garlic cloves, crushed

1 tablespoon dried oregano
1 bay leaf, crumbled
Freshly ground white pepper

Squeeze the lemon directly into a bowl. Whisk in the remaining ingredients, adding a liberal amount of pepper. Marinate the meat on both sides for a few hours or overnight. When ready to broil, drain the meat. Use the marinade to baste the meat frequently as it broils.

**Nutrients and calories are negligible
for this marinade.**

Hot Pepper Sauce

Zesty and spicy, this hot pepper sauce can be stored indefinitely in your refrigerator, ready for you to drizzle over soups, tacos, and sandwiches. It's a great salt substitute. What a *hot* gift for a friend! You can even label the jar with the nutrients as a convenience.

For about ½ cup

12 small, dried, red chilies or
   8 large, fresh, hot chilies
1 shallot or ½ small onion,
   minced

1 large garlic clove, minced
⅓ cup vinegar or Spiced
   Vinegar (page 13)

1. Seed, and chop the chilies. Drop them into a saucepan with the shallot or onion and garlic. Add enough water to cover, and simmer until water has evaporated to about 3 tablespoons, approximately 10 minutes.

2. Turn the mixture into a blender or mortar and beat, gradually adding the vinegar. Continue beating until smooth. Transfer to a jar. Cover, and store in the refrigerator.

Nutrients for ½ tablespoon.

Calories: 7
Exchange: ½ vegetable

g	mg
carbohydrate: 2	potassium: 58
protein: negligible	sodium: 1
fat: 0	cholesterol: 0
fiber: negligible	

Spiced Vinegar

This tart-spicy seasoning can be easily made as a treat for yourself and friends. One tablespoonful has only *2 calories!* Keep it in an attractive cruet to pass at the table.

For 1 cup

1 cup vinegar, preferably
   white
4 whole cloves
5 whole allspice
Pinch mace, salt, and sugar

1 teaspoon celery, minced, or
   pinch celery seed
¼ teaspoon mustard seed
1 tablespoon brandy

In a jar, combine the vinegar and remaining ingredients. Cover with a tight lid. Shake thoroughly. Store for 3 weeks before using. Strain and store indefinitely in the jar.

Nutrients for 1 tablespoon.

Calories: 2
Exchange: free

g	mg
carbohydrate: 0	potassium: 16.5
protein: 0	sodium: negligible
fat: 0	cholesterol: 0
fiber: 0	

Vietnamese Nuoc Mam Sauce

Nuoc Mam is the staple seasoning and dipping sauce for Vietnamese cuisine. Plain nuoc mam (fish sauce) could be a descendant of *garum*, the ancient fermented fish seasoning used by early Greek and Roman cooks. The Filipino version is called *bagoong*; the Thai counterpart is *nam pla*. This dazzling recipe is practically calorie-free. But the salt in the fish sauce does increase the sodium content. Check the label, and use the amount suitable for your own dietary needs. Store it in the refrigerator, and try the sauce with Vietnamese Cha Gio (pages 249–51).

For about ½ cup

1–3 fresh or canned chilies, seeded and chopped
2 garlic cloves, crushed
Few drops noncaloric sweetener (optional)
Juice of ½ lime or lemon

3 tablespoons rice wine vinegar
2 teaspoons carrot, finely grated
3 tablespoons plain nuoc mam (Vietnamese or Thai fish sauce, such as Tiparos)

Begin cautiously with 1 chile, and add more after tasting. Grind all ingredients in a mortar or blender. Taste, and adjust seasonings until you reach the subtle blend of flavors that pleases you. Serve cold.

Nutrients for 1 tablespoon without fish sauce.

Calories: 3
Exchange: free

g	mg
carbohydrate: 1	potassium: 21.5
protein: negligible	sodium: negligible
fat: 0	cholesterol: 0
fiber: negligible	

Sambal (Hot Pepper Sauce)

When Indonesian people acknowledge that their dishes are *hot*, they certainly have sambal in mind. Drops of this sauce will liven bland dishes, and it is lower in calories than Sambal Bajak (page 21).

For about 1 cup

2 ripe tomatoes, peeled and
   chopped
2 teaspoons trassi (Indonesian
   shrimp paste)
1 medium onion, chopped

2 garlic cloves
Pinch sweetener (optional)
Juice of ½ lemon
Dried red pepper seeds

In a blender or mortar, grind together all ingredients to make a smooth sauce. Add as many red pepper seeds as you can bear. Serve cold with rice and sate dishes.

Nutrients for 1 tablespoon. Calculations do
not include trassi shrimp paste. Read the
label, and add the sodium content.

Calories: 10
Exchange: ½ vegetable

g	mg
carbohydrate: 2	potassium: 73
protein: negligible	sodium: 4
fat: negligible	cholesterol: 0
fiber: negligible	

Harissa (Tunisian Hot Sauce)

Harissa is the Tunisian word for *red hot pepper!* You may use fresh or dried chilies or ground pepper. A dash of harissa in Tunisian dishes—red hot in color and flavor—goes a long way! Rasika Mezmi, diplomat with the Tunisian Mission in New York, offers you her own easy version.

For about ½ cup

1 tablespoon corn oil	Pinch salt
1 small onion, minced	Black pepper
1 small can (6 ounces) tomato paste	Cayenne

1. In a saucepan, heat the oil, and sauté the onion. Stir in the tomato paste, and gradually add 6 tablespoons water to make a thick paste. Gently simmer for 10 minutes.

2. Season lightly with salt, liberally with black pepper and cayenne. Cool, and refrigerate in a covered jar.

Nutrients for ½ tablespoon.

Calories: 19

Exchange: ½ vegetable

g	mg
carbohydrate: 2	potassium: 108
protein: negligible	sodium: 91
fat: 1	cholesterol: 0
fiber: negligible	

Mexican Salsa Picante

Use as a table dipping sauce with any Mexican dish. For a milder sauce, cut back on the chilies.

For about 1½ cups (12 tablespoons)

1 tablespoon garlic, chopped
Pinch salt
½ cup Spanish onion, chopped
3 fresh jalapeño or hot yellow
   chilies

1 tablespoon fresh coriander
   (cilantro), chopped
3 ripe tomatoes, peeled and
   diced
Pinch sugar (optional)

1. In a mortar or blender, grind the garlic with the salt.
2. Add the onion, and beat to blend.
3. Continue beating, and add the chilies, coriander, and tomatoes.
4. Taste, and enhance the seasonings to please yourself, adding a pinch of sugar only if necessary.

Nutrients for 1 tablespoon.

Calories: 8

Exchange: ½ vegetable

g	mg
carbohydrate: 2	potassium: 67
protein: negligible	sodium: 11
fat: negligible	cholesterol: 0
fiber: negligible	

Indonesian Peanut Sauce

Crunchy peanut sauce, zesty with spices, will liven Indonesian meals or any dishes that complement its flavor. If you want to avoid the fat calories from coconut milk (25 calories and ½ fat exchange in ½ tablespoon), make the sauce without the coconut. If you prefer a creamy version, use creamy peanut butter.

For about 1½ cups

½ cup chunky peanut butter   Dash ground cayenne
1 garlic clove, finely minced   ½ cup Coconut Milk
                                  (pages 30–31)

1. In a saucepan, gradually heat the peanut butter, stirring constantly. Season with garlic and cayenne.
2. Gradually add ½ cup water and the coconut milk. Cook over low heat until sauce flavors blend. Taste, and adjust seasonings. Serve warm or cold.

Nutrients for ½ tablespoon with coconut milk.

Calories: 83
Exchanges: ½ vegetable; 1½ fat

g	mg
carbohydrate: 2	potassium: 89
protein: 3	sodium: 54
fat: 6	cholesterol: NA
fiber: negligible	

Homemade Tomato Sauce

Here's a luscious topping for pizza, linguine, and any pasta, or whenever you need tomato sauce.

For about 3 cups

1 tablespoon unsaturated oil
1 onion or 2 shallots, chopped
1–2 garlic cloves, chopped
8 large ripe tomatoes (2½ cups drained) or 10 canned tomatoes
1 tablespoon tomato paste
½ cup dry white wine

1 cup White Chicken Stock (page 98) or water
2 tablespoons dry nonfat milk
Herbs: 1 tablespoon each fresh parsley, thyme, and basil, 1 bay leaf
Freshly ground white pepper

1. In a saucepan, heat the oil, and sauté the onion or shallots and garlic until soft. Stir in the tomatoes, tomato paste, and wine. Simmer for 5 minutes.

2. Add the chicken stock or water, dry milk, and herbs. Simmer for 15 minutes, stirring frequently, or until the sauce is thickened and reduced to about 3 cups. Taste, and adjust the seasonings. Cool, and freeze in ½-cup portions.

Nutrients for ½ cup.

Calories: 55
Exchanges: 1 vegetable; ½ fat

g	mg
carbohydrate: 5	potassium: 217
protein: 1.5	sodium: 40
fat: 3	cholesterol: 0
fiber: negligible	

Beef-Tomato Sauce/Gravy

Here's a pasta-loving topping—superb on all shapes of macaroni or spaghetti. Many Italian-Americans call this a "gravy" rather than a "sauce" because it is cooked with meat. When seasoned with cinnamon (another Greek idea!) and herbs, it transforms a serving of brown rice or bulgur into a fetching meal! Serve with a crispy raw salad.

For 6–8 servings

1 pound ground beef
2 tablespoons olive or other
  vegetable oil
4 garlic cloves, minced
2 pounds fresh or canned
  plum tomatoes, chopped
  and drained
1 bay leaf
2–3 sprigs fresh or 1 teaspoon
  dried basil

1 small cinnamon stick
  (optional)
Salt (optional)
¼ cup dry wine (optional)
1 teaspoon dried oregano
Freshly ground pepper
Fresh parsley and basil, or
  oregano, chopped, for
  garnish

1. Drop the beef into a skillet over medium heat. Mash with a fork while adding 1 cup water. Keep mashing until the beef lumps separate into grains, and the color changes from red to light brown.

Lower heat, and simmer for 5 minutes to release the fat. (To eliminate the fat in meat: Place a strainer over a large bowl; pour all beef and liquid into strainer; drain for a minute or so; use the meat, and refrigerate the liquid; when the fat congeals on top, discard only the fat and use the liquid in cooking grain dishes.)

2. Meanwhile, in a 2-quart casserole, make a tomato sauce: Heat the oil, and gently sauté the garlic without browning. Stir in the tomatoes, bay leaf, basil, and cinnamon stick. Simmer for 15 or 20 minutes until thickened. Taste, and adjust seasonings with more basil and some pepper (you won't need any salt if you are using canned tomatoes; they have added sodium).

3. While tomato sauce is simmering, return the beef to the skillet. Add the wine (if you are using it), and cook for a few minutes until the alcohol evaporates. Season beef with oregano, crushed between your fingers, and pepper. Taste, and adjust seasonings for beef before combining with the tomato sauce. It should be spicy. Discard the bay leaf and cinnamon stick. (You may rinse and dry the cinnamon stick to reuse.)

4. Stir the beef into the tomato sauce. Heat thoroughly, and taste for seasonings. Serve hot with chopped parsley and basil or oregano on top.

Sambal Bajak
(Indonesian Relish with Nuts)

Hot—hot—hot. A dab will do. Highly seasoned curries and condiments called sambal originated in Malaysia and spread to neighboring Indonesia.

For 10 servings

¼ cup ground cayenne or hot
  red pepper
12 macadamia or kemiri nuts,
  chopped
1 teaspoon ground paprika
1 medium onion, chopped

1 medium tomato, chopped
1 garlic clove, chopped
½ teaspoon brown sugar
  (optional)
2 tablespoons unsaturated
  vegetable oil

1. In a small bowl, mix all ingredients except the oil.
2. Heat the oil in a skillet. Stir the spice mixture into the skillet, lower the heat, and sauté for 20 minutes, stirring almost constantly, until the liquid has been absorbed. Cool, and store, covered, in the refrigerator.

Mint Chutney

Wherever you find Indian curries, a chutney of pickled fruits and vegetables can't be too far away. After all, chutneys originated in India and their worldwide popularity is their greatest selling point. Wonderfully fragrant mint will make a memorable chutney for a memorable meal. You may use any mint variety you like, but do try it!

Makes about 2 cups

1 cup fresh mint, chopped
2 fresh green chilies, seeded and chopped
1 garlic clove, chopped
3 green onions, chopped
¼ cup lemon juice, more to taste

1 teaspoon Garam Masala (page 2), more to taste
1 teaspoon raisins, soaked in 1 tablespoon water
Pinch salt (optional)

1. Grind together all the ingredients in a mortar or blender until smooth. Taste, and adjust seasonings.
2. Transfer the chutney to a serving bowl or jar. Cover, and refrigerate until ready to serve.

Nutrients for 2 tablespoons.
Negligible calories and nutrients. Only 10 calories in ½ cup.

Pesto Genovese

Originating in Genoa, pesto is made exactly as the Italian word *pesto* describes—ground, crushed, pounded. It has become very popular and exciting tossed on freshly drained pasta and served with crisp salad. This reduced-calorie version has been adapted from the recipe of Sloane Elliott, editor in chief of *The Athenian* magazine, Athens, Greece.

For about ½ cup (6 servings)

2 large garlic cloves
1 handful fresh basil leaves
  (about ¼ cup), washed and
  dried
1 tablespoon pine nuts
  (optional)

2 tablespoons Parmesan,
  Romano, or kefalotyri
  cheese, grated
3 tablespoons fine olive oil

1. Using a mortar and pestle or a blender, pound the garlic, basil, pine nuts, and cheese. Continue to pound or grind. Gradually add the oil. Beat until smooth. Store in the refrigerator, or freeze in small portions (use ice-cube trays or other small containers).

2. When you cook the noodles or spaghetti, be sure to save a little of the cooking liquid. When you add the pesto, add some liquid to make a smooth consistency. After tossing the pasta with the pesto, divide into 6 portions. Add the pasta exchange to the following calculations.

Nutrients for 1 tablespoon with pine nuts.

Calories: 77
Exchanges: ½ vegetable; 1½ fat

g	mg
carbohydrate: negligible	potassium: 16
protein: 1	sodium: 31
fat: 8	cholesterol: 1
fiber: 0	

Crème Fraîche

Here's a creamy and very rich seasoning for pepper steaks, baked potatoes, vegetable soups, and quick pasta dishes. *Crème Fraîche* means
"fresh cream" in French. By adding buttermilk or yogurt, the cream thickens into a delicious condiment.

For 1 cup

1 cup heavy cream   4 tablespoons buttermilk or
                                        low-fat yogurt

1. Mix the cream and buttermilk or yogurt in a glass bowl or jar. Cover,
and let stand at room temperature overnight, or for at least 8 hours, until
thickened.
2. Refrigerate, covered, and use within 3 weeks.

Nutrients for 1 tablespoon.

Calories: 54
Exchange: 1 fat

g	mg
carbohydrate: negligible	potassium: 17
protein: negligible	sodium: 10
fat: 5.5	cholesterol: 21
fiber: 0	

Tofu (Soybean or Bean Curd)

Tofu—custardlike curd of fermented soybeans—is no longer a mysterious food confined to Asiatic menus. And for good reason. It is high in protein, keeps well in water in the refrigerator (if the water is changed daily), and is versatile to steam, stir-fry, stew, or braise. Try Spicy Tofu (page 49), Tsel Dofu (page 137), and the suggestions below, and you'll soon dream up more.

For 1 tofu or bean curd (2½ x 2¾ x 1 inches)

1 tofu (4 ounces/120 g)

1. Use tofu uncooked as you buy it. Or drain, and steam tofu for 5 minutes. Slice or cube as you wish: Slice horizontally into thirds without separating. Then slice downward into cubes, strips, or rectangles. Steaming it briefly before stir-frying makes it firmer and less likely to crumble, but steaming is not necessary.

2. Sprinkle tofu lightly with soy sauce or with your favorite dressing for salad. Or serve in a cup of chicken broth for a quick soup, sprinkled with chopped chive or coriander. Or stir tofu into other vegetable dishes or combinations you cook.

Nutrients for 1 tofu.

Calories: 86

Exchange: 1 medium-fat meat

g	mg
carbohydrate: 2	potassium: 50
protein: 9	sodium: 8
fat: 5	cholesterol: 0
fiber: negligible	

Uncle Bill's Homemade Yogurt

Smooth and sourly delicious, easy to make at home, and an excellent ingredient in many dishes—that's yogurt! This fermented milk product also answers to many other names: *leban* to Arabic-speaking people, *mast* to Persians, *madzoon* to Armenians, *koumis* to Mongols, *yaourti* to Hellenes. I learned from my mother how to make yogurt and brought up three children using her easy method. When I was writing this book, her brother, William G. Lagakos, showed me how he makes yogurt. I find his recipe foolproof and have used it ever since. Uncle Bill is a talented professional chef and instructor, and more recently, our family historian; he wrote *Profile of a Family*, a chronicle of our family since my grandparents emigrated to the United States from Greece in the first decade of this century. Try his recipe, and keep some starter to make a fresh batch. Share it with friends. You'll surely be continuing a tradition that began with ancient Greeks and Romans, according to some historians. Remember, high-fat milk makes richer yogurt with more fat calories than the low-fat version suggested below.

For 4 cups

4 cups (1 quart) low-fat milk	**3 tablespoons plain low-fat yogurt starter (commercial yogurt, any of the types mentioned above, or saved from a previous batch)**

1. Rinse a heavy 2-quart saucepan with cold water; shake out excess but do not wipe dry (this prevents milk from sticking to pan as it heats). Pour in the milk, and gradually bring to a boil, stirring occasionally in an X or S motion (to keep skin from forming on top).

2. While milk is heating, select 4 or 5 cups or a large bowl in which you plan to make the yogurt. Place on a tray in a warmed oven with the heat turned off.

3. When the milk begins to boil, set your timer, and boil the milk for 3 minutes. Remove from heat, but keep the milk in the saucepan. Place food thermometer in the milk if you have one. Cool the milk to 115°F (or until you can hold your small finger in the milk to the count of 10). Shake a few drops of milk on your wrist to sensitize yourself to the temperature for future times.

4. Place yogurt starter in a small bowl. Scoop a cupful of the 115°F milk, and gradually stir into the starter, stirring with a whisk. Keep adding

milk and stirring until smooth. Then stir the milk-yogurt mixture into the remaining milk in the saucepan.

5. Remove tray with warmed cups or bowl from the oven. Ladle one cup of the milk-yogurt mixture into each cup. If you are using the bowl, you can measure as much yogurt as you need after it thickens. Place tray in a warm spot in your kitchen or in the oven with heat turned off. Cover with wax paper, a wool blanket, and 2 or 3 dry kitchen towels, and tuck in the edges. Leave undisturbed for at least 6 hours or overnight (the length of time determines the sourness—the longer, the sourer).

6. When thickened, cover with plastic wrap. Refrigerate and use within 3 days for best flavor. Use plain or mixed with fruit or in any recipe in this book that requires plain yogurt. Save 3 tablespoons of starter for your next batch.

Nutrients for 1 cup.

Calories: 144
Exchange: 1 low-fat milk

g	mg
carbohydrate: 16	potassium: 531
protein: 12	sodium: 159
fat: 3.5	cholesterol: 14
fiber: 0	

Afghan Yogurt Chaka

A velvety, minty yogurt sauce adds a touch of ancient Afghanistan to soups (Maushauwa, pages 93–95) and vegetable dishes or as a dip with raw vegetables and unsalted crackers. So I'm including nutrients for 1 tablespoon or 1 cup, depending on how much you need. I learned to make this excellent sauce when researching my earlier book, *The New York Ethnic Food Market Guide & Cookbook*, and it became a favorite for us. Try it!

For 1 cup

1 cup plain low-fat yogurt	**2 tablespoons fresh mint,**
2 garlic cloves, finely minced	**chopped**

1. In a bowl, mix the yogurt and garlic. Cover, and store in the refrigerator until ready to serve.

2. Mix half the mint into the Yogurt Chaka before you drop a dollop into the food. Sprinkle the remaining mint on top.

Nutrients for 1 tablespoon.

Calories: 18
Exchange: ½ vegetable

g	mg
carbohydrate: 2	potassium: 68
protein: 1.5	sodium: 20
fat: negligible	cholesterol: 2
fiber: 0	

Nutrients for 1 cup.

Calories: 148
Exchanges: 1 vegetable; 1 low-fat milk

g	mg
carbohydrate: 17	potassium: 543
protein: 12	sodium: 160
fat: 3.5	cholesterol: 14
fiber: 0	

Kadhi (Yogurt Relish)

Vegetarians of India are among the most inventive cooks, combining legumes, vegetables, and the inevitable yogurt relishes with distinctive spices. This recipe comes from Yogentra Chokshi of India. He suggests kadhi with vegetable curries, chutneys, and chapati for dipping. And it's *hot*.

For 2 cups

2 cups plain low-fat yogurt
2 garlic cloves, crushed
2 teaspoons corn oil
½ teaspoon ground turmeric

1 teaspoon ground coriander
1 teaspoon ground cumin
¼ teaspoon mustard seed
5 fresh red chilies, chopped

1. In a bowl, mix the yogurt and garlic.
2. Heat the oil in a small skillet. Stir in all the spices and chilies. Cook over low heat for a few minutes until the mustard seed begins to pop.
3. Stir a little of the yogurt into the spices. Then add the remaining yogurt, and cook gently until thoroughly heated. Store in the refrigerator for up to 5 days.

Nutrients for 2 tablespoons.

Calories: 24
Exchange: 1 vegetable

g	mg
carbohydrate: 2	potassium: 71.5
protein: 1.5	sodium: 20
fat: 1	cholesterol: 2
fiber: 0	

Coconut Water, Milk, and Cream

The ancient coconut palm offers startling variety in many Indian, Indonesian, Thai, Chinese, Caribbean, and Hawaiian curries and desserts. You can pour refreshing coconut water from the coconut, squeeze milk and cream from the pulp, using water or milk.

The delicious coconut meat, unfortunately high in saturated fat, must be relished in tiny portions. For example, a 2-inch piece equals 3 fat exchanges. Use this recipe as a guide when you are buying a fresh brown coconut—not the green water or jelly coconut, which is usually available only in West Indian markets.

For 1 coconut (4⅝ inches in diameter, 4⅞ inches high, 1⅔ pounds)

1 fresh coconut   **Low-fat milk (optional)**

1. To empty the coconut water: Poke a hole in one or two of the brown spots on the coconut top. Invert coconut over a glass and pour out the liquid (a really fresh coconut can hold a very large glassful). Use as a beverage or in cookery (check nutrients below).

2. Tap the coconut with a hammer or on a stone floor to crack open. (If you want to use part of the shell for a container, saw the shell.) Heat the coconut sections in the shell over the burner or in a slow oven for 15 minutes. Pry off the outer shell, and scrape off the inner skin.

3. Finely grate the coconut pulp with a food processor, blender, or by hand. You should have 5 cups, loosely packed, or 3 packed cups. (At this point you can freeze the grated coconut and keep it indefinitely.)

4. To make *thick* coconut milk: Drop the grated coconut in the top of a double boiler, and heat gently over hot water. Pour in ½ cup warm water, and let soak for a few minutes. Strain through a fine sieve or cheesecloth into a bowl, squeezing by hand. You should have about ¾ cup *thick* coconut milk. (You can freeze this in small, measured quantities for later use.)

5. To make *thin* coconut milk: Drop the residue coconut into a bowl. Add 3 cups warm water. Soak for a few minutes. Then strain, and squeeze as described in step 4. Use in cookery.

6. To make coconut *cream*, follow steps 4 and 5 using warm milk instead of water.

Nutrients for coconut water, milk, and cream.
Calculations for fiber, potassium, sodium, and cholesterol
are not available.

Coconut water	*Coconut milk*	*Coconut cream*
1 cup	*1 cup*	*1 tablespoon*
calories: 53	calories: 605	calories: 48
exchange: 1 fruit	exchanges: 12 fat	exchange: 1 fat
carbohydrate: 11 g	carbohydrate: 12.5 g	carbohydrate: 1 g
protein: negligible	protein: 8 g	protein: negligible
fat: negligible	fat: 60 g	fat: 4.5 g
	1 tablespoon	
	calories: 38	
	exchange: ¾ fat	
	carbohydrate: negligible	
	protein: negligible	
	fat: 4 g	

Panir
(Homemade Cheese of India)

Thick white cheese as made in India has the freshest imaginable flavor. Panir (also called *surati*) is undoubtedly the most popular cheese of buffalo's or cow's milk—especially in Gujarat. Try it at home. After straining the curd, you'll also have the whey. In India, this whey is often served to invalids. Some cooks use it as the liquid when mixing bread.

LIME PANIR

For 1 cup cheese and 3 cups whey

4 cups (1 quart) low-fat (1%)   **Juice of 1 medium lime**
milk

1. Rinse the inside of a 2-quart saucepan with cold water. Pour in the milk, and bring to a boil over low heat, stirring occasionally to prevent a skin from forming on the surface. Remove from heat.

(continued)

2. Stir the lime juice into the boiled milk. The milk will soon separate into curds and whey.

3. Drape a cheesecloth bag or cloth over a strainer, and set over a bowl. Pour the curds and milk into the cheesecloth. Lift corners and hang over the bowl. Drain for 15 or 20 minutes until you have 3 cups whey and 1 cup curds in the cheesecloth.

4. Transfer curds to a plate; cover, and refrigerate. Use as cheese, in salads and vegetable dishes, or in recipes requiring panir. Refrigerate whey separately. Use curds and whey within 2 or 3 days for freshest flavor.

Nutrients for 1 tablespoon.

Calories: 26
Exchange: ¼ low-fat milk

g	mg
carbohydrate: 3	potassium: 98
protein: 2	sodium: 31
fat: 1	cholesterol: 2.5
fiber: 0	

LEMON PANIR

Make lemon panir exactly like lime panir but substitute 3 tablespoons lemon juice for the lime juice. For color and flavor, New Delhi nutritionist Rekha Sharma suggests adding a pinch of saffron and sweetener to the milk when bringing it to a boil. The result is Shree Khand (also spelled Shrikhand), a fine dessert or snack, with or without fruits.

Nutrients for 1 tablespoon.

Same as those for Lime Panir, above.

Kefir (Polish Homemade Cheese)

Kefir originated in the Caucasus made of camel's and later of goat's milk. It is velvety and creamy like cream cheese, but a bit tarter and without the high fat content. You'll really enjoy it. Kefir is easy to make and needs no supervision while turning into cheese. This recipe comes from Ingrid Bolski, a native of Poland who lives in New York. Begin 3 or 4 days before you plan to use it.

For 2 cups (16 tablespoons)

1 quart (4 cups) low-fat (1%) milk

3 tablespoons plain low-fat yogurt or low-fat sour cream for starter

1. In a heavy saucepan, bring milk to a boil. Remove from heat, and cool slightly.

2. Pour milk into a bowl or jar. Stir in the yogurt or sour cream. Cover bowl or jar, and rest at room temperature for 2 to 3 days until thickened (less in warm weather, more for a sourer cheese).

3. To thicken the cheese: Drain through a dampened cheesecloth draped over a bowl for about 20 minutes. Transfer, and drain overnight in the refrigerator. Save the whey for a beverage or soup.

4. To serve: Chill, and slice or spread on raw vegetables. For a snack or lunch, try Cheese and Fruit Open Sandwich (page 61).

Nutrients for 1 tablespoon.

Calories: 27

Exchange: ¼ low-fat milk

g	mg
carbohydrate: 3	potassium: 102
protein: 2	sodium: 33
fat: negligible	cholesterol: 3
fiber: 0	

Persian Spice Blend

Store this unusual herb-spice blend in a covered jar. Use it to season your soups and stews.

For about ¼ cup

4 tablespoons dried mint
1 teaspoon ground cinnamon

1 teaspoon freshly ground
   white pepper

1. Crush the mint in your palms directly into a small bowl.
2. Add the cinnamon and pepper.
3. Mix and transfer to a small jar. Cover tightly. Label the jar and store with the rest of your spices.

Nutrients for any amount.

No calories. Use freely.

APPETIZERS

If I had cheese, I wouldn't ask for appetizers.
HELLENIC PROVERB

Onion-Lime Appetizer, Indian Style

Snappy flavor and crisp texture! A splendid accompaniment to serve with hot curries as I first tasted it in Agra, India, near the Taj Mahal. A *thali* (round serving tray) was spread with fresh green leaves, which held small dishes filled with various dals, curries, vegetables, and chutney.

For 4 servings

1 large red onion (about 6 ounces)

2–3 tablespoons lime juice
1 tablespoon fresh coriander, very finely minced

1. Peel, and finely slice the onion into rings. Cut the larger rings in half. Drop into a bowl.
2. Sprinkle onion rings with the lime juice and coriander. Mix thoroughly. Taste, and adjust seasonings. Cover, and marinate in the refrigerator before serving. Divide into 4 portions. Serve cold.

Nutrients for 1 serving.

Calories: 22
Exchange: 1 vegetable

g	mg
carbohydrate: 5	potassium: 101.5
protein: negligible	sodium: 1
fat: negligible	cholesterol: 0
fiber: 2	

Persian Onion Appetizer

Here's a great onion appetizer with mint and vinegar. And try these seasonings on any raw vegetable in season—cabbage, celery, cauliflower, lettuce.

For 2 servings

1 cup Spanish-type onion, diced	**1 tablespoon fresh mint, minced**
1–2 tablespoons vinegar	**Fresh mint leaves for garnish**

In a small bowl, thoroughly mix the onion, vinegar, and minced mint. Taste, and adjust the seasonings, adding more vinegar, if you like. Serve chilled, garnished with mint leaves.

Nutrients for ¼ cup.

Calories: 27
Exchange: 1 vegetable

g	mg
carbohydrate: 6	potassium: 124
protein: negligible	sodium: 1.5
fat: negligible	cholesterol: 0
fiber: 2.5	

Bagna Cauda

An herby-nutty Italian dipping sauce served hot with raw or blanched vegetables—broccoli, cauliflower, zucchini or squash, cucumber, palm hearts, fennel, red or green bell pepper, artichoke hearts . . . Bagna means gravy or thickened sauce in a dialect of Piedmont, Italy. Some Italian cooks use overwhelming amounts of garlic in it. When served, it is almost an Italian counterpart of Swiss fondue with vegetables replacing the bread. Try it for a party.

For about 1 cup

2 tablespoons olive oil
1 tablespoon unsalted
   margarine
2 tablespoons pine nuts or
   almonds, slivered and
   toasted
2 medium pimientos, chopped
1 anchovy fillet, thoroughly
   rinsed and chopped
   (optional)

1 small garlic clove, chopped
1 tablespoon fresh or
   1 teaspoon dried basil
3 tablespoons fresh parsley,
   chopped
½ cup fresh or canned
   mushrooms, chopped

In a saucepan, combine all ingredients except the herbs and mushrooms. Heat gently until the flavors blend, stirring frequently. Stir in the herbs and mushrooms—with some of the liquid if you are using canned mushrooms. Cook until mushrooms are tender, adding water or liquid, if necessary, to make 1 cup of sauce. Serve hot with cold vegetables.

Nutrients for 1 tablespoon without anchovy fillet.

Calories: 60
Exchanges: ½ vegetable; 1 fat

g	mg
carbohydrate: 2	potassium: 44
protein: negligible	sodium: negligible
fat: 6	cholesterol: 0
fiber: negligible	

Guacamole

Pick up an avocado and seasonings, an attractive bowl, and a fork for mashing and mixing, and out comes guacamole! Serve this exciting Mexican appetizer with crisp tortilla chips for dipping. Also excellent with fresh celery, cucumber, or lettuce.

For about 1 cup

1 ripe avocado
½ small onion, grated
1 small ripe tomato, chopped
2 teaspoons lemon juice

1 tablespoon fresh coriander
   (cilantro), chopped
Drops of hot sauce
1–2 teaspoons jalapeño chile,
   chopped

1. Peel the avocado, cut in half, and discard the seed (or save to start a plant).

2. In a bowl, mash the avocado until soft but still quite lumpy.

3. Stir in the onion, tomato, lemon juice, coriander, and enough hot sauce and chile to please your own taste.

4. Chill for an hour to allow the flavors to blend. Serve cold.

Nutrients for ¼ cup.

Calories: 88
Exchanges: 1 vegetable; 1½ fat

g	mg
carbohydrate: 6	potassium: 354
protein: 1	sodium: 8
fat: 8	cholesterol: 0
fiber: 1.5	

Tzatziki (Herbed Yogurt)

Cool Tzatziki features yogurt with vegetables—a healthy dish and far more suitable for people with diabetes than the many sweetened yogurts that appear in the stores. Tzatziki originated in the Middle East and spread to Greece where it is amazingly popular as a salad. This recipe also appeared in my cookbook *The Food of Greece*. You can serve four as an appetizer and two as a salad. Tzatziki is also good with zucchini, eggplant, fish, or as a condiment in pita sandwiches.

For 4 servings

2 cups Uncle Bill's Homemade
    Yogurt (pages 26–27) or
    store-bought plain low-fat
    yogurt
1 medium cucumber, peeled,
    seeded, and diced or grated

1 garlic clove, minced
1 tablespoon white vinegar
1 tablespoon fresh dill or mint,
    finely chopped

1. Combine all ingredients in a glass or earthenware bowl. Chill to allow flavors to penetrate the cucumber.
2. Serve as a dip, or on lettuce leaves as a salad.

Nutrients for ½ cup.

Calories: 78
Exchanges: ½ vegetable; ½ low-fat milk

g	mg
carbohydrate: 9.5	potassium: 315
protein: 6	sodium: 80
fat: 2	cholesterol: 7
fiber: negligible	

Marinated Celery, Hellenic Style

A cool vegetable appetizer, doubled, becomes a fine lunch dish. Use the same recipe for other vegetables—artichokes, mushrooms, leeks, wax or green beans. . . .

For 8 servings

1 bunch Pascal celery (4 cups)
⅓ cup olive oil
Juice of 1 lemon
2 tablespoons fresh fennel
   leaves, chopped
1–2 sprigs fresh thyme,
   chopped

2 sprigs fresh parsley, chopped
1 small bay leaf
Freshly ground white pepper
Lemon slices and fennel leaves
   for garnish

1. Scrape celery lightly. Using a sharp knife, cut stalks diagonally into 1½-inch pieces. Cut larger pieces in half lengthwise.

2. To make the marinade: In a saucepan, combine the oil, lemon juice, herbs, seasonings, and ½ cup water. Bring to a boil.

3. Drop the celery into the marinade. Stir, and add only enough water to half cover the celery. Invert a dish over the celery. Cover pan and simmer for 10 minutes or until crisp-tender. Cool in the marinade.

4. Store, marinade and all, in a covered glass jar in the refrigerator. Serve cold, garnished with the lemon and fennel.

Nutrients for ½ cup.

Calories: 37
Exchanges: ½ vegetable; ½ fat

g	mg
carbohydrate: 2	potassium: 122
protein: negligible	sodium: 38
fat: 3	cholesterol: 0
fiber: 1	

Pinchos
(Spanish Broiled Mushrooms)

The Spanish word *pincho* has many meanings—thorn, goad, prod, skewer. In this recipe of marinated mushrooms broiled on skewers, the word *pincho* tells you how to make them. A gentle whiff of wine and mushrooms from these pinchos will lure your guests for more and more.

For 8 servings

2 cups button mushrooms
2 tablespoons olive oil
1 tablespoon dry red wine

1 small garlic clove, crushed
Salt (optional) and freshly
  ground pepper

1. Wipe off the mushrooms with a kitchen towel.
2. In a small bowl, whisk together the oil, wine, garlic, and a pinch of salt (you really don't need any) and pepper to make a tangy marinade.
3. Drop mushrooms into the marinade, and mix to coat thoroughly. Marinate for at least an hour before broiling.
4. To broil, slide the mushrooms onto skewers, preferably bamboo (that have been soaked in water for 15 minutes to prevent burning). Broil, and turn after a few minutes until just brown. Serve immediately.

Nutrients for ¼ cup.

Calories: 42
Exchanges: ½ vegetable; ½ fat

g	mg
carbohydrate: 2	potassium: 157
protein: 1	sodium: 1
fat: 4	cholesterol: 0
fiber: 2	

Caponatina

Caponatina (also known as caponata in Italy) has many fans. A student of mine in a foods class was so enthralled by his grandmother's recipe of caponatina, he became a chef. Serve it on unsalted crackers or toast squares.

For 12 servings

1 pound eggplant	1 teaspoon capers, rinsed and
3 tablespoons olive oil	drained (optional)
1 large onion, chopped	4 green olives, pitted and
3 stalks celery, sliced or	chopped
chopped	2 garlic cloves, slivered
4 fresh or canned tomatoes,	¼ cup vinegar
peeled and chopped	Pinch sugar (optional)

1. Wash, and dry the eggplant. Cut into ½-inch cubes with skin on.
2. Heat 1 tablespoon of the oil in a saucepan. When it is almost smoking, add the eggplant. Stir, and cook over high heat to avoid eggplant soaking up too much oil. Add the remaining oil, and continue frying until eggplant is browned on all sides.
3. Drop the remaining ingredients and ¼ cup water into the pan. Cook over medium heat for 10 minutes. Cool in the pan. Spoon caponatina into a container. Cover, and refrigerate. Serve cold as an appetizer.

Nutrients for ¼ cup.

Calories: 50
Exchanges: 1 vegetable; ½ fat

g	mg
carbohydrate: 4	potassium: 163.5
protein: negligible	sodium: 33
fat: 4	cholesterol: 0
fiber: 1	

Ratatouille

Of all the fabulous vegetable creations, this delectable French ratatouille is probably most famous of all. Many variations appear on other Mediterranean tables, too, including those throughout Greece. You may prefer to slice vegetables and layer them in a casserole and bake slowly a day in advance. Be generous with seasonings. Delicious for an appetizer, picnic, or main dish. But be careful not to overcook it.

For 4 servings

½ pound eggplant (1 slender violet type), diced
½ pound baby zucchini, scraped and diced
1 large red bell pepper, seeded and diced
1 large green bell pepper, seeded and diced

2 teaspoons olive oil
1 onion or green onion, minced
2 garlic cloves, crushed
1 large ripe tomato
Fresh basil or thyme, chopped
Freshly ground pepper
Fresh parsley for garnish

1. Keep eggplant, zucchini, and peppers separated until sautéed. Heat ½ teaspoon of the oil in a nonstick saucepan. Sauté the onion and garlic until soft. Add the eggplant, and sauté for 3 minutes. Transfer eggplant, onion, and garlic to a bowl.

2. If the pan is dry, add ½ teaspoon oil, and sauté the zucchini for 3 minutes. Lift, and add to the eggplant. Sauté the peppers until crisp-tender, about 2 minutes. Combine them with the eggplant and zucchini.

3. Pour remaining oil into the pan. Add the tomato, cook, and stir, adding water or tomato juice to make a thick sauce.

4. Gently mix the sautéed vegetables into the tomato sauce. Season with basil or thyme and some pepper. Taste, and enhance the seasonings. Serve warm or cold, garnished with fresh parsley.

Nutrients for ½ cup.

Calories: 51
Exchanges: 1½ vegetable; ½ fat

g	mg
carbohydrate: 7	potassium: 295
protein: 1	sodium: 6
fat: 2.5	cholesterol: 0
fiber: 3	

Shrimp Tapas

Tapas are Spanish appetizers and snacks. Eating tapas with family and friends is a national custom, a chance to socialize and nibble. Succulent shrimps make tempting tapas. Easy to marinate in advance.

For 4–6 servings

1 tablespoon olive oil
2 shallots, minced
1 garlic clove, crushed
½ cup dry red wine

20 large shrimps, cleaned and
　cooked
Freshly ground pepper
Fresh parsley for garnish

1. In a saucepan, heat the oil, and sauté the shallots and garlic until soft.
2. Stir in the wine, and simmer until thickened, mixing frequently.
3. Drop in the shrimps, and coat with the marinade. Simmer briefly. Remove from heat. Cool shrimps in the marinade, and then refrigerate. If serving warm, reheat just before serving. Adjust the seasonings. Drain shrimps before serving. Serve warm or cold with chopped parsley.

Nutrients for 2 shrimps.

Calories: 54

Exchange: 1 lean meat

g	mg
carbohydrate: 1	potassium: 103
protein: 8	sodium: 57
fat: 2	cholesterol: 60
fiber: negligible	

Marinated Octopus

If you haven't tasted octopus, you're missing a treat and an excellent low-fat, high-protein food. You can eat almost twice as much octopus (1¾ ounces) as you can a lean meat (1 ounce) for a lean meat exchange. And there's no waste. Octopus can be cooked in a stew or tomato sauce. Marinating is only one delicious method.

For 8–10 servings

1 small octopus (1 pound)
2 tablespoons red wine vinegar
2 tablespoons lemon juice
3 garlic cloves, minced
1 medium onion or 2 green
    onions, minced (optional)

Freshly ground white pepper
2 tablespoons fine olive oil
Herbs: dried rosemary, thyme,
    or oregano, fresh parsley,
    bay leaf

1. Buy a fresh octopus, and ask if it has been tenderized. For a really old-fashioned touch, you can pound it forty times on a stone or rough surface. This is good exercise, and helps tenderize it, but isn't absolutely necessary. Wash thoroughly.

2. Place octopus in a saucepan only large enough to hold it. Cover, and steam octopus over low heat *without adding any water*. Check after about an hour, and check tenderness. The octopus will turn bright red, get stiff at first, then limp, and secrete a dark red liquid. Continue cooking until tender. The liquid will jell in the refrigerator and has a strong taste. You can discard the liquid.

3. When cool enough to handle, rub off the outer skin of the octopus. Slice octopus into bite-size pieces, and place them in a glass jar with a lid or in a bowl. (If you prefer to use the octopus in another dish, read the nutrients below for unmarinated octopus.)

4. Add all the remaining ingredients, using your own taste and favorite herbs to flavor the octopus (garlic, vinegar, and herbs give lots of flavor). Cover the jar, shake it gently to mix thoroughly, and store in the refrigerator. Marinate from 2 to 3 days for delicious results. Serve cold within a week.

Nutrients for 100 g (3.5 ounces or about ½ cup) unmarinated octopus.

Calories: 73
Exchanges: 1½ lean meat

g	mg
carbohydrate: 0	potassium: NA
protein: 15	sodium: NA
fat: negligible	cholesterol: NA
fiber: NA	

Nutrients for marinade.

Calories: 35
Exchanges: ½ vegetable; ½ fat

g	mg
carbohydrate: 1	potassium: 245
protein: negligible	sodium: 1
fat: 3	cholesterol: 0
fiber: negligible	

Moules (Mussels, French Style)

Try this appetizing mussels dish for an instant trip to Bretagne (Brittany). It was offered by the French chef of a charming restaurant in New York.

For 4 servings

24 mussels
1 tablespoon dried bread
   crumbs, preferably from
   French bread

2 garlic cloves, crushed
1 tablespoon unsalted
   margarine or butter, melted

1. Scrub the mussels, and clip off the beards. Place mussels in a pan with 2 cups water. Cover the pan, and steam the mussels over low heat for 10 minutes until the shells open. Discard any unopened shells.

2. When cool enough to handle, lift the mussels, and discard the half shell without the mussel. Reserve the liquid for a fish soup. Arrange the mussels close together in a casserole or on snail dishes.

3. Sprinkle the bread crumbs, garlic, and margarine over the mussels. Broil for 2 to 3 minutes until golden brown. Serve hot.

Nutrients for 6 mussels.

Calories: 62
Exchanges: ½ lean meat; ½ fat

g	mg
carbohydrate: 3	potassium: 101
protein: 4	sodium: 94
fat: 4	cholesterol: 11
fiber: 0	

Spicy Tofu

When you need an intriguing and very nutritious appetizer, plan this one with confidence. Make a day in advance for better flavor (and convenience).

For 2 servings

2 tofu (bean curds)	½ teaspoon peppercorns
1 tablespoon soy sauce	4 green onions, sliced into
1 tablespoon orange juice	rings
½ orange rind, diced	1–2 teaspoons lemon juice

1. Steam the tofu for 10 minutes.
2. While the curds are steaming, make the marinade: In a saucepan, mix the soy sauce, orange juice, rind, peppercorns, and half the green onions. Add ½ cup water. Bring to a boil, and simmer for 5 minutes.
3. Cut each tofu into 18 pieces with this quick trick: First, slice in half crosswise, keeping the halves together as they were; next, slice from the top down into thirds; turn the knife, and slice down in thirds perpendicular to the earlier slices. You should have 18 cubes.
4. Gently mix in the marinade, and soak the tofu cubes. Cool thoroughly. Chill until ready to serve.
5. Drain off the marinade and remove the peppercorns.
6. Arrange the tofu cubes in a serving bowl. Sprinkle with the lemon juice and remaining green onions. Divide between two plates. Serve cold.

**Nutrients for 1 serving without soy sauce.
Check the label for sodium content.**

Calories: 94
Exchanges: 1 medium-fat meat; 1 vegetable

g	mg
carbohydrate: 7	potassium: 197
protein: 9	sodium: 11
fat: 4	cholesterol: 0
fiber: 2	

Curried Eggs

Zesty to taste when seasoned discreetly, curried eggs are also lovely to look at. The recipe is from a guide at the United Nations who was born in Karikal, a coastal city south of Madras. He calls the eggs *rost a morta*.

For 4 servings

1 tablespoon corn oil	½ teaspoon ground turmeric
1 medium onion, minced	2 teaspoons ground cumin
½ teaspoon mustard seed	4 hard-cooked eggs
½ medium green bell pepper	4 fresh coriander leaves for
¼ teaspoon cayenne pepper	garnish (optional)
1 inch fresh ginger, chopped	

1. In a small skillet, heat the oil. Add the onion, and sauté until translucent, about 2 minutes.

2. Move onions to one side, and drop the mustard seed into the warm oil. Stir until the mustard begins to pop.

3. Stir in the green pepper, cayenne, ginger, turmeric, and cumin. Cook for 2 minutes over low heat, stirring constantly to avoid browning. Stir in the onion and enough water to make a sauce (it may spatter).

4. Peel the eggs, and roll them in the curry until thoroughly coated. Garnish before serving, if you like. Serve warm or cold with chapati or other Indian bread.

Nutrients for 1 curried egg.

Calories: 120

Exchanges: ½ medium-fat meat; ½ vegetable; 1½ fat

g	mg
carbohydrate: 2	potassium: 108
protein: 6	sodium: 70
fat: 9	cholesterol: 274
fiber: negligible	

Pickled Beet Eggs

Such a delightful Pennsylvania Dutch recipe belongs in a collection of international recipes. It's fun to take on a picnic and surprise your friends with. Be sure to save the cooking liquid from red beets next time you cook some, and try this one.

For 4 servings

4 hard-cooked eggs	1 garlic clove, slivered
4 whole cloves	Small bay leaf
1 cup cooking liquid from red beets, strained	½ teaspoon coriander seeds
¾ cup cider vinegar	Fresh thyme sprig

1. Peel the eggs. Stud the more pointed end of each egg with a clove. Place in a quart-size jar with a lid.

2. Make a marinade in a saucepan. Combine the liquid from beets, vinegar, and remaining ingredients. Bring to a boil. Pour over the eggs, and cool. Cover and refrigerate for 10 days to 2 weeks. The white turns beet color, and the yellow slightly pink. Serve cold.

Nutrients for ½ egg.

Calories: 40
Exchange: ½ medium-fat meat

g	mg
carbohydrate: negligible	potassium: 34
protein: 3	sodium: 35
fat: 3	cholesterol: 137
fiber: 0	

Quesadilla Especial

Quesadilla is named for the Spanish word for cheese—*queso*. Serve this dish piping hot from the oven with the cheese melting as we enjoyed it in JJ's Oasis Latino restaurant in Palm Springs. Owners Doré and Gladys Reyes also inspired the recipe for Guacamole (page 39).

For 4 servings

1 flour tortilla
¼ cup jack cheese, grated
¼ cup yellow American cheese, grated
¼ cup cooked chicken, shredded

1 lettuce leaf, shredded
1 small ripe tomato, slivered
1 small onion, finely sliced
2 green onions (including green parts), minced
Fresh coriander (cilantro)

1. Place the tortilla on a preheated griddle. Immediately strew the tortilla evenly with the cheese, chicken, lettuce, tomato, onion, green onions, and coriander.

2. Grill over medium-hot heat until cheese melts, but don't let the tortilla brown. Fold the tortilla in half to make a half-moon. Slice across into 4 portions. Serve immediately.

Nutrients for ¼ quesadilla.

Calories: 170
Exchanges: ½ starch/bread; 1½ lean meat; 1 fat

g	mg
carbohydrate: 7	potassium: 170
protein: 12	sodium: 294
fat: 10	cholesterol: 39
fiber: 1	

Hummus with Tahini

Hummus—a creamy specialty celebrated in the Middle East—has become very popular in Western countries, especially among vegetarians. *Hummus* is the Arabic word for chick-peas, the major ingredient. You may prefer to substitute canned chick-peas when you are in a hurry. Serve with crispy raw vegetables and unsalted crackers.

For 6 servings

⅔ cup dried chick-peas
1 tablespoon tahini (sesame
   seed paste)
4 tablespoons lemon juice
1 tablespoon olive oil
2 garlic cloves, crushed

½ teaspoon ground coriander
   (optional)
¼ teaspoon ground cumin
   (optional)
Fresh parsley, minced, for
   garnish

1. Wash chick-peas, cover with water in a bowl, and soak overnight. Next day, drain and cover with fresh water in a saucepan. Cook until tender, about 1½ hours. Drain, and sieve through a food mill into a bowl.

2. In a small bowl, beat the tahini with 2 to 3 tablespoons water to make a smooth paste.

3. Gradually add the tahini to the chick-peas, alternating with the lemon juice and olive oil. Then mix in the garlic and spices (if you are using them). Taste, and adjust seasonings. Refrigerate before serving. Divide into 6 servings. Serve cold, sprinkled with parsley.

Nutrients for ⅓ cup.

Calories: 122

Exchanges: 1 starch/bread; 1 fat

g	mg
carbohydrate: 14	potassium: 189
protein: 5	sodium: 8
fat: 6	cholesterol: 0
fiber: 3	

BREAKFAST, BRUNCH, AND LUNCH DISHES

Over the egg, quick, quick.
PERUVIAN PROVERB

Birchermuesli

This crunchy, high-fiber breakfast food originated in a Swiss clinic run by Dr. R. Bircher-Benner. The original combination featured oatmeal and raw apple. Muesli is probably the forerunner of the popular granola. You can vary the types of flakes you mix into it. Store the dry muesli indefinitely to serve as a quick breakfast or snack.

For about 4½ cups dry muesli

1 cup wheat flakes
1 cup oat flakes
⅓ cup bran flakes
½ cup wheat germ

2 dried apple rings, chopped
4 apricot halves, chopped
4 tablespoons raisins
1 fresh apple (optional)
¼ cup low-fat milk (optional)

1. Mix the wheat, oat, and bran flakes, wheat germ, dried apple rings, apricots, and raisins in a jar. Shake to mix. Store in a dry place.

2. When ready to serve, shake the mixture to distribute it evenly. Measure ⅓ cup into a serving bowl.

3. Swiss style: Cover with cold water, and rest it for 15 minutes or longer until flakes are swollen. Add the grated fresh apple and the milk. (Add the fruit and milk exchanges as indicated below, if you do.) Enjoy Birchermuesli cold.

**Nutrients for ⅓ cup with dried fruit
without apple and milk.**

Calories: 86
Exchanges: 1¼ starch/bread

g	mg
carbohydrate: 18	potassium: 198
protein: 4	sodium: 2
fat: 1	cholesterol: 0
fiber: 3	

Nutrients for 1 medium apple.

Calories: 62
Exchange: 1 fruit

g	mg
carbohydrate: 16	potassium: 122
protein: negligible	sodium: 1
fat: negligible	cholesterol: 0
fiber: 2	

Nutrients for ¼ cup low-fat milk (1%).

Calories: 25
Exchange: ½ low-fat milk

g	mg
carbohydrate: 3	potassium: 95
protein: 2	sodium: 31
fat: negligible	cholesterol: 0
fiber: 0	

Strapatsada
(Mediterranean Vegetable-Egg Dish)

Moira Beaton, nutritionist at the Diabetic Clinic in Paphos, Cyprus, who contributed this savory recipe, calls it a Mediterranean omelet, and for good reason. It includes "really any fresh vegetables in season (except root vegetables) bound together with eggs." You can easily adapt the idea no matter where you live, using 1 cup raw vegetables of your choice, if you do not have those suggested here.

For 6 servings

½ teaspoon unsaturated oil
1 small onion or 2 green onions, finely chopped
1 cup red or green bell peppers, zucchini, green beans, mushrooms, etc., chopped (a single vegetable or several mixed, as you like)

1 medium tomato, finely chopped
6 eggs, lightly beaten
1 slice halloumi (Cypriot) cheese, diced (optional)
Pinch salt (optional) and freshly ground pepper
Lemon wedges for garnish

1. Heat the oil in a nonstick omelet pan or skillet. Sauté the onion until soft.

2. Add the vegetables, except the tomatoes. Cover the pan, and allow the vegetables to "sweat" over low heat until tender but not mushy.

3. Stir in the tomato with the beaten eggs. If you are using the cheese, add it as well. Season lightly (you won't need salt if you are using the cheese, because it is salty enough).

4. Stir and cook quickly over medium heat until the eggs are lightly scrambled. Divide evenly into 6 servings. Serve hot with lemon wedges and a green, leafy salad.

Nutrients for 1 serving without cheese.

Calories: 71
Exchanges: ½ medium-fat meat; ½ vegetable; ½ fat

g	mg
carbohydrate: 3	potassium: 119
protein: 5	sodium: 68.5
fat: 5	cholesterol: 205
fiber: negligible	

Tortilla (Spanish Omelet)

Tortilla is one of those Spanish words that has different meanings in Spain and Mexico. The famous tortilla of Mexico used to make Mexican Tacos (page 69) and Crab Enchiladas (pages 202–3) is really a thin flat bread of cornmeal or wheat. It has been the Mexican staple food since pre-Columbian times. But a Spanish tortilla is like an Italian *frittata* or a Hellenic *kayania*—a round pancake of fried eggs and other aromatics; it is not folded, omelet-style, into a half-moon. Speckled with diced potatoes, this Spanish tortilla provides a hearty brunch or lunch dish.

For 4 servings

1 teaspoon olive oil	1 tablespoon fresh parsley,
1 large onion, chopped	chopped, more for garnish
2 medium potatoes, cooked	4 eggs
and diced	Pinch salt and freshly ground
	pepper

1. Heat the oil in a nonstick omelet pan or skillet. Add the onion, and sauté until soft and transparent. Stir in the potatoes, and cook for 2 minutes until golden brown. Add the parsley.

2. In a bowl, lightly beat the eggs, and season with a little salt and pepper. Raise heat under the pan or skillet, and pour the eggs over the potatoes, tilting pan to spread the eggs evenly. Reduce heat, and keep tilting pan to allow egg to flow to the sides until it sets. Slide tortilla onto a large plate. Invert directly into the pan to cook the bottom side. Slice evenly into 4 portions. Serve warm or cold, garnished with fresh parsley.

Nutrients for 1 serving.

Calories: 176

Exchanges: 1 starch/bread; 1 medium-fat meat; ½ fat

g	mg
carbohydrate: 16	potassium: 350
protein: 8	sodium: 103
fat: 9	cholesterol: 274
fiber: 2.5	

Appelpannekoeken
(Dutch Apple Pancakes)

Steaming hot and fragrant with apple, they are delicious for breakfast or brunch. Enjoy these pancakes as do the Dutch people, who introduced pancakes to other American settlers.

For 6 round pancakes (6 inches in diameter)

½ tablespoon (½ package)
   active dry yeast
¼ teaspoon sugar (optional)
2 cups all-purpose flour
¼ teaspoon salt
1¼–1½ cups milk, warmed
6 teaspoons unsalted
   margarine, melted

2 small apples, cored, peeled,
   and sliced (8 circles per
   apple)
Brown sugar replacement or
   dietetic maple syrup for
   topping

1. In a small, warm bowl, dissolve the yeast and sugar (if you are using it) in ½ cup warm water. Cover, and set aside until doubled in bulk.

2. In a large bowl, mix the flour and salt. Make a well in the middle. Pour in the swollen yeast, and add 1¼ cups of the milk to the well. Mix with a wooden spoon, adding only enough of the remaining milk to make a nice, fairly thick batter. Set aside in a warm place for about 30 minutes until bubbles begin to appear.

3. Meanwhile, slowly heat the largest griddle you have. When it is very hot, pour ½ teaspoon of the margarine on the griddle. Pour ½ cup of the batter on the griddle. Place 4 or 5 slices of apple on the top (uncooked side). When pancake bottom browns, turn over and brown the apple side. Be sure pancakes are ready; they bake more slowly than baking powder pancakes.

4. Serve immediately with remaining half tablespoon margarine for each pancake, plain or with brown sugar replacement.

Nutrients for 1 (6-inch) pancake.

Calories: 238
Exchanges: 2 starch/bread; 1 fruit; ½ fat

g	mg
carbohydrate: 43.5	potassium: 191
protein: 7	sodium: 50
fat: 4	cholesterol: 3
fiber: 2	

Cheese and Fruit Open Sandwich

Contrasts offered by fibrous bread, fresh cheese, and seasonal fruit are exciting to the palate and very easy to serve.

For 1 serving

1 slice pumpernickel bread
2 tablespoons low-fat cottage
  cheese

1 tablespoon Berry/Fruit Sauce
  (pages 300–301)

Place bread on a plate. Spread with the cheese, and top with berry or fruit sauce. Serve immediately or wrap for a picnic or lunch basket.

Nutrients for 1 serving with Peach Sauce.

Calories: 115

Exchanges: 1 starch/bread; ½ fruit

g	mg
carbohydrate: 23	potassium: 133
protein: 6	sodium: 161
fat: negligible	cholesterol: 1
fiber: 5	

Pan Bagnat
(Sandwiches, Monaco Style)

Pan Bagnat is the name for this stuffed sandwich in Monaco and in France (where the name is hyphenated). The fillings can vary. For example, Bordeaux-born Celine Beteta Wong, who works in the office of the Consulate of Monaco in New York, says she always fills her Pan Bagnat with tuna. It can be a complete meal—great for a picnic or bag lunch. This recipe is from the late Princess Grace of Monaco, who graciously shared it with me many years ago.

For 4 servings

4 round rolls	1 hard-cooked egg, sliced
1 teaspoon olive oil	2 anchovies, rinsed and
1 medium onion, minced	chopped (optional)
1 green bell pepper, finely	2 small black olives, rinsed,
sliced	pitted, and chopped
1 ripe tomato, sliced	1 tablespoon vinegar

1. Slice the rolls in half horizontally. Remove part of the inside of the bread to allow space for the filling.

2. Divide all the filling evenly among the 4 rolls. Begin by drizzling the bottom of the rolls with a little oil. Drop some onion, bell pepper, tomato, egg, anchovy (if you are using it), and olives into each roll bottom (the filling amounts are personal choices).

3. Season to your taste with vinegar. Cover the roll with the top half. Serve cold.

Nutrients for 1 Pan Bagnat without anchovies.

Calories: 141
Exchanges: 1½ starch/bread; ½ fat

g	mg
carbohydrate: 21	potassium: 227
protein: 5	sodium: 194
fat: 5	cholesterol: 68
fiber: 2	

Chinese Shrimp Toast

Here's a favorite Chinese dim sum or lunch dish.

For 8 toasts

½ pound shrimp, shelled,
  cleaned, and finely chopped
5 water chestnuts, finely
  chopped
1 egg white
Pinch salt or ½ teaspoon soy
  sauce

1 teaspoon cornstarch
¼ teaspoon fresh ginger,
  minced
8 slices bread
Peanut or corn oil for frying

1. In a bowl, combine the shrimp, water chestnuts, egg white, salt or soy sauce, cornstarch, and ginger, and mix thoroughly.

2. Divide the mixture into 8 portions. Spread each portion on the bread slices.

3. Heat the oil to 325°F. Slip the toast into the hot oil, shrimp side up, and fry until golden brown on both sides. Drain thoroughly on paper towels. While it is still hot, cut each slice into 4 strips (if you are serving it as an appetizer, cut into 8 squares). Serve immediately. Or you can freeze the toasts after they cool, and reheat before serving another time.

Nutrients for 1 toast.

Calories: 172
Exchanges: 1 starch/bread; 1 lean meat; 1 fat

g	mg
carbohydrate: 16	potassium: 108
protein: 8	sodium: 202
fat: 8	cholesterol: 43
fiber: negligible	

Pizza Margherita

Prof. G. M. Molinatti, of the Clinica Medica 2, Università di Torino in Torino, Italy, sent this recipe of the famous pizza. It is the name for pizza without anchovies (the latter is called Pizza Napoletana). If you can't use all the pizza during one meal, freeze the slices to microwave or reheat when you need them.

For 12 servings

1 package active dry yeast or .6 ounce cake compressed yeast
1 pound (4 cups) all-purpose flour
Pinch salt (optional)
1 pound fresh tomatoes (6 fresh plum) or 2½ cups Homemade Tomato Sauce (page 19)

Herbs: 1 bay leaf; 1 teaspoon fresh parsley, chopped; pinch dried thyme or basil
4 ounces, mozzarella, grated
2 tablespoons olive or other unsaturated oil
Dried oregano

1. For the dough: Mix the yeast with ¼ cup warm water in a small bowl. Cover, and proof until doubled in bulk.

2. Measure the flour into a large bowl. Make a well in the middle. Add the swollen yeast, a pinch of salt (if you are using it), and enough warm water (about 1½ cups) to make a soft dough. If the dough is too stiff, dampen your hands with warm water, and work the dough to soften it. Knead dough for 5 minutes. Cover, and keep warm until doubled in bulk, about 1½ hours.

3. To make the sauce: If you are using fresh tomatoes, chop them and simmer in a saucepan, stirring frequently, for about 15 minutes. Add the herbs. If you are using Homemade Tomato Sauce, heat it, and taste for seasonings; remove bay leaf.

4. To assemble the pizza: Roll out the dough to fit a pizza pan or another shallow baking pan. (You can flip the dough and stretch it over the back of your hands as a pizza maker does.) Flute the edges neatly.

5. Spread the tomato sauce over the dough, sprinkle with mozzarella and the oil, and top with oregano.

6. Bake in a moderately hot oven at 375°F for 20 to 25 minutes until the dough is golden brown, and the cheese melts. Cut into 12 slices. Serve hot.

Cottage Cheese–flecked Hamburgers

Hamburgers, the number-one favorite in the United States, were introduced by German immigrants. Now this cottage cheese–flecked version, for a meaty lunch, is contributed by Zentralinstitut für Diabetes in East Germany.

For 4 servings

6 ounces lean ground beef	1 small onion, minced
6 ounces lean ground pork	Pinch salt and freshly ground
1 egg, lightly beaten	pepper
½ cup low-fat cottage cheese	1 teaspoon sunflower oil

1. In a bowl, knead the beef, pork, egg, cottage cheese, and onion. Season lightly with salt and pepper.

2. Divide into 4 sections. Shape each section into flat hamburgers.

3. Brush with oil. Grill over charcoal, broil in the oven, or fry in a nonstick skillet on both sides to the desired doneness. Boiled potatoes and steamed vegetables make a good side dish. Serve hot.

Pita Sandwich Medley

For a quick and easy Middle Eastern lunch, here's a great one. Use fresh pitas, and for more flavor, warm gently before slicing and filling them.

For 4 servings

2 pitas (each 6 inches across)
4 ounces cooked chicken
   breast or lean meat, slivered
1 ripe medium tomato, thinly
   sliced

1 small cucumber, grated or
   slivered
½ cup low-fat yogurt or
   Tzatziki (page 40)
4 teaspoons vinegar for garnish
Dried oregano for garnish

1. Heat the pitas slightly for more flavor, if you like. Cut in half cross-wise. Place each half on a plate.

2. Divide the chicken or meat equally into 4 parts and drop into the pita halves.

3. Divide the tomato and cucumber evenly among the 4 pita halves.

4. Season each filling with 2 tablespoons yogurt or Tzatziki, 1 teaspoon vinegar, and crushed oregano. Serve immediately.

Nutrients for 1 pita.

Calories: 136
Exchanges: 1 lean meat; 3 vegetable

g	mg
carbohydrate:16	potassium: 287.5
protein: 14	sodium: 211
fat: 1.5	cholesterol: 26
fiber: 1	

Slatit Blanquit
(Tunisian Open-Faced Sandwiches)

Soak bread slices in dressing and top with various morsels for a delicious sandwich.

For 4 servings

1 tablespoon olive oil plus
  1 teaspoon for sprinkling
3 tablespoons or more flavorful
  vinegar
Harissa (page 16) (optional) or
  hot sauce
4 slices day-old bread, cut
  ½-inch thick

1 hard-cooked egg, sliced
¼ cup tuna fish (canned in
  water), crumbled
1 ounce feta or other cheese,
  crumbled or grated
2 olives, pitted, rinsed, and
  chopped
4 fresh parsley sprigs, chopped

1. In a wide soup bowl, whisk the oil with enough vinegar and hot sauce to make a tasty dressing.

2. Dip each bread slice into the dressing just long enough to soak up some dressing. Place the slices on a platter or individual plates.

3. Dot each bread slice with one-fourth of the egg slices, tuna, cheese, and olives. Top with chopped parsley. Serve immediately.

Nutrients for 1 sandwich.

Calories: 165
Exchanges: 1 starch/bread; ½ medium-fat meat; 1 fat

g	mg
carbohydrate: 15	potassium: 95
protein: 8	sodium: 366
fat: 8	cholesterol: 82
fiber: negligible	

Italian Hero Sandwich

Make heros—also called submarines, hoagies, grinders, po'boys—for a quick lunch!

For 4 servings

1 small onion, sliced
4 slices canned red roasted peppers, including 1 teaspoon oil
2 tablespoons vinegar
4 round rolls or 2 long hero rolls

1 ounce prosciutto or ham, sliced paper thin
2 ounces mozzarella, thinly sliced
4 lettuce leaves
2 medium tomatoes, sliced in 8 circles

1. In a small bowl, combine the onion slices, peppers, and oil. Drizzle with the vinegar. Marinate for 15 minutes or longer.

2. Slice rolls in half lengthwise to make tops and bottoms. If you are using long hero rolls, slice crosswise in half to make 4 servings. If you are using round rolls, use one per serving.

3. To stuff the heros: Divide the onion-pepper mixture into 4 parts, and spread each part in a roll half; spread a slice of prosciutto, mozzarella, and lettuce, and 2 slices tomato in each half roll. Serve immediately.

Nutrients for 1 hero.

Calories: 168

Exchanges: 1 starch/bread; ½ medium-fat meat; 1 vegetable; ½ fat

g	mg
carbohydrate: 21	potassium: 293
protein: 8	sodium: 310
fat: 6	cholesterol: 12
fiber: 2	

Mexican Tacos

Thanks are due to Mexicans for conceiving these hearty, folded sandwiches, which you can munch out of hand. Tacos are now popular on
restaurant and home menus wherever we live. This recipe features traditional fillings—meat, jack cheese, and shredded vegetables with seasonings. You can substitute diced leftover meat, 1 ounce per taco, instead of
the ground beef.

For 4 servings

¼ pound lean ground beef
1 small onion, grated
Pinch salt
Freshly ground pepper
1 teaspoon fresh coriander or
  parsley, chopped
4 corn tortillas

1 ounce jack cheese, shredded
  (optional)
1½ cups lettuce, shredded
1 tomato, sliced
1 teaspoon unsaturated
  vegetable oil
Taco sauce

1. In a skillet over medium heat, mash the beef with ¼ cup water,
stirring with a fork until the grains are separated and raw color changes to
light brown. Drain off all the fat.

2. Stir in the onion, salt, pepper, and coriander or parsley. Cook for 4
to 5 minutes until tender. Keep warm.

3. Meanwhile, make taco shells by heating the tortillas on a griddle or
skillet. When they are hot, turn them one at a time to soften; then quickly
bend in half to form shells.

4. Divide the beef, cheese (if you are using it), lettuce, and tomato into
4 equal parts. To serve tacos, fill the shells with 1 portion of each filling
ingredient, a few drops of oil, and a dash or two of taco sauce, if you like
it hot. Serve immediately.

Nutrients for 1 taco without cheese.

Calories: 170

Exchanges: 1 starch/bread; 1 medium-fat meat; ⅕ vegetable

g	mg
carbohydrate: 16	potassium: 261
protein: 10	sodium: 83
fat: 8	cholesterol: 26
fiber: 2	

Vegetarian Tacos

Tacos with vegetables are favorites with my family. You can use all kinds of crispy or leftover vegetables to vary the fillings—bean sprouts, carrots, beets, pea pods, spinach, zucchini, etc. . . . Be liberal. One cup of raw or a half cup of cooked vegetables equals only 25 calories and 1 vegetable exchange.

For 4 servings

4 corn tortillas
1 large or 2 medium celery stalks, finely sliced
1 medium onion, shredded
½ cucumber, shredded and squeezed
4 large crisp lettuce leaves, finely sliced
1 medium red or green bell pepper, seeded and finely sliced

1 ripe, juicy tomato, finely sliced
1 ounce jack cheese, shredded
4 tablespoons Mexican Salsa Picante (page 17) (optional)
4 tablespoons Guacamole (page 39) (optional)
Hot taco sauce

1. On a hot, ungreased skillet, heat the tortillas on both sides for about 1 minute. Bend in half to make taco shells. Place each shell on a plate, and set aside to cool.

2. Prepare the celery, onion, cucumber, lettuce, pepper, and tomato, and set out in separate dishes for guests to help themselves.

3. Each one adds vegetables and cheese, and seasons to his own taste.

Nutrients for 1 taco without salsa or guacamole.

Calories: 126
Exchanges: 1 starch/bread; ½ medium-fat meat; ½ vegetable

g	mg
carbohydrate: 20	potassium: 409
protein: 5	sodium: 145
fat: 3.5	cholesterol: 7
fiber: 4	

SOUPS AND

STEWS

Know, cabbages, that
there is spinach in the stew.
SPANISH PROVERB

Monegasque Basil Soup

Enriched with pesto sauce, this delicious recipe was shared with me by the late Princess Grace of Monaco. When your fresh basil and summer vegetables are abundant, treat your family and friends. (I have reduced the amount of olive oil in the original recipe.)

For 8 servings

1 pound string beans and wax beans mixed, sliced

3 medium potatoes, diced

4 carrots, sliced

2 medium zucchini, scraped and diced

¾ teaspoon salt and freshly ground pepper

3 tablespoons noodles

3 garlic cloves

¼ cup fresh basil leaves, chopped

2 tablespoons and 2 teaspoons olive oil

2 tablespoons grated cheese

1. Pour 2 quarts water into a soup pot. Add the beans, potatoes, and carrots. Bring to a boil, and cook for about 10 minutes. Add the zucchini, a little salt and pepper, and the noodles. Continue cooking until all are al dente. (This is the challenging part of the soup—to master the cooking time.)

2. Meanwhile, in a small bowl or mortar, crush the garlic and add the basil. Continue beating as you add the oil. Mix thoroughly. Sprinkle with the grated cheese.

3. Add this preparation to the soup, mix, and serve.

Nutrients for 1 cup.

Calories: 88

Exchanges: ½ starch/bread; ½ vegetable; 1 fat

g	mg
carbohydrate: 10	potassium: 271
protein: 2	sodium: 40
fat: 5	cholesterol: 4
fiber: 3	

Spinatsuppe
(Norwegian Spinach Soup)

Mellow and wholesome, this Norwegian favorite is quick to prepare, low in calories, and high in vitamin A.

For 4 cups

8 ounces (½ pound) fresh or
  frozen spinach
4 cups White Chicken Stock
  (page 98)
1 small onion, minced
1 tablespoon unsalted
  margarine or butter

1 tablespoon all-purpose flour
Pinch sugar (optional)
½ teaspoon nutmeg, freshly
  grated
Pinch salt

1. Wash, drain, and coarsely chop the fresh spinach; if you are using frozen spinach, partially thaw before chopping.

2. In a medium saucepan, bring the stock with the onion to a boil. Stir in the spinach, lower heat, and cook uncovered for 5 minutes. Remove from heat.

3. To thicken and flavor the soup: Make a roux in a small saucepan by melting the margarine. Add the flour, and stir over low heat for a few minutes without browning. Remove from heat, and gradually add about a cup of the soup liquid, stirring constantly. When dissolved, stir the mixture into the soup.

4. Return to the heat and slowly bring to a boil. Stir, and cook until the soup thickens.

5. Season with a speck of sugar (if you like), nutmeg to suit your taste, and a pinch of salt.

Nutrients for 1 cup.

Calories: 71

Exchanges: ½ starch/bread; ½ vegetable; ½ fat

g	mg
carbohydrate: 8	potassium: 265.5
protein: 3	sodium: 65
fat: 3	cholesterol: 1
fiber: 1.5	

French Onion Soup

Such a fragrant soup served on a wintry day will make your friends beam. All you need is *patience* when cooking the onions.

For 6 servings

4 large onions
2 tablespoons unsalted butter
2 tablespoons fine olive oil
3 tablespoons all-purpose flour
6 cups White Beef Stock
  (page 99)

6 slices crisp toast (preferably
  from homemade bread)
3 tablespoons Swiss cheese,
  grated

1. Peel, and finely grate or sliver the onions in a food processor or with a sharp knife.

2. Heat the butter and oil in a heavy casserole. When the butter begins to bubble, add the onions, and lower the heat. Gently sauté the onions over very low heat until golden, about 30 minutes, stirring frequently. Avoid rushing or browning the onions.

3. Sprinkle the flour over the onions, and cook for 2 minutes.

4. Stir in the stock, and simmer for 20 to 30 minutes. Taste, and continue simmering if the onions aren't tender enough.

5. To serve: Use an earthenware tureen or individual earthenware bowls. Ladle the very hot soup into the tureen or bowls. Top with the toast. Sprinkle 1 teaspoon cheese on each toast.

6. Broil until the cheese melts. Serve immediately.

Nutrients for 1 cup.

Calories: 243
Exchanges: 1½ starch/bread; 1½ vegetable; 2 fat

g	mg
carbohydrate: 30	potassium: 251
protein: 6	sodium: 206
fat: 11	cholesterol: 15
fiber: 3	

Frühlingssuppe (Spring Soup)

When you want a bright, low-calorie soup that is also quick to make, try this one. The recipe is adapted from *Diät bei Zuckerkrankheit*, diabetic recipes from Dr. P. Dieterle of Munich. This recipe is high in vitamin A.

For 4 servings

2 medium carrots, cut into fine strips
½ pound fresh peas
2 small stalks celery, cut into fine strips
1 small cauliflower, broken into florets, sliced in half

4 cups White Chicken Stock (page 98)
Pinch salt
Grated nutmeg
4 tablespoons fresh chive, finely chopped

1. Combine the carrots, peas, celery, cauliflower, and the chicken stock in a soup pot. Simmer until the vegetables are just tender. Add a little water, if necessary, to make 4 cups.

2. Season lightly with salt and nutmeg. Serve warm with 1 tablespoon chive on each serving.

Nutrients for 1 cup.

Calories: 73
Exchanges: ½ starch/bread; 1 vegetable

g	mg
carbohydrate: 13	potassium: 420
protein: 4.5	sodium: 110
fat: .5	cholesterol: 1
fiber: 5	

Vegetable Borscht

Bright beety borscht is a staple throughout Russia, the Ukraine, and Poland. Instead of cooking borscht with the usual rich beef broth and meat, this version focuses on vegetables—thick as a casserole. Serve it with a traditional dollop of sour cream. Freeze cup-size portions for quick meals and snacks.

For 6 servings

4 beets
2 stalks celery
3 carrots
2 parsnips
2 medium onions
8 cups water or White Chicken Stock (page 98)
1 medium cabbage, shredded (about 4 cups)

½ cup fresh tomatoes, strained, or canned tomato juice
2 tablespoons fresh dill, chopped
¼ teaspoon salt
Fresh parsley for garnish
2 tablespoons diet sour cream

1. Peel or scrape the beets, celery, carrots, and parsnips. Cut into julienne strips. Slice the onions thin and again into halves or quarters. (There should be 1½ cups beets, 1 cup celery, 1 cup carrots, ½ cup parsnips, and ¾ cup onions.)

2. In a casserole, bring the stock or water to a boil. Add the beets, celery, carrots, parsnips, and onions. Cover pan, and simmer for about 15 minutes until almost tender.

3. Stir in the cabbage, and continue cooking for 15 or 20 minutes until vegetables are tender but not mushy. Add the tomatoes or tomato juice during the last 10 minutes. Remove from heat.

4. Season with the dill and a little salt, and sprinkle on the parsley. Serve hot or cold with a dollop of sour cream, 1 teaspoon per serving.

Nutrients for 1 cup.

Calories: 94
Exchanges: 4 vegetable

g	mg
carbohydrate: 21	potassium: 716
protein: 3	sodium: 187
fat: negligible	cholesterol: 0
fiber: 7	

Japanese Soup

An appetizing soup with a subtle blend of ginger, soy sauce, and dashi, this one is beautiful to serve in a Japanese soup bowl. You can prepare the stock in advance and freeze it.

For 4 servings

1 piece dashi kombu (kelp leaf)
½ cup dried fish flakes (optional)
1 bean curd or 4 shrimps

4 leaves fresh spinach, rape blossoms, or other leafy green
1 teaspoon Japanese soy sauce
1 teaspoon fresh ginger, minced

1. To make dashi stock: Wipe the kombu with a damp cloth. Cut into 4-inch strips, and slash near the edges. Place kombu in a soup pot, and add 4 cups water. Heat over medium heat, and immediately remove the kombu before the liquid boils. For more flavor, add the fish flakes, and heat to the boiling point. Remove from heat, and strain. Use as a soup stock.

2. For this soup, if you're using the bean curd, cut into small cubes. If you are using the shrimps, clean and wash, leaving only the tail on. (Tail is discarded after eating.)

3. Add the bean curd or shrimps to the stock. Simmer for a few minutes. Drop in the leafy green you are using. Season with soy sauce and taste.

4. Divide the broth, curd or shrimps, and vegetable leaves among 4 bowls. Serve hot, seasoned with the ginger.

Nutrients for 1 cup.

Calories: 22
Exchange: ½ vegetable

g	mg
carbohydrate: negligible	potassium: 32
protein: 2	sodium: 5
fat: 1	cholesterol: 0
fiber: negligible	

Alecha (Ethiopian Vegetable Stew)

Colored yellow with *erd* (turmeric), studded with veggies, and spiced with ginger and garlic, this is a relatively mild Ethiopian dish. "Alecha contrasts with our hot dishes," says an Ethiopian member of the Ethiopian Mission to the United Nations. Alecha is a traditional abstinence dish for the Coptic Christians who avoid meat and meat products before taking Communion.

For 5 servings

2 tablespoons unsaturated
    vegetable oil
2 medium onions, chopped
1 teaspoon *erd* (fresh) or
    ground turmeric
2–3 garlic cloves, minced
2–3 teaspoons fresh ginger,
    minced

4 carrots, scraped and
    chopped
1 large green bell pepper,
    seeded and chopped
3 potatoes, peeled and sliced
½ small cabbage, cut in
    chunks
Pinch salt (optional) and
    freshly ground white pepper

1. Heat the oil in a casserole and sauté the onions, adding the *erd*, garlic, and ginger after a few minutes.

2. Stir in the carrots, green pepper, potatoes, and cabbage. Cover the casserole, and cook over low heat to allow the vegetables to sweat for 5 minutes or so.

3. Uncover, and add just enough water to make a thick stew. Simmer until just tender but not mushy. Taste, and enhance seasonings to please your taste. Serve warm.

Nutrients for 1 cup.

Calories: 128
Exchanges: 1 starch/bread; 1 vegetable; ½ fat

g	mg
carbohydrate: 24	potassium: 506
protein: 3	sodium: 69
fat: 3	cholesterol: 0
fiber: 5	

Berner Linsensuppe
(Lentil Soup, Bern Style)

Now here's a pureed soup, spicy with nutmeg, to nourish you and also bring you near the Swiss Alps (at least, in spirit). Thanks are due to Myrtha Frick, Swiss nutritionist, who offers you the recipe.

For 4 servings

½ cup lentils
4 cups White Chicken Stock
   (page 98)
½ tablespoon unsalted
   margarine or butter

1 medium onion, finely
   minced
2 teaspoons vinegar
¼ teaspoon salt and freshly
   ground pepper
Grated nutmeg

1. In a soup pot, boil the lentils in the chicken stock for about 45 minutes or until tender.
2. Grind in a blender, and pour back into the pot.
3. Meanwhile, in a small skillet, heat the margarine, and sauté the onion until soft. Stir into the soup.
4. Season the soup with the vinegar, a pinch of salt and pepper, and some nutmeg. Taste to adjust seasonings. Heat thoroughly. Serve hot.

Nutrients for 1 cup.

Calories: 91
Exchanges: 1 starch/bread; ½ vegetable

g	mg
carbohydrate:13	potassium: 250
protein: 6	sodium: 141
fat: 2	cholesterol: 1
fiber: 2.5	

Faki (Hellenic Lentil Soup)

Spiced with herbs, faki is almost like a soul food for many Hellenes, including ancient poets. "For bulb-and-lentil soup is like ambrosia in the chilly cold," wrote Chrysippus in the third century B.C. Tomatoes found their way into the soup after Columbus's discovery of America. This recipe also appeared in my cookbook, *The Food of Greece.*

For 8 servings

1 cup lentils
1 medium onion, chopped
2–3 garlic cloves, chopped
1 stalk celery, chopped
3 fresh or 5 Italian-type plum
   tomatoes and juices
1 large bay leaf
4 sprigs fresh parsley

Fresh mint or basil or other
   favorite herb
¼ cup fine olive oil
Pinch salt and freshly ground
   pepper
3 tablespoons fine quality
   vinegar
Dried oregano for garnish

1. Wash lentils in a soup pot. Cover with 8 cups cold water, and bring to a boil. Cover the pot, turn off the heat, and let stand for an hour.

2. Bring to a boil, and stir in the onion, garlic, and celery. Cover, and simmer for 30 minutes.

3. Add the tomatoes, bay leaf, parsley, your favorite herb, and half the oil. Simmer for 30 minutes, stirring occasionally. Add enough water to make 8 cups. Remove the bay leaf.

4. Season the soup, and add the remaining oil. Taste, and adjust the seasonings. Serve hot with vinegar, and garnished with oregano rubbed between your palms.

Nutrients for ⅔ cup.

Calories: 129
Exchanges: 1 starch/bread; 1 fat

g	mg
carbohydrate: 13	potassium: 282.5
protein: 5	sodium: 21
fat: 7	cholesterol: 0
fiber: 2.5	

Cool Tropical Fruit Soup

This is a gem of a soup on a hot day. The blend of tropical fruits is ravishing. Serve in small bowls placed over lustrous green leaves and decorated with fresh flowers, if you have some.

For 4 servings

1 fresh mango	8 ice cubes
1 very ripe banana	4 slices fresh or canned
½ cup unsweetened pineapple	unsweetened pineapple
juice	Fresh mint leaves for garnish

1. Peel the mango and push the fruit without the pit through a food mill or strainer (about 1 cup puree). (You may save chopped mango to add later for some texture.) Place mango puree in a blender or food processor.

2. Peel, and mash the banana. Add to the mango puree.

3. Pour the pineapple juice into the blender or processor. Add the cubes, and grind until thoroughly mixed; measure, and pour enough ice water to make 4 cups. Divide among 4 chilled serving bowls.

4. Finely chop the pineapple, and divide into 4 portions. Stir each portion into the fruit puree. Dice the mango, if you have reserved any. Garnish each bowl with mint leaves. Serve chilled.

Nutrients for 1 cup.

Calories: 115
Exchanges: 2 fruit

g	mg
carbohydrate: 29	potassium: 323
protein: 1	sodium: 2
fat: negligible	cholesterol: 0
fiber: 3	

Sayur Lodeh
(Indonesian Eggplant Soup)

Indonesian herbs enhance this unusual eggplant soup, enriched with coconut milk. Plan Sayur Lodeh when you can afford to use a fat exchange in your diet.

For 4 servings

1 medium eggplant
1 medium onion, sliced
¼ teaspoon garlic, sliced
2 tablespoons shrimp or meat, chopped
½ tablespoon unsalted warm margarine
1 green bell pepper, sliced

1 medium tomato, chopped
1 daun salam or bay leaf
1 slice laos (galingale) (optional)
Pinch salt
1 cup White Chicken Stock (page 98) or water
½ cup Coconut Milk (pages 30–31)

1. Peel the eggplant, and cut into small cubes. Cover with water, and set aside to soak.

2. In a casserole, sauté the onion, garlic, and shrimp or meat in the warm margarine.

3. Add the green pepper, tomato, daun salam or bay leaf, and laos (if you are using it), a pinch of salt, and the stock. Stir in the coconut milk. Bring to a boil.

4. Drain the eggplant, and add to the soup with enough water to make 4 cups, if necessary. Simmer until tender. Serve hot.

Nutrients for 1 cup.

Calories: 81

Exchanges: 1 vegetable; 1 fat

g	mg
carbohydrate: 6	potassium: 171
protein: 3	sodium: 41
fat: 6	cholesterol: 11
fiber: 1.5	

Turkish Yogurt Soup

This scrumptious yogurt soup is like the one I tasted a long time ago in a Turkish restaurant in London that I cannot forget. I had eaten yogurt all my life but never thought of it in a soup. What an idea! What's more, the appetizer Tzatziki (page 40) is probably a related offspring—popular by different names throughout the Middle East.

For 4 servings

4 cups plain low-fat yogurt
1 large cucumber (preferably seedless), grated
1–2 garlic cloves, crushed
2 green onions, including green parts, chopped
1 tablespoon fresh parsley, finely chopped

1 tablespoon fresh mint, finely chopped
8 crushed ice cubes or 1 cup ice water
Freshly ground white pepper (optional)
Fresh parsley and mint leaves for garnish

1. Thicken the yogurt by draining through a dampened cheesecloth for about 15 minutes. Save the whey for a beverage.

2. Combine the yogurt, cucumber, garlic, onions, parsley, and mint in a bowl. Add the ice cubes or ice water. Stir, and refrigerate for a few hours.

3. Taste, and adjust the seasonings. If the mixture is too thick, add a few tablespoons of yogurt, milk, or ice water.

4. Spoon into chilled soup bowls. Garnish with parsley and mint leaves. Serve cold.

Nutrients for 1 cup.

Calories: 150
Exchanges: 1 vegetable; 1 low-fat milk

g	mg
carbohydrate: 17	potassium: 589
protein: 12	sodium: 160
fat: 3.5	cholesterol: 14
fiber: negligible	

Tom Yum Goong (Sour Shrimp Soup)

Seductively aromatic with magrood leaves, lemon grass, and kalanga (Thai seasonings), Tom Yum Goong is simply unforgettable. It is also hot! The recipe is from Prayong Voraragsa, a native of Bangkok, who re-creates delicious Thai dishes at Siam Orchid, his restaurant in Scarsdale, New York. If you cannot find these Thai ingredients, ask at a Thai restaurant or Asian market.

For 4 servings

18 small shrimps
1 stalk fresh lemon grass (or dried lemon grass)
2 magrood leaves (shiny green leaves, no substitute)
1 cup canned straw mushrooms, drained, or button mushrooms
1–2 tablespoons nampla (Tiparos fish sauce)

2–3 tablespoons lime or lemon juice
2 pieces kalanga (dried root, no substitute)
3–4 fresh red and green chilies, sliced, including seeds
2 sprigs fresh coriander or 2 green onions, chopped for garnish

1. Wash and shell the shrimps. Discard the veins, but don't remove the tails. (These are left on by many cooks, to add flavor to the stock, and thrown away after eating.)

2. Peel outer skin of the lemon grass, and cut into 1½-inch slices. If you are using the dried variety, soak the lemon grass in cold water.

3. In a saucepan, bring 4 cups cold water to a boil. Add the lemon grass, magrood leaves, and shrimps. Simmer for 3 minutes. Remove from heat. Add the mushrooms.

4. Season with nampla, lime juice, kalanga, and chilies. Bring to a boil, and simmer for a minute. Taste, and adjust seasonings. Serve hot, garnished with coriander or green onions.

**Nutrients for 1 cup without nampla fish sauce.
Check the label.**

Calories: 28
Exchange: 1 vegetable

g	mg
carbohydrate: 4	potassium: 205
protein: 4	sodium: 220.5
fat: negligible	cholesterol: 21
fiber: 2	

Aljotta (Maltese Fish Soup)

This delicious dish for a complete meal (soup and entrée) was contributed by the Consulate-General of Malta in New York.

For 6 servings

1 pound nonoily fish of any
  kind, left all in one piece
1 tablespoon unsaturated
  vegetable oil
1 large onion, chopped
Sprig fresh parsley, chopped,
  more for garnish

Sprig fresh mint, chopped,
  more for garnish
2 tomatoes, chopped, or
  1 tablespoon tomato paste
Salt and freshly ground white
  pepper
¼ cup long-grain rice
Lemon wedges for garnish

1. Wash, and dry the fish. Reserve while making the sauce.

2. Heat the oil in a casserole, and sauté the onion, parsley, and mint until the onion softens.

3. Stir in 6 cups hot water and the tomatoes. Simmer for 5 minutes. Season lightly with salt and pepper.

4. Add the fish. Continue simmering gently only until the fish is just tender, about 7 minutes. Test with a fork. Very carefully remove the fish to a warm platter.

5. Strain the cooking liquid into a soup pot. You should have 6 cups. Bring to a boil, and gradually add the rice. Cook for about 10 minutes until just tender. Divide into 6 soup cups. Serve hot, garnished with mint and parsley. Cut the fish into 6 equal parts. Serve fish as a separate course with the lemon and a crisp salad.

Nutrients for 1 cup.

Calories: 148
Exchanges: ½ starch/bread; 1½ lean meat; 1 vegetable

g	mg
carbohydrate: 10	potassium: 387
protein: 13	sodium: 87
fat: 6	cholesterol: 28
fiber: 1	

Sancocho Panameno
(Spicy Panamanian Stew)

Spicy with chilies and coriander, this is a rib-sticking stew and fun to serve with chunks cut from ears of corn—wonderful for a party! The recipe is from Maria Kanellopoulos, who was born in Panama of Hellenic parents, adaptable wherever you live. If you don't have cassava (manioc), which is available in Hispanic and Asian shops fresh or frozen, use potatoes.

For 10 servings

2 pounds chicken, segmented	2 green bell peppers, chopped
2 large onions, chopped	Salt and freshly ground white
2 fresh or canned green chilies	pepper
2 sprigs fresh coriander or	2 large ears fresh or frozen
parsley	corn
2 teaspoons dried oregano	1 pound zucchini, cut into
2 garlic cloves, minced	chunks
1 pound potatoes or cassava	10 small lemon wedges
4 tomatoes, chopped	

1. Wash the chicken pieces, and drop into a soup pot or casserole. Pour 10 cups water into the pot. Bring to a boil, and skim off all foam and fat rising to the surface. Lower heat, cover pot, and cook chicken for 10 minutes.

2. Add the onions, chilies, coriander or parsley, half the oregano, the garlic, cassava or potatoes, tomatoes, green peppers, and some salt and pepper. Simmer for 15 minutes.

3. Meanwhile, cut each ear of corn into 5 pieces. (Use a strong knife or cleaver; position it where you want to cut into the ear, and give the blunt edge a sharp whack with a mallet or the side of a wooden board.) Add the corn segments and zucchini to the stew. Continue cooking for about 10 minutes until chicken and vegetables are just tender. The stew should be soupy with lots of broth.

4. Crush the remaining oregano into the soup. Divide into 10 servings in soup bowls with broth, chicken, and vegetables in each serving. Serve hot, garnished with lemon wedges.

Nutrients for 1 cup.

Calories: 197
Exchanges: 2 lean meat; 1 vegetable; 1 fruit

g	mg
carbohydrate: 20.5	potassium: 610.5
protein: 15	sodium: 156
fat: 7	cholesterol: 40
fiber: 5	

Bermuda Mussel Stew

Jill Kempe of the Bermuda Diabetic Association shares this mussel stew. "As a diabetic person," she says, "I know the value of having [nutritional] information in a cookbook."

For 6 servings

2 teaspoons unsaturated
  margarine or unsalted butter
1 large onion, chopped
1 ounce salt pork, diced

1 pound shucked mussels
Pinch salt and freshly ground
  pepper
Fresh parsley, chopped

1. Heat the margarine in a saucepan, and sauté the onion and salt pork.
2. Add the mussels. Season with a little salt and pepper.
3. Pour in 6 cups water. Stew until mussels are tender, about 8 minutes. Divide evenly into 6 portions. Serve hot, sprinkled with parsley.

Nutrients for 1 cup.

Calories: 130
Exchanges: 1½ lean meat; 1 vegetable; 1 fat

g	mg
carbohydrate: 5	potassium: 310
protein: 12	sodium: 306
fat: 7.5	cholesterol: 33
fiber: 1	

Soupa Avgolemono (Egg-Lemon Soup)

The classic lemon-flavored soup of Greece is also popular in Cyprus. From the Diabetic Clinic in Paphos, nutritionist Moira Beaton sends a Cypriot recipe with a message: "A traditional Greek soup, it is usually made with the stock from a freshly boiled chicken. The chicken meat is eaten with the soup."

For 4 cups

4 cups White Chicken Stock (page 98) or 4 chicken bouillon cubes diluted in 4 cups water
4 tablespoons short-grain rice, washed
2 egg yolks
¼ cup (4 tablespoons) lemon juice
Salt and freshly ground pepper

1. In a saucepan, bring the stock to a boil; if you are using bouillon cubes, dissolve 4 in 4 cups water. Gradually add the rice, and simmer until just tender. Remove from heat.

2. In a bowl, beat the yolks until thick. Gradually add the lemon juice, and then, a spoonful at a time, some of the hot stock. Stirring constantly, gradually pour the egg-lemon mixture into the hot soup. Heat but do not boil (soup will curdle). Taste soup and season, adding more lemon juice, if necessary. Serve hot as a first course or shred the cooked chicken into the soup and serve as a principal luncheon dish.

Nutrients for 1 cup.

Calories: 90
Exchanges: ½ starch/bread; ½ medium-fat meat; ½ fruit

g	mg
carbohydrate: 12	potassium: 73
protein: 3	sodium: 39
fat: 3	cholesterol: 137
fiber: negligible	

Classic Chicken Soup

There's something about chicken soup! This easy and very flavorful version was sent to me by Golda Meir in 1972 when she was Prime Minister of Israel. The recipe here, her favorite chicken soup, is exactly as she offered it. Incidentally, many groups around the world enjoy this type of meal—a stew with meat or poultry and vegetables cooked in the same broth. They wouldn't dream of throwing away the food or the broth. You can remove the vegetables before they overcook.

For 10 servings

1 chicken (about 2½ pounds)
2 sprigs fresh parsley
1 stalk celery, cut in segments
2 medium onions, quartered
Pinch salt and freshly ground
   pepper

Pinch paprika
¼ cup long-grain rice
   (optional)
Knaidlach (page 90)

1. Wash the chicken, and place in a soup pot. Cover with 10 cups cold water, and bring to a boil. Skim off any foam that rises to the surface.

2. Drop in the parsley, celery, and onions. Season with a little salt, pepper, and a pinch of paprika. Simmer over low heat until the chicken is tender, about 1 hour.

3. Remove the chicken, and keep warm on a platter. Arrange the vegetables around the chicken.

4. Strain the broth, and skim off any fat on the surface. If you are serving rice, add it, and bring soup to a boil for another quarter of an hour.

5. Serve the soup hot with Knaidlach. Serve the chicken and vegetables separately.

Nutrients for 1 cup.

Calories: 107
Exchanges: 1½ lean meat; 1 vegetable

g	mg
carbohydrate: 5	potassium: 144
protein: 14	sodium: 56
fat: 3	cholesterol: 40
fiber: negligible	

Knaidlach

This is the recipe that the late Golda Meir generously contributed with her chicken soup. You can use them with any soup or with her own (page 89).

For 8 (1-inch) Knaidlach

2 matzoth
1 teaspoon vegetable oil
1 large onion, minced
1 tablespoon fresh parsley,
  chopped

2 eggs, lightly beaten
Pinch salt and freshly ground
  pepper

1. Crush the matzoth in a bowl; reserve 1 tablespoon matzo meal to use later. Cover matzoth in the bowl with cold water, and soak until soft; then squeeze dry, discarding the excess water. Place the soaked matzoth in a bowl, and reserve.

2. In a small skillet, heat the oil, and sauté the onion until translucent.

3. Add the onion to the soaked matzoth. Stir in the parsley, eggs, and pinches of salt and pepper. Mash with a fork to mix thoroughly.

4. Add enough matzo meal that the mixture can be formed into balls. Shape into small balls, and let stand for one hour.

5. Half an hour before you are planning to serve, drop the balls into the boiling soup. Cook for ½ hour. Serve hot.

Nutrients for 2 Knaidlach.

Calories: 176

Exchanges: 1½ starch/bread; ½ medium-fat meat; ½ vegetable

g	mg
carbohydrate: 25	potassium: 129
protein: 6	sodium: 229
fat: 4.5	cholesterol: 137
fiber: 10	

Scotch Broth

Enriched with barley, peas, and meat, and brightened with many vegetables, this "broth" is a really nutritious meal! It's wonderful to cook when you have the various vegetables on hand. Freeze cup portions for quick meals.

For about 10 cups

¼ cup dried peas
3 tablespoons barley
½ pound lean beef or lamb,
    cut into small cubes
1 large leek, washed and sliced
2–3 turnips, peeled and diced
2 carrots, scraped and diced

¼ pound kale, washed and
    finely chopped
Pinch salt and freshly ground
    pepper
½ carrot, grated, for garnish
2 tablespoons fresh parsley,
    chopped for garnish

1. The night before you cook, wash the peas and barley in separate bowls. Cover with cold water, and soak overnight. (If you forget to do this, cover the peas and barley with water, bring to a boil, turn off heat, and soak for 1 hour before cooking.)

2. Wash the beef or lamb in hot water. Then place the meat in a soup pot with about 5 cups cold water. Bring to a boil, and lower heat. Skim off foam and fat. Cook for 30 minutes.

3. Add the remaining ingredients according to how long each one takes to cook: First, add 5 cups water with the peas and barley; cook for 30 minutes. At that point, add the leek, turnips, and carrots; cook for 15 minutes. Then stir the kale into the soup when meat, peas, and barley are tender. Simmer for 5 minutes. (Total cooking time is 50 minutes.)

4. Taste, and adjust seasonings. Serve in a soup tureen, garnished with the grated carrot and chopped parsley.

Nutrients for 1 cup.

Calories: 97
Exchanges: ½ medium-fat meat; 2½ vegetable

g	mg
carbohydrate: 14	potassium: 245
protein: 7.5	sodium: 44
fat: 1	cholesterol: 13
fiber: 4	

Kenya Stew

The following typical stew of Kenya is a favorite recipe of Catherine Gatungo, a native of Kenya, who works in the Kenya Mission to the United
Nations in New York. Be sure to try her recipe of Kale and Red Peppers
(page 132) as an accompaniment. Catherine cooks the stew in both versions, with either beef or pinto beans and vegetables. You have the same
options.

For 6 servings

½ pound chuck beef or ½ cup
    pinto beans, soaked
    overnight
2 teaspoons unsaturated oil
2 large onions, chopped
Seasonings: 2 garlic cloves,
    1 bay leaf, paprika, curry
    powder

2 carrots, sliced
2 large stalks celery, sliced
1 very small potato
1 tablespoon tomato paste
    (optional)

1. If you are using the beef, cut it into bite-size cubes. If you are making
the stew of beans, cook them until almost tender. Drain the beans.

2. Begin the stew: In a casserole, heat the oil, and sauté the onions
until soft. Stir in the garlic, bay leaf, paprika, and curry powder to make
a flavorful mixture.

3. Drop the cubes of beef or the drained beans into the seasonings. Stir,
and cook over medium heat until thoroughly coated, about 4 minutes. Pour
in 6 cups water to cover the beans or meat. Simmer for 15 minutes.

4. Add the carrots, celery, and potato (as a thickener for the sauce).
Cook until beans or meat and vegetables are tender. Dilute the tomato
paste with a little of the stew liquid, and stir into the stew toward the end
of the cooking, for color and flavor. Mash the potato to thicken the sauce.
Serve hot with kale or plain.

Nutrients for 1 cup.

Calories: 129
Exchanges: 1 medium-fat meat; 2 vegetable

g	mg
carbohydrate: 9	potassium: 302
protein: 10	sodium: 71
fat: 6	cholesterol: 30
fiber: 2	

Maushauwa (Afghan Soup)

An exotic soup with extraordinary contrasts: colors dark, red, and white, textures thick and smooth, temperatures hot and cold. Yet it is made of ordinary ingredients. There's a base of assorted beans and rice, covered with a spicy tomato sauce featuring tiny meatballs (both hot), and a topping of Afghan Yogurt Chaka (nice and cold), garnished with mint.

You can make the bean mixture in advance and freeze it, to cut down last-minute preparation. Do the same for the meatball sauce. Cook the rice in the beans when you're ready to serve.

Since this is a rich soup, nutrients for both 6- or 8-portion sizes are included for the recipe. You can decide how to divide the soup on the basis of how many guests you have and how large each portion should be. Enjoy this unusual dish!

For 6–8 servings

¼ cup dried red kidney beans
¼ cup green split peas or mung beans
¼ cup lentils or yellow split peas
6 ounces extra lean ground beef
1–1½ teaspoons ground cinnamon
½–¾ teaspoon ground red pepper
Freshly ground black pepper
1 teaspoon unsaturated vegetable oil

1 medium onion or 3 green onions, minced
1 cup fresh tomatoes or canned, chopped
¼ cup white rice
Pinch salt
1–2 cups Afghan Yogurt Chaka (page 28)
¼ cup fresh mint leaves, chopped, or 1 tablespoon dried mint

1. Soak the beans, peas, and lentils by either method but soak them separately because they cook at different speeds. (a) Evening before you cook, in separate bowls: wash, cover with water, and soak overnight. Or (b) the same day you plan to cook: cover with water in pans, bring to boil, cook for 2 minutes, remove from heat, and soak for 1 hour.

2. Drain the kidney beans. Cover with 4 cups cold water and bring to a boil. Simmer for 20 minutes. Drain the peas, add them to the kidney beans along with 1 cup water. Cook for 20 minutes, stirring frequently. Drain lentils, and add to the beans and peas. Continue cooking until almost

(continued)

tender, about 20 to 25 minutes, adding water, if necessary to keep the mixture soupy. (Total cooking time is 60–65 minutes.)

3. While bean mixture cooks, make a meatball sauce with the next 7 ingredients. First, make the meatballs. In a bowl, mix the beef with enough cinnamon and red and black peppers to make a spicy flavor; knead thoroughly to distribute the spices. Break off tiny pieces and roll into 30 or 40 balls ½ inch in diameter, depending on whether you plan 6 or 8 servings (an easy way to do this is to line them up on your board in tens as you roll to keep track of the number).

4. Now make the tomato sauce: Heat the oil in a small skillet and sauté the onion. Add half to the bean mixture (for flavor). While skillet is still hot, sauté the tiny meatballs, shaking steadily to brown on all sides. Stir the tomatoes into the skillet. Add a little water, if needed to half-cover the meatballs. Lower heat, and simmer for 10 minutes, until sauce thickens. Taste, and season with more cinnamon and pepper. (It should be very spicy because the bean mixture is bland.)

5. To complete the maushauwa, stir the rice into the beans with enough water to cook the rice, and cook for 15 minutes, stirring frequently to prevent sticking, until rice is tender, about 15 minutes (don't overcook the rice). You should have 3 cups of the beans and rice; add water, if necessary. Taste the beans and rice, and if they are too bland, sprinkle with cinnamon and a pinch of salt.

6. To serve, ladle hot beans and rice into 6 or 8 bowls. Top each bowl with 5 meatballs and some sauce, divided among the bowls. Spoon 1 or 2 tablespoons Chaka over the top (remember to add the calories to your total) and sprinkle liberally with fresh or dried mint. Serve immediately.

**Nutrients for ⅙ recipe without
the Afghan Yogurt Chaka.**

Calories: 204
Exchanges: 1½ starch/bread; 1½ lean meat

g	mg
carbohydrate: 24	potassium: 472
protein: 14	sodium: 47
fat: 6	cholesterol: 24
fiber: 5	

Nutrients for ⅛ recipe without the Afghan Yogurt Chaka.

Calories: 153

Exchanges: 1 starch/bread; 1 lean meat; ½ vegetable

g	mg
carbohydrate: 18	potassium: 354
protein: 11	sodium: 35
fat: 4	cholesterol: 18
fiber: 4	

Ashe Reshte
(Persian Meatball-Noodle Soup)

Meatballs in many countries allow cooks to use their own distinctive seasonings. Tiny meatballs can be served as a main course, or as this recipe
suggests, in a hearty soup. By decreasing the amount of meat in the soup
and increasing the legumes and noodles, you can lower the proportion of
fat in this nutritious soup.

For 6 servings

¼ cup black-eyed peas
¼ cup lentils
¼ pound lean ground beef
1 small onion, grated
1 tablespoon Persian Spice
   Blend (page 34)

4 cups White Beef Stock
   (page 99) or water
¼ cup noodles
Small handful fresh parsley,
   chopped

1. In a small bowl, wash the black-eyed peas and cover with cold water.
Soak overnight.

2. When you are ready to cook, put lentils in a small saucepan and
cover with cold water. Bring to a boil. Remove from heat. Cover pan, and
let lentils swell while you make the meatballs.

3. Mix the ground beef, onion, and 1 teaspoon of the spice blend in a
small bowl. Work mixture for a few minutes to blend ingredients. Then
divide meat into 18 parts, and roll each part into a small meatball.

4. In a saucepan, bring 2 cups water to a boil. Add the meatballs and
very slowly simmer for 15 minutes. Life meatballs with a slotted spoon
and keep warm. Discard the cooking water. (This step eliminates much of
the fat.)

5. To cook the soup: Bring the stock or water to a boil. Drain the black-
eyed peas, and add to the stock. (Discard the water the peas have soaked
in.) Simmer for 15 minutes or until almost tender.

6. Add the lentils and their soaking water, and cook for 25 minutes
longer.

7. Drop the meatballs and noodles into the soup. Season with 1 teaspoon of the spice blend. Simmer until noodles are tender but not mushy.

8. Stir in half the parsley. Taste soup, and flavor it to please your taste
and needs. Ladle soup into 6 bowls with 3 meatballs in each. Serve hot,
garnished with the remaining parsley, and pass the spice blend at the
table.

Nutrients for 1 cup.

Calories: 170

Exchanges: ½ starch/bread; 1 medium-fat meat; 2 vegetable

g	mg
carbohydrate: 19	potassium: 348
protein: 13	sodium: 25.5
fat: 5	cholesterol: 23
fiber: 5	

White Chicken Stock

A rich, low-calorie stock without fat for your soups and sauces. By keeping homemade stocks in your freezer, you can quickly prepare soups and snacks without the high sodium in canned broth.

For 2 quarts (8 cups)

3–3½ pounds chicken necks,
  backs, wings, bones
1 stalk celery, chopped
1 medium onion or 2 shallots,
  chopped
½ leek, chopped
1 small carrot

8–10 mushroom stems
1 scant teaspoon white
  peppercorns
Herbs: 2 small bay leaves,
  2 fresh parsley and thyme
  sprigs

1. Chop the chicken parts into small pieces. Wash, and place in a soup pot. Cover with 4 quarts cold water. Gradually bring to a boil. Skim off all foam and fat that rise to the surface.

2. Add the remaining ingredients. Simmer for 40 minutes. Degrease the fat on the surface.

3. Dampen a double cheesecloth, and drape over a strainer. Set the strainer over a 3-quart saucepan. Pour the stock and bones directly into the cheesecloth, and let the stock drip into the pan. Discard the bones and save remaining chicken and vegetables for another use.

4. Boil the stock until it is reduced to 2 quarts. Cool and refrigerate. Discard all fat that congeals on the surface. Use within 3 days. Or freeze in 1-cup portions. Be sure to label the stock, and date it. Use within 3 months.

Nutrients for 1 cup.

Calories: 11
Exchange: ½ vegetable

g	mg
carbohydrate: 1	potassium: 21
protein: negligible	sodium: 4
fat: negligible	cholesterol: 0
fiber: 0	

White Beef Stock

I learned to make this clarified beef stock from Hermann Reiner, executive chef of the Windows on the World restaurants at the World Trade Center in New York. This excellent chef, who was born in Austria and worked in many countries before coming to the United States, suggests this method of rinsing the bones in hot water and pouring off the first boiled water to produce a clear stock. Freeze this and other stocks; be sure to label and date the stock and to use it within 3 months.

For 1½ quarts (6 cups)

3 pounds beef bones, chopped
    in small pieces
1 stalk celery, chopped
1 leek, chopped
1 carrot, chopped
1 medium onion, chopped

Herbs: 1 large bay leaf,
    2–3 fresh parsley stems,
    2 thyme sprigs
2 ripe tomatoes
1 teaspoon white peppercorns

1. Wash the bones with hot water. In a soup pot, cover bones with cold water. Bring to a boil. Pour off the water. Add 3 quarts (12 cups) cold water. Bring to a boil, and skim off all foam rising to the surface.

2. Add the remaining ingredients, and very slowly bring to a boil. Simmer for 1½ hours. From time to time, degrease the stock.

3. Strain stock through double cheesecloth draped over a strainer directly into another pot.

4. Boil stock until reduced to 1½ quarts. Cool, and refrigerate. Discard all fat that congeals on the surface. Use within 3 days. Or freeze in 1-cup portions, and use within 3 months. Be sure to label the stock, and date it.

Nutrients for 1 cup.

Calories: 13
Exchange: ½ vegetable

g	mg
carbohydrate: 1.5	potassium: 24
protein: negligible	sodium: 5
fat: negligible	cholesterol: 1
fiber: 0	

White Fish Stock

Use this stock to make delicious fish soups and sauces. Your local fish market will have fish bones (from filleted fish) and heads for a nominal (if any) charge.

For 1½ quarts (6 cups)

3 pounds nonoily fish bones and heads, cut into small pieces (sole, flounder, snapper, etc.)
½ cup dry white wine
3 small shallots, chopped
½ small carrot, chopped

1 stalk celery, chopped
½ leek, chopped (optional)
7–8 mushroom stems
½ teaspoon white peppercorns
Herbs: 2 bay leaves, 2 sprigs fresh parsley, 2 sprigs fresh thyme

1. Wash the fish bones and heads, and drop into a soup pot. Add 3 quarts (12 cups) cold water. Slowly bring to a boil. Skim off all foam rising to the surface.

2. Add the wine, shallots, carrot, celery, leek (if you have one), mushroom stems, peppercorns, and herbs. Simmer stock for 30 minutes.

3. Dampen a double cheesecloth, and drape it over a fine strainer. Set the strainer over another saucepan. Strain the stock directly into the cheesecloth. Let it drip into the pan. Discard remains in the cheesecloth.

4. Boil the stock over medium heat until reduced to about half the original amount, or 6 cups. Cool the stock. Discard any fat on the surface. Freeze in 1-cup portions. (This is a very flavorful stock. You can add salt when you use the stock, but you probably won't need to.)

Nutrients for 1 cup.

Calories: 11
Exchange: ½ vegetable

g	mg
carbohydrate: 1	potassium: 20
protein: negligible	sodium: 4
fat: negligible	cholesterol: 1
fiber: 0	

SALADS AND
DRESSINGS

**Eat and drink,
and put what is left
in a palmetto bag.**
MOORISH PROVERB

Mesclun

Mesclun is a beautiful salad of *raw* leafy greens, blossoms, and herbs for you to serve during "high season" when such varieties are plentiful. The salad has recently become popular in some upscale restaurants. Where did Mesclun originate? In Nice, France—among people of Italian ancestry, according to Romeo de Gobbi of Le Cirque restaurant in New York. The salad "has been around a long time," he says. The word *mesclun* comes from the Italian word *mescolare* (to mix). That definition tells the story! To mix Mesclun, toss together many different color and flavor combinations—tender or rough, crisp, mild, peppery, nutty, red, yellow, light green, deep green, and more. Toss your own masterpiece. Double and triple the amounts for a larger party.

For 4 servings

1 cup loose-leaf salad (butterhead, garden, Boston, Bibb)

1 cup spinach or a mixture of dandelion greens and carrot tops (deep green)

½ cup amaranth, young beet leaves, red cabbage (red)

1 cup Chinese (bok choy) or celery cabbage or cabbage leaves

1 cup young turnip or mustard leaves, chicory (curly-leaf endive), escarole (bitter)

1 cup romaine or iceberg lettuce

1 cup watercress or arugula

½ cup sorrel or sour dock

1 cup herb leaves and blossoms: basil, mint, parsley, coriander, oregano, thyme, tarragon, chervil, nasturtium, etc.

Lemon Dressing (page 121) seasoned lightly with salt and pepper, or plain lemon juice or vinegar

1. Wash, dry, and snip or tear the leafy greens into bite-size pieces. Wrap in a dry kitchen towel, and refrigerate until ready to serve.

2. Select a very simple dressing, and season lightly with salt and pepper.

3. Just before serving, toss salad in a bowl. Divide into 4 servings. Serve cold.

**Nutrients for 1 serving (2 cups)
without dressing.**

Calories: 32

Exchange: 1 vegetable

g	mg
carbohydrate: 6	potassium: 412
protein: 3	sodium: 31
fat: negligible	cholesterol: 0
fiber: 5	

Carrot Salad

A refreshing salad and quick to make, this recipe is inspired by one in Israel. The carrots make this salad high in vitamin A.

For 6 servings

2 cups carrot, shredded
¼ cup black raisins
1 small apple, peeled and slivered

1 cup sliced cantaloupe or melon, slivered
3 tablespoons orange juice

Combine all ingredients in a bowl. Refrigerate for a few hours until the raisins absorb the juice. Divide into 6 parts on salad plates on crisp lettuce. Serve cold.

Nutrients for 1 serving.

Calories: 58

Exchange: 1 fruit

g	mg
carbohydrate: 14	potassium: 283
protein: negligible	sodium: 16
fat: negligible	cholesterol: 0
fiber: 2	

Horiatiki Salata
(Hellenic Village Salad)

The most colorful raw salad of Greece can be your favorite whenever these vegetables are in season.

For 8 servings

4–5 firm, ripe tomatoes
1 garlic clove, cut
1 large cucumber, peeled and cut in chunks
2 medium green bell peppers, seeded and sliced
3 green onions or 1 large onion, sliced
Greek olives, preferably Kalamata type, rinsed

2 ounces feta, broken into small chunks
1 tablespoon fine olive oil
2 tablespoons vinegar (optional)
Freshly ground pepper (optional)
Dried oregano for garnish

1. Peel and slice the tomatoes in eighths, and place in a large salad bowl that has been rubbed with the cut garlic.

2. Drop the cucumber, peppers, onions, olives, and feta into the bowl.

3. Whisk the oil and vinegar (if you are using it) and pepper (if you are using it) to make a dressing. Toss into the salad. Rub the oregano into your palms over the salad. Divide into 8 equal portions. Serve cold.

Nutrients for 1 serving with vinegar.

Calories: 61
Exchanges: 1 vegetable; 1 fat

g	mg
carbohydrate: 5.5	potassium: 237
protein: 2	sodium: 113
fat: 4	cholesterol: 6
fiber: 1.5	

Salade Sabzi (Persian Salad)

The fresh herbs and radishes stimulate flavor surprises in this crisp raw salad.

For 4 servings

1 garlic clove, cut in half	3 radishes, finely sliced
1 head crisp lettuce (romaine, iceberg, etc.)	½ cup fresh parsley, chopped
	¼ cup fresh dill, chopped
2 ripe medium tomatoes, sliced or quartered	½ cup fresh mint, chopped
	Lemon Dressing (page 121) or
3 green onions, finely sliced	another dressing

1. Rub a salad bowl with the cut garlic.
2. Wash the lettuce, and dry thoroughly. Break into small pieces, and drop into the salad bowl. Add the tomatoes, onions, radishes, parsley, dill, and mint.
3. Toss with the dressing. Divide into 4 portions, and serve immediately.

Nutrients for 1 serving without dressing.

Calories: 29
Exchange: 1 vegetable

g	mg
carbohydrate: 6	potassium: 317.5
protein: 2	sodium: 14
fat: negligible	cholesterol: 0
fiber: 2	

German Endive Salad

Delicately slivered endive and onion are livened by a simple and flavorful dressing. It is the extremely fine slicing of endive that makes the salad unusual, and also reduces the toughness of the leaves.

For 4 servings

1 bunch crisp curly-leaf
  endive
1 small onion
2 tablespoons olive or other
  unsaturated vegetable oil

3 tablespoons lemon juice,
  more to taste
Salt (optional) and freshly
  ground pepper

1. Trim endive, separate leaves, and wash thoroughly. Drain, and dry the leaves. With a very sharp knife or processor, very finely slice the endive, and place in a bowl.

2. Very finely sliver the onion, and add to the endive. Toss until well mixed.

3. To make the dressing, whisk together the oil and lemon juice. Mix in a pinch of salt (if you are using it) and pepper. Just before serving, drizzle over the salad, and toss lightly. Taste, and adjust seasonings. Divide into 4 portions, and arrange on salad plates. Serve cold.

Nutrients for 1 serving.

Calories: 77
Exchanges: ½ vegetable; 1½ fat

g	mg
carbohydrate: 4	potassium: 209
protein: negligible	sodium: 43
fat: 7	cholesterol: 0
fiber: 2	

Chinese Sprout Salad

This salad is a great use for bean sprouts—homemade or store-bought. To make your own sprouts: Rinse a small handful of mung beans or soybeans in a jar; cover with cheesecloth; place jar on its side in a kitchen closet near the sink; rinse beans 2 to 3 times daily and drain off all the water. The beans will sprout in a few days and triple in volume. Store in the refrigerator.

For 2 servings

1 cup fresh bean sprouts
1 teaspoon peanut oil
5–6 white peppercorns
1–2 tablespoons rice wine
   vinegar

Pinch sugar (optional)
2 teaspoons soy sauce
1 green onion, including green
   part, thinly sliced

1. You may serve the sprouts raw or steamed. If you steam them, cook in a steamer for about 5 minutes. Chill the sprouts quickly in ice water. Drain, and transfer to a bowl.

2. Heat the oil in a very small pan, and add the peppercorns. Cook gently for a few minutes. Then add the vinegar, sugar (if you are using it), and soy sauce. Stir thoroughly. Remove the peppercorns.

3. Pour sauce over the sprouts. Add the green onion, and toss to mix thoroughly. Serve cold.

Nutrients for 1 serving.

Calories: 54
Exchanges: 1½ vegetable; ½ fat

g	mg
carbohydrate: 11	potassium: 215
protein: 1.5	sodium: 8.5
fat: 2.5	cholesterol: 0
fiber: 2	

Salada de Abacate
(Brazilian Avocado Salad)

Unforgettable when it was served to us in Brazil by a friend who is also a fine cook, this salad is easy to make at home and delicious with fish and seafood dishes.

For 2 servings

1 ripe medium avocado, peeled and diced
1 medium onion, minced
2 garlic cloves, minced or crushed

Juice of 1 lemon, strained, more if necessary
1 tablespoon fresh dill, chopped
Lettuce or cabbage leaves for garnish

1. In a bowl, combine all the ingredients except the lettuce. Taste, and add more lemon juice, if you like.

2. Cover salad, and refrigerate for several hours.

3. To serve: Place the lettuce or cabbage leaves on 2 salad plates. Scoop half the salad on each leaf. Serve cold.

Nutrients for 1 serving.

Calories: 130
Exchanges: ½ vegetable; ½ fruit; ½ fat

g	mg
carbohydrate: 11	potassium: 552
protein: 2	sodium: 18
fat: 10	cholesterol: 0
fiber: 3	

Carrot, Celery, and Apple Salad

A crispy and fiberful salad, very easy to whip up, is suggested by the Zentralinstitut für Diabetes in East Germany.

For 4 servings

3½ cups carrots, peeled and
  grated
2 medium stalks celery, peeled
  and grated

1 large apple, grated
2 tablespoons lemon juice
Noncaloric sweetener

1. In a bowl, combine the carrots, celery, and apple.
2. Drizzle with lemon juice and sweetener to suit your taste, and toss. Divide among 4 salad plates. Serve cold.

Nutrients for 1 serving.

Calories: 66
Exchanges: ½ vegetable; 1 fruit

g	mg
carbohydrate: 16	potassium: 421
protein: 1	sodium: 55
fat: negligible	cholesterol: 0
fiber: 4	

Tabbouleh

Lebanese mint-and-parsley salad is beautiful and edible and looks like a mosaic. Serve tabbouleh on lettuce that can be rolled around the salad and eaten with fingers—and watch it disappear.

For 8 servings

⅓ cup medium bulgur (cracked wheat)

4 cups firm ripe tomatoes, peeled and finely diced

1 cup green onions including green parts, finely cut

1 cup fresh mint, finely minced

¾ cup fresh parsley, finely minced

1 tablespoon fine olive oil

¼ cup fresh lemon juice

Pinch salt (optional) and freshly ground pepper

8 romaine lettuce leaves

Fresh mint and parsley leaves for garnish

1. Spread the bulgur in a bowl. Pour in only enough boiling water to cover bulgur. Let stand for 15 minutes until bulgur is swollen, and water is absorbed. If the water is not absorbed, drain thoroughly.

2. Combine the tomatoes, green onions, mint, parsley, and swollen bulgur in a serving bowl.

3. Make a dressing using the oil, lemon juice, pinch of salt (if you are using it), and pepper. Toss the dressing with the salad. Taste, and adjust the seasonings.

4. Set the romaine leaves on 8 plates. Divide the salad evenly. Serve chilled, garnished with fresh mint and parsley leaves.

Nutrients for ½ cup.

Calories: 48

Exchanges: 1 vegetable; ½ fat

g	mg
carbohydrate: 7	potassium: 163
protein: 1	sodium: 20
fat: 2	cholesterol: 0
fiber: 1	

Salade Niçoise

When I first enjoyed Salad Niçoise in Paris, I immediately wrote notes about it. That was on my first visit to Paris. I had only been married for a few years, and we lived in Europe at the time. It may have been that recipe that started me off as a food researcher and writer.

Although this salad originated in Nice, it is made throughout France and also in other countries. When I first sampled it, I thought it would make a wonderful meal. It does. I hope you agree. Plan it for a large family or neighborhood gathering. They'll love it.

For 8 servings

1 garlic clove, cut
4 ripe tomatoes, peeled and quartered
1 seedless cucumber, peeled and sliced
1 cup green onions, thinly sliced
2 potatoes, cooked, peeled, and thinly sliced

½ cup tuna fish (packed in water)
8 black olives, preferably Niçoise
1 hard-cooked egg, sliced
2 tablespoons olive oil
Pinch salt and freshly ground pepper
Fresh basil leaves, chopped
4 anchovies (optional)

1. Rub a salad bowl with the cut garlic. Combine tomatoes, cucumber, onions, potatoes, tuna, olives, and egg in the bowl.

2. In a cup, mix the oil, pinch of salt, pepper, and basil to make a dressing. Toss lightly with the salad. Chill for a few hours.

3. Divide the salad evenly among 8 plates. Garnish each with ½ anchovy, if you wish. Serve cold.

Nutrients for 1 serving with 1 anchovy.

Calories: 94
Exchanges: ½ starch/bread; ½ lean meat; ½ fat

g	mg
carbohydrate: 8	potassium: 333
protein: 5	sodium: 159
fat: 5	cholesterol: 41
fiber: 2	

Lotus Rhizome Salad

All parts of the lotus are used by the Chinese cook. The huge and graceful leaf is often used to wrap meat and rice fillings before steaming them. Lotus seeds make savory snacks. But the rhizome is probably the most useful, eaten steamed and marinated. In cross-sections, the flesh can be seen lacy and white, the texture crisp.

Lotus rhizomes are available in Chinese markets. If you don't see them, be sure to ask. Lotus rhizomes are kept refrigerated in shops during warm weather.

For 4 servings

1 lotus rhizome (about 7 inches   Soy Dressing (page 123) or
    long) or 2 smaller ones   another dressing

1. When ready to cook: Wash, and peel the lotus. Cut across into very thin slices, and plunge these immediately into a bowl filled with cold water to prevent discoloration.

2. In a saucepan, bring to a boil enough water to cover the lotus. As soon as the water boils, drain the lotus, and pour the boiling water over it. Soak for 5 minutes.

3. Drain the lotus, and rinse in cold water. Dry on a towel. You may use it in soups or stir-fries. In salads, pour dressing over the lotus, and marinate in the refrigerator before serving. Serve cold.

Nutrients for 10 slices (3 ounces).

Calories: 59
Exchange: 1 starch/bread

g	mg
carbohydrate: 14	potassium: 323
protein: 1	sodium: 40
fat: negligible	cholesterol: 0
fiber: negligible	

Salada de Palmito e Batatas
(Brazilian Palm Heart and Potato Salad)

Enjoy the whiteness of palm hearts and potatoes dappled with green peas, fresh dill, and black olives in a smooth, lemony dressing. Make a day in advance.

For 4 servings

2 medium potatoes
2 cups hearts of palm, thinly
  sliced
2 Spanish black olives, rinsed,
  pitted, and chopped
1 hard-cooked egg, chopped
¼ cup fresh or frozen green
  peas, cooked
1 onion, diced

1 tablespoon fresh dill,
  chopped
2 tablespoons reduced-calorie
  mayonnaise
1 tablespoon lemon juice,
  more to taste
Garnish: fresh dill, chopped;
  2 olives, rinsed, pitted, and
  sliced

1. Cook the potatoes in their jackets in lightly salted water. Peel, and dice. Place in a bowl.

2. Gently mix in the next 6 ingredients.

3. Stir together the mayonnaise and lemon juice in a cup. Toss into the salad. Chill the salad in the refrigerator overnight.

4. When ready to serve, divide into 4 portions on plates. Garnish attractively with the dill and the olive slices.

Nutrients for 1 serving.

Calories: 74
Exchanges: ½ starch/bread; 1 vegetable

g	mg
carbohydrate: 12	potassium: 158 (without the palm)
protein: 3	sodium: 71 (without the palm)
fat: 2	cholesterol: 32
fiber: 2	

Boiled Vegetable Salad

"This recipe makes good use of Cyprus's famous vegetables. The beets give the dish its rosy color," says Moira Beaton, nutritionist in the Diabetic Clinic in Paphos, Cyprus, who generously contributed her version of the colorful and delicious recipe for this book. She suggests you serve it as a main dish for lunch or as a salad with another meal. This is another salad high in vitamin A.

For 6 servings

2 medium potatoes, scrubbed
2 beets, unpeeled
2 carrots, scraped
2 onions
2 medium stalks celery with leaves
2 small zucchini, thickly sliced
Salt and freshly ground pepper

2 tablespoons low-calorie French dressing
1–2 garlic cloves, crushed
2 hard-cooked eggs, finely chopped
1 tablespoon fresh parsley, finely chopped

1. Combine all the vegetables except the zucchini in a large saucepan. Add water to cover, season with a little salt and pepper, and cook until vegetables are somewhat tender but still firm.

2. Tuck the zucchini into the pan, and continue cooking until all vegetables are al dente. Drain and cool the vegetables.

3. When you are ready to serve, peel the potatoes and beets, and cut into chunks or slices. Slice the carrots thickly, and dice the onions. Chop the celery and leaves. Place all the vegetables in a salad bowl.

4. To season the vegetables: Mix the dressing and garlic in a cup, and gently toss with the vegetables.

5. With your fingers, lightly blend the chopped eggs and parsley. Sprinkle over the vegetables. Divide salad among 6 plates. Serve cold.

Nutrients for 1 serving.

Calories: 124
Exchanges: 1 starch/bread; ½ medium-fat meat; ½ vegetable

g	mg
carbohydrate: 18.5	potassium: 576
protein: 4	sodium: 153
fat: 4	cholesterol: 91
fiber: 5	

Spinach with Tofu, Japanese Style

Akiyo Tsukahara of Tokyo and Osaka, currently living in New York, offers this cool green salad studded with crumbled tofu and bonito. Spinach makes this recipe high in vitamin A.

For 4 servings

10 ounces fresh or frozen
  spinach
Salt
2 tablespoons shaved bonito
  (kezuribushi) (optional)

1 tofu (4 ounces) (momendofu)
2 tablespoons low-sodium soy
  sauce for dipping

1. Wash, and trim fresh spinach. If you are using frozen spinach, partially thaw before cooking. Boil spinach in salted water until just tender, about 2 minutes. Drain, and rinse immediately in cold water. Cut in 1-inch pieces.

2. In a bowl, thoroughly mix the spinach with the shaved bonito. Refrigerate until ready to serve.

3. Discard excess water from the tofu. Refrigerate tofu until ready to serve.

4. Just before serving, crumble the tofu with your fingers, and mix with the spinach and bonito (if you are using it). Divide into 4 portions. Serve immediately, and pass the soy sauce.

Nutrients for 1 serving without bonito with ½ tablespoon soy sauce for each serving.

Calories: 48
Exchanges: ½ medium-fat meat; ½ vegetable

g	mg
carbohydrate: 5	potassium: 463.5
protein: 6	sodium: 365
fat: 1	cholesterol: 0
fiber: 2	

Kartoffelsalat
(Potato Salad, German Style)

I adapted the universally popular potato salad from a recipe originally published in Dr. P. Dieterle's book, *Diät bei Zuckerkrankheit*, in Munich by the German Diabetes Association.

For 4 servings

4 medium potatoes
Pinch salt
1 medium onion, finely
  minced
1 medium dill pickle, chopped
½ teaspoon capers, rinsed
  (optional)

½ cup White Chicken Stock
  (page 98) or water
1 tablespoon vegetable oil
2 teaspoons spicy mustard
1 tablespoon vinegar or lemon
  juice
Freshly ground pepper

1. Cook the potatoes in their jackets in lightly salted water.
2. When the potatoes are cooked and cool enough to handle, peel and slice them, and drop them into a bowl.
3. In a small bowl, whisk the remaining ingredients. Taste, and adjust seasonings. Pour dressing over the potatoes, and marinate for 30 minutes before serving the salad. Serve warm or cold.

Nutrients for 1 serving without capers.

Calories: 146

Exchanges: 1½ starch/bread; ½ vegetable; ½ fat

g	mg
carbohydrate: 26	potassium: 473
protein: 3	sodium: 298
fat: 4	cholesterol: 0
fiber: 3	

Asparagus with Tomato

Everyone enjoys asparagus. Try this attractive arrangement described by Angela Vera, a dietitian with the Association of Diabetics of Uruguay.

For 4 servings

1 pound asparagus	1 tablespoon unsaturated
4 medium ripe tomatoes	vegetable oil
2 hard-cooked eggs	Juice of 1 lemon
	Salt and freshly ground pepper

1. Trim the asparagus. Place asparagus on a steamer, and steam until bright green and tender but not mushy. Arrange asparagus on a platter.

2. Slice the tomatoes in circles or quarters. Set them around the asparagus. Peel, and slice the eggs in half. Tuck eggs between tomato slices.

3. In a small bowl, mix the oil, lemon juice, and a pinch of salt and pepper. Pour over the vegetables. Divide equally among 4 plates with a half egg per serving. Serve cold.

Nutrients for 1 serving.

Calories: 128

Exchanges: ½ medium-fat meat; 2 vegetable; 1 fat

g	mg
carbohydrate: 12	potassium: 671.5
protein: 7	sodium: 80
fat: 7	cholesterol: 137
fiber: 4	

Russian Cucumber Salad

One of the many tempting salads of the *zakuska* (Russian appetizer tray), this is a New World adaptation of the Old World favorite.

For 4 servings

2 medium cucumbers	1 teaspoon prepared mustard
2 tablespoons vinegar,	(not too hot)
preferably white wine	⅓ cup diet sour cream
1 hard-cooked egg	Freshly grated white pepper
	Fresh dill for garnish

1. Peel, halve, and seed the cucumbers (if the seeds are large). Slice cucumbers thin, and drop into a bowl. Sprinkle with 2 tablespoons of the vinegar, and marinate for about 30 minutes.

2. Meanwhile, separate the egg. Slice the white into thin strips, and set aside until later.

3. For the dressing: Rub the egg yolk through a sieve directly into a small bowl. Gradually beat in the remaining vinegar, the mustard, sour cream, and a generous grating of pepper. Refrigerate until ready to toss.

4. When ready to serve, drain the cucumber slices on paper towels. Toss cucumbers in a bowl with the egg white strips and the dressing. Serve cold, garnished with chopped dill.

Nutrients for 1 serving.

Calories: 49

Exchanges: ½ medium-fat meat; ½ vegetable

g	mg
carbohydrate: 4	potassium: 105
protein: 3	sodium: 54
fat: 2.5	cholesterol: 68
fiber: negligible	

Cucumber Raita

This is an absolutely superb mate for curries and flat breads. If you like the raita even spicier, shower it with more cumin and cayenne than indicated.

For 2 servings

1 cucumber, peeled, seeded, and coarsely grated
½ small onion, finely chopped
1 cup plain low-fat yogurt
½ teaspoon unsaturated vegetable oil
¼ teaspoon ground cumin
Pinch of cayenne pepper
¼ teaspoon mustard seed
Fresh coriander, chopped

1. In a bowl, mix the cucumber, onion, and yogurt.

2. Heat the oil in a small skillet. Fry the cumin, cayenne, and mustard, stirring constantly over low heat for a few minutes until the mustard seed begins to pop.

3. Remove skillet from the heat, and quickly add a spoonful of the yogurt mixture. Mix this into the remaining yogurt mixture in the bowl. Serve chilled, topped with coriander.

Nutrients for ½ cup.

Calories: 97
Exchanges: 1½ vegetable; ½ low-fat milk

g	mg
carbohydrate: 11	potassium: 382
protein: 6.5	sodium: 82.5
fat: 3	cholesterol: 7
fiber: 1	

Vinaigrette

Here is Escoffier's classic formula! It's a balancing act—between oil and vinegar. If you reduce the proportion of tablespoons of oil to vinegar, you'll cut fat and calories. Many contemporary chefs prefer 50/50 for oil and vinegar. Experiment, especially if you are using balsamic vinegar.

For 8 servings

3 tablespoons olive or other
  unsaturated vegetable oil
1 tablespoon vinegar
Pinch salt and freshly ground
  pepper

Herb (parsley, tarragon,
  chervil, etc.) when
  appropriate (optional)

Mix 3 parts oil with 1 part vinegar. Season with salt, pepper, and herb (if you are using it).

Nutrients for ½ tablespoon.

Calories: 90
Exchanges: 2 fat

g	mg
carbohydrate: negligible	potassium: 4
protein: 0	sodium: 27
fat: 10	cholesterol: 0
fiber: 0	

Spicier Vinaigrette

Here's a zestier version with a lower proportion of fat calories. Make in advance, and keep in your refrigerator.

For 8 servings

4 tablespoons olive oil
3 tablespoons red wine vinegar
Dash Dijon or Dusseldorfer
  mustard

1 garlic clove, cut in half
  lengthwise
Pinch dried oregano or thyme
Pinch salt and freshly ground
  pepper

Mix all ingredients in a jar or bowl. Taste, and adjust seasonings. Store in refrigerator. Pour as much as you need into the bowl. For even more punch, rub your salad bowl with cut garlic before tossing the salad.

Nutrients for ½ tablespoon.

Calories: 61
Exchanges: 1½ fat

g	mg
carbohydrate: negligible	potassium: 11
protein: 0	sodium: 15
fat: 7	cholesterol: 0
fiber: 0	

Lemon Dressing

Here's a delicious lemony dressing for any crisp salad.

For 8 servings

¼ cup olive oil
3 tablespoons lemon juice
1 garlic clove, crushed
   (optional)

Pinch salt and freshly ground
   pepper

Mix all ingredients in a jar or bowl. Taste, and adjust seasonings. Shake or whip just before tossing salad.

Nutrients for ½ tablespoon with garlic.

Calories: 61
Exchanges: 1½ fat

g	mg
carbohydrate: negligible	potassium: 7
protein: negligible	sodium: 15
fat: 7	cholesterol: 0
fiber: 0	

Yogurt Dressing

Here's a dressing that's zippier and lower in calories than mayonnaise. You may double the recipe if you have the yogurt on hand and can use it in a few days.

For 4 servings

½ cup low-fat plain yogurt
1 garlic clove, crushed or
    minced
Small piece cucumber, diced
    or grated (optional)
1 tablespoon fresh parsley,
    chopped

1 tablespoon fresh mint,
    chopped
Dash hot mustard
Small piece red or green bell
    pepper, diced
Freshly ground white pepper

1. In a small bowl, mix all the ingredients. Add just enough crushed ice or ice water to create a pouring consistency for the dressing.

2. Refrigerate for a few hours before serving to allow the seasonings to permeate the yogurt. Serve chilled over crisp salads.

Nutrients for 2 tablespoons.

Calories: 20
Exchange: ½ vegetable

g	mg
carbohydrate: 2	potassium: 74
protein: 2	sodium: 23
fat: negligible	cholesterol: 2
fiber: negligible	

Soy Dressing

Keep this flavorful dressing on hand for bean sprouts, lotus root, and other seasonal vegetables.

For about ½ cup

4 tablespoons peanut oil
6 tablespoons rice wine vinegar
1 teaspoon black peppercorns
Pinch sugar

1 small green onion, minced
1 tablespoon low-sodium soy sauce

In a jar with a lid, shake all the ingredients. Store in the refrigerator until needed. Strain, and drizzle over the salad.

Nutrients for 1 tablespoon.

Calories: 45
Exchanges: 1 vegetable; ½ fat

g	mg
carbohydrate: 6	potassium: 102
protein: negligible	sodium: 39
fat: 3.5	cholesterol: 0
fiber: negligible	

VEGETABLES
AND STARCHY
VEGETABLES

Every pumpkin is known by its stem.
HEBREW PROVERB

Dutch Red Cabbage

Spicy red cabbage is a Dutch favorite with or without the golden apple rings.

For 4 servings

3 cups red cabbage, shredded
3 whole cloves
Pinch salt
2 teaspoons unsalted
    margarine or butter
Pinch sugar (optional)

1 tablespoon apple cider
    vinegar
½ teaspoon cornstarch
Dutch Apple Rings (page 145)
    (optional)

1. In a casserole, combine the cabbage with ½ cup water, the cloves, a pinch of salt, margarine, and the sugar (if you are using it). Bring to a boil, and cover the casserole. Lower the heat, and simmer for about 10 minutes or until just tender, not mushy.

2. Taste, and season with vinegar. To thicken the sauce, dissolve the cornstarch in 1 tablespoon cold water. Stir into the sauce. Cook until thickened. Divide into 4 portions. Serve hot with an apple slice on the cabbage or plain.

Nutrients for 1 serving.

Calories: 35
Exchanges: ½ vegetable; ½ fat

g	mg
carbohydrate: 4	potassium: 108
fat: 2	sodium: 32
protein: negligible	cholesterol: 0
fiber: 2	

Chinese Kale

Succulent and crispy flower stalks heighten the pleasures of Chinese kale *(kai lan tsoi)*, and its many varieties provide a long growing season. Kale, available in Asian markets, is delicious steamed, stewed, or stir-fried.

For 4 servings

1 pound Chinese kale	**Chinese oyster sauce**
Salt (optional)	

1. Wash the Chinese kale. Drop into a saucepan with just enough water to cover bottom of the pan. Partially cover, and bring to a boil to create steam. Cook for 3 or 4 minutes until leaves collapse, and kale is still crisp, seasoning lightly with salt, if you wish.

2. Chop kale fine, and while it is still hot, place in a bowl. Drizzle with oyster sauce, and cook in the sauce. Serve warm or cold.

Nutrients and calories not available for Chinese kale.

Exchange (for ½ cup cooked): 1 vegetable

Okra Curry, Bombay Style

Okra inspires inventive recipes in many lands. People of India curry their okra pods and flavor the sauce imaginatively with spices. African and Creole cooks like the slippery texture and call it gumbo, which is the Bantu word for okra. But Hellenes drizzle okra with vinegar before cooking to *avoid* having a gummy stew. Others fry it. This recipe is like one I enjoyed in Bombay. If you don't like okra, use squash or snake gourd, zucchini, or another vegetable, cubed, in step 4.

For 4 servings

1 pound fresh or frozen okra	1 teaspoon ground coriander
2 garlic cloves	1 teaspoon ground cumin
2 hot green chilies, seeded and chopped	½ teaspoon ground turmeric
2 tablespoons fresh coriander, chopped	2 small potatoes, peeled and cubed
1 teaspoon corn oil	Freshly ground pepper

1. Wash the okra, and trim the stem end. Cut crosswise into 1-inch sections.

2. In a blender or mortar, grind together the garlic, chilies, and fresh coriander.

3. Heat the oil in a saucepan. Add the ground garlic, chilies, and coriander to the oil. Cook, and stir for 2 to 3 minutes over medium heat without burning. Sprinkle the ground coriander, cumin, and turmeric into the seasonings and cook for 2 minutes.

4. Drop the okra and potatoes into the seasonings and stir until well coated. Add almost enough water to cover the vegetables. Cover the pan, and simmer until tender and sauce has thickened. If sauce is too thin, transfer okra and potatoes to a warm bowl, and cook sauce down, stirring, until thick. Pour over the vegetables. Grind some pepper over the top. Serve warm with chapati.

Nutrients for 1 serving.

Calories: 92

Exchanges: 1 starch/bread; ½ vegetable

g	mg
carbohydrate: 19	potassium: 388
protein: 3	sodium: 6
fat: 2	cholesterol: 0
fiber: 4	

Calabaza (West Indian Pumpkin)

Bright orange calabaza is always available in Hispanic and Caribbean markets. It is usually sold in slices when the calabaza is very large. And it is always delicious when eaten freshly cooked. You can estimate that a ¾-pound piece yields 2 cups of chunks. Boil the chunks in very lightly salted water, and serve as chunks or mashed with a dab of margarine or butter or just plain. Calabaza is also delicious in soups mixed with other vegetables.

Nutrients for ½ cup cooked calabaza.

Calories: 40.5

Exchange: 1 starch/bread

g	mg
carbohydrate: 10	potassium: 294
protein: 1	sodium: 2.5
fat: negligible	cholesterol: 0
fiber: 1.5	

Spanish Marinated Cauliflower

Bland cauliflower erupts into a new taste sensation when you marinate the florets. Spanish people usually dip the marinated cauliflower into beaten egg and deep-fry it (tasty but high in calories), but it is also delicious raw or steamed and served with your favorite dipping sauce.

For 6 servings

4 cups cauliflower florets
2 tablespoons olive oil
2 tablespoons red wine vinegar
1 tablespoon lemon juice

1 small garlic clove, crushed
Freshly ground pepper
Pinch dried thyme or oregano

1. Wash, and trim the cauliflower. Break it into florets, the smaller, the better. (You'll have about 5 cups, loosely packed.)

2. In a bowl large enough to hold the cauliflower, whisk together the oil, vinegar, lemon juice, garlic, pepper, and herb to make a marinade. Taste, and add more vinegar and herb, if you like.

3. Drop the cauliflower into the marinade. Flip to coat the cauliflower. Cover, and refrigerate overnight or as long as you can.

4. Taste, and see if you like it raw. If so, serve the cauliflower in a salad. Or steam the marinated cauliflower for 10 minutes or until just crisp-tender. Divide into 6 portions. Serve hot or cold.

Nutrients for 1 serving.

Calories: 62
Exchanges: 1 vegetable; 1 fat

g	mg
carbohydrate: 4.5	potassium: 276
protein: 2	sodium: 6
fat: 5	cholesterol: 0
fiber: 2	

Amaranth

It's impossible to pass amaranth without admiring its brilliant leaves—splashy beet-red centers and bright green edges. Amaranth originated in tropical Africa and is also called "amaranthus spinach" and "Chinese spinach." You are likely to find it in Asian markets. The long stems are very tender steamed, so don't discard them. Steam as a vegetable or chop into soups. Toss raw amaranth into Mesclun (page 102) and other salads.

Nutrients for 1 cup raw amaranth.

Calories: 7
Exchange: free

g	mg
carbohydrate: 1	potassium: 171
protein: negligible	sodium: 5
fat: negligible	cholesterol: 0
fiber: negligible	

Nutrients for 1 cup cooked, drained amaranth.

Calories: 28
Exchange: 1 vegetable

g	mg
carbohydrate: 5	potassium: 846
protein: 3	sodium: 28
fat: negligible	cholesterol: 0
fiber: 2	

Kale and Red Peppers,
Kenya Style

Bright and healthful, this recipe is shared by Catherine Gatungo of the Kenya Mission to the United Nations. She suggests it as a cooked salad accompaniment with Kenya Stew (page 92) and other meals. The flavor and texture blend well with the stew.

For 4 servings

1 pound kale, cooked and
  chopped
Pinch salt

1 red bell pepper, seeded and
  diced

Mix the kale, a pinch of salt, and red bell pepper. Divide into 4 equal portions. Serve warm or cold.

Nutrients for 1 serving.

Calories: 53
Exchanges: 2 vegetable

g	mg
carbohydrate: 9	potassium: 148
protein: 6	sodium: 54
fat: negligible	cholesterol: 0
fiber: 1	

Sweet-Sour Mustard Greens

Raw mustard greens taste bitterly delicious mixed with sweeter salad greens. When cooked in this recipe, mustard greens team well with corn, poultry, or game dishes.

For 4 servings

4 cups boiled or steamed
    mustard greens, drained
½ teaspoon unsaturated
    vegetable oil (optional)

1–2 garlic cloves, crushed
    (optional)
Salt and freshly ground pepper
3 tablespoons cider vinegar
Noncaloric sweetener to taste

1. Chop the greens, and keep warm.
2. Heat the oil in a small pan, and sauté the garlic for a minute. Stir a small portion of the greens into the garlic. Then add to the larger amount, and mix thoroughly. Season with a little salt, pepper, vinegar, and sweetener to please your taste. Divide into 4 portions. Serve warm or cold.

Nutrients for 1 serving.

Calories: 35
Exchange: 1 vegetable

g	mg
carbohydrate: 4	potassium: 294
protein: 35	sodium: 22
fat: 2	cholesterol: 0
fiber: 3	

Stewed Tomatoes,
American Indian Style

This American Indian recipe would be easy to make anywhere in the world, especially in peak tomato season.

For 4 servings

1 slice bacon, chopped
3 green or 6 wild onions,
  chopped
1 garlic clove, crushed
½ stalk celery, chopped
3 pounds ripe tomatoes,
  peeled and chopped

Pinch sugar (optional)
Freshly ground white pepper
1 tablespoon yellow cornmeal
1 tablespoon fresh thyme
  leaves, chopped

1. Fry the bacon in a nonstick skillet until crisp. Drain on a paper towel. Crush the bacon, and reserve. Pour off all fat.

2. Heat the skillet, and drop in the onion, garlic, and celery. Stir, and cook for 3 to 4 minutes.

3. Add the tomatoes and juices, and bring to a boil. Lower heat, and simmer, partially covered, for 15 minutes, stirring occasionally. Taste, and season to suit your needs.

4. Mix the cornmeal into the tomatoes, and continue simmering for 5 minutes or until the tomatoes thicken, and the cornmeal is cooked. Flavor with the thyme. Serve warm, sprinkled with the crushed bacon.

Nutrients for 1 serving.

Calories: 54
Exchanges: ½ starch/bread; ½ vegetable

g	mg
carbohydrate: 10	potassium: 348
protein: 2	sodium: 51
fat: 1	cholesterol: 1
fiber: 2	

Carrots Lyonnaise

Superbly simple when you need a fragrant side dish—easy and inexpensive. The carrots (deep yellow-orange vegetables) make the recipe high in vitamin A.

For 4 servings

1 teaspoon unsalted margarine
  or butter
1 medium onion, very finely
  sliced

½ teaspoon dried thyme
2 cups carrots, very thinly
  sliced crosswise

1. In a saucepan just large enough to hold the ingredients, heat but do not brown the margarine or butter.
2. Quickly mix in the remaining ingredients, crumbling the thyme.
3. Cover pan, and lower heat to minimum. Cook gently without uncovering the pan for 10 minutes. Holding the lid tightly, shake the pan back and forth frequently to mix without losing the steam inside the pan. Serve warm.

Nutrients for 1 serving.

Calories: 46
Exchanges: 2 vegetable

g	mg
carbohydrate: 10	potassium: 217
protein: 1	sodium: 54
fat: negligible	cholesterol: 0
fiber: 3	

English Steamed Cucumbers

Here's an easy and festive use for large cucumbers. I adapted this recipe from an old English one, substituting bulgur for the traditional bread crumbs.

For 4 servings

2 large, firm cucumbers
1 medium onion, minced
4 tablespoons bulgur, soaked
in ¼ cup boiling water
2 dry sage leaves, crumbled

Pinch salt and freshly ground
white pepper
1 teaspoon unsalted margarine
or butter, melted
Fresh parsley and thyme sprigs
for garnish

1. Peel, and slice the cucumbers in half lengthwise. Using a small spoon, scoop out and discard the seeds.

2. For the stuffing: In a small bowl, mix the onion, the swollen bulgur, and sage. Stuff the cucumbers, dividing the mixture evenly. Season very lightly with salt and pepper.

3. Place the cucumbers on a steamer. Steam for 20 minutes.

4. Transfer the cucumbers to a serving dish. Drizzle with the melted margarine or butter. Garnish with parsley and thyme between the cucumber halves. Serve warm.

Nutrients for ½ cucumber.

Calories: 37
Exchange: ½ starch/bread

g	mg
carbohydrate: 6	potassium: 182
protein: 1	sodium: 30.5
fat: 1	cholesterol: 0
fiber: 1.5	

Tsel Dofu
(Tibetan Vegetables and Bean Curd)

Dofu is the Tibetan spelling for tofu. A wonderful dish steaming hot from the wok, I've enjoyed it again and again at the Tibetan Kitchen in New York. I developed this recipe without suggestions from the chef. You'll like it, too. This recipe is high in vitamins A and C.

For 4 servings

2 tofu (bean curd)
1 tablespoon corn oil
2 medium onions, slivered
1 medium tomato, sliced
1 large red bell pepper, cut
    into chunks

2 cups fresh whole spinach
    leaves
4 cups bok choy (Chinese
    white cabbage), cut into bite-
    size pieces
Chinese light soy sauce

1. Steam the bean curd for about 5 minutes. Cut into pieces 1¼ × 1¼ × ¼ inches. Set aside while sautéing the vegetables.

2. Heat the oil in a wok or skillet. Sauté the onions until soft. Add the tomato, pepper, spinach, and bok choy. Stir-fry until soft but still very crisp with a nice sauce. Season the sauce with soy sauce to your taste.

3. Slip the bean curd into the sauce, and cook for a minute to heat and flavor. Then lift the bean curd to the top. Divide into 4 equal portions. Serve immediately.

Nutrients for 1 serving.

Calories: 94
Exchanges: ½ medium-fat meat; 1½ vegetable; ½ fat

g	mg
carbohydrate: 9.5	potassium: 850
protein: 7	sodium: 89
fat: 4	cholesterol: 0
fiber: 6	

Balsam Pear or Bitter Gourd

Also called the bitter melon or *fu kwa* in Chinese (its scientific name is *Momordica charantia*), the balsam pear has bumpy ridges from the stem to the tapering tip and can be lovely light green or darker, tinged with yellow or red. The Indian variety is yellow-orange, and some are white. But they are all bitter. Either parboil or soak in lightly salted water before cooking.

For 2 servings

1 bitter gourd (8 ounces)   Pinch salt

1. Wash and lightly scrub the gourd (the skin is edible). Cut in half lengthwise, and discard the seeds (not edible).
2. Cover with cold water in a saucepan. Add a pinch of salt, and soak for 15 minutes; or bring to a boil, boil for 2 minutes, and drain.
3. Slice into pieces 1¼ by ¼ inches (you'll have 2 cups). Steam or stir-fry with other vegetables.

Nutrients for 1 cup.

Calories: 24

Exchange: 1 vegetable

g	mg
carbohydrate: 5	potassium: 398
protein: 1	sodium: 8
fat: negligible	cholesterol: 0
fiber: 1	

Chayote Salad

You'll find this pear-shaped, creamy or deep green gourd in Asian, Hispanic, and West Indian markets. Among the Chinese, the chayote is called *fa chon kwa* or Buddha's palm melon. It is bland enough to flavor with your favorite seasonings.

For 4 servings

2–3 chayotes (1 pound)   Dressing (optional)
Fresh oregano, coriander, or
  basil, chopped

1. Wash the chayotes. In a saucepan, cook in water to cover until tender, from 5 to 20 minutes depending on the size of the chayotes you are cooking. Drain, and cool the chayotes.
2. Quarter the small chayotes or chop the large ones, including the edible seeds.
3. In a small bowl, mix the chayotes, stir in the herb and dressing you are using. Taste, and adjust the seasonings. Divide into 4 portions. Serve warm or cold.

Nutrients for 1 cup sliced in 1-inch pieces.

Calories: 38
Exchanges: 1½ vegetable

g	mg
carbohydrate: 8	potassium: 276
protein: 1	sodium: 1
fat: negligible	cholesterol: 0
fiber: negligible	

Mashed Rutabaga

This large, yellow turnip takes its name from the Swiss dialect word for "bag root." It is very popular among Northern Europeans and is as easy to cook as a potato. For friends who prefer livelier flavors, serve it with a dipping sauce, or dice and cook in a curry!

For 4 servings

1 pound rutabaga
Pinch salt (optional)
2 teaspoons unsalted
  margarine or butter
  (optional)

¼ cup low-fat milk (optional)
Freshly ground pepper
  (optional)

1. Wash the rutabaga. Place in a saucepan, and cover with water, adding a pinch of salt if you wish. Cook until fork-tender.
2. Peel rutabaga, and mash in a bowl. Beat in the margarine and milk and pepper, to your own taste. Divide into 4 portions. Serve hot.

**Nutrients for 1 serving cooked in water
without any optional ingredients.**

Calories: 40
Exchanges: 2 vegetable

g	mg
carbohydrate: 9	potassium: 189.5
protein: 1	sodium: 4.5
fat: negligible	cholesterol: 0
fiber: NA	

Asparagus and Almonds,
Chinese Style

You can use any fresh vegetable (cabbage, bok choy, celery, sprouts, mustard greens, etc.) instead of asparagus.

For 4 servings

1 pound slender asparagus	Pinch salt or ¼ teaspoon soy
2 green onions	sauce
½ teaspoon peanut or other	Pinch sugar
vegetable oil	6 blanched almonds, slivered
	and toasted

1. Wash and trim the asparagus. Slice diagonally into 2-inch pieces.
2. Slice the green onions the same size as the asparagus.
3. In a wok or skillet, heat the oil over high heat, and drop in the green onions. Stir-fry for a few seconds, and add the asparagus. Continue stir-frying until the asparagus turns bright green. Season, and remove from heat.
4. Sprinkle with the almonds, and serve immediately. Can also be served cold.

Nutrients for 1 serving.

Calories: 50
Exchanges: 1 vegetable; ½ fat

g	mg
carbohydrate: 7	potassium: 401
protein: 3	sodium: 34
fat: 2	cholesterol: 0
fiber: 3	

Gazpacho
(Andalusian Vegetable Dish)

Beautifully diced and seasoned with verve, gazpacho looks and tastes perfect for a summer lunch. Each serving has 1.8 mg riboflavin and 55 mg vitamin C in addition to nutrients listed below.

For 4 servings

4 ripe small tomatoes, peeled, seeded, and finely diced

1 seedless cucumber, peeled and finely diced

1 small green bell pepper, seeded and finely diced

1 medium onion, minced

1 tablespoon olive oil

2 tablespoons lemon juice or vinegar

1 small garlic clove, crushed

Cayenne pepper

Pinch salt

1 very juicy tomato

Fresh parsley for garnish

½ cup croutons for garnish

1. In a bowl, gently mix the diced tomatoes, cucumber, pepper, and onion. Refrigerate while making the dressing.

2. In a jar or bowl, mix the oil, lemon juice, garlic, and a dash of cayenne pepper and salt. Whisk or shake to mix. Drizzle over the salad while carefully mixing with a fork.

3. Mash the very juicy tomato through a strainer or food mill. Add enough cracked ice to the tomato juice, if necessary, to make 1 cup. Stir the juice into the diced vegetables. Taste, and adjust the seasonings.

4. Refrigerate before serving the gazpacho. Divide into 4 portions. Serve cold, garnished with a parsley leaf and croutons.

Nutrients for 1 serving.

Calories: 93

Exchanges: ½ starch/bread; 1 vegetable; ½ fat

g	mg
carbohydrate: 14	potassium: 487
protein: 3	sodium: 78
fat: 4	cholesterol: 0
fiber: 3	

Acar Kuning
(Indonesian Pickled Vegetables)

Planning a party? Mix these vegetables and refrigerate a day in advance. Serve on toast or chapati. Daun salam and laos (galingale) are available in Indonesian or other Asian markets. Recipe is adapted from one offered by the Information Division, Embassy of Indonesia, Washington, D.C.

For 6 servings

1 large onion	⅓ cup white vinegar
1 garlic clove	½ teaspoon brown sugar
1 tablespoon corn oil	6 shallots, peeled whole
1 slice ginger about ¼ inch thick	½ cup green beans, sliced lengthwise 1¼ inches long
¼ teaspoon ground turmeric	½ cup carrots, sliced
2 hot green chilies, split and seeded	½ cup cauliflower florets
2 daun salam or 1 bay leaf	1 small cucumber, peeled and seeded, cut into strips 1¼
2 slices laos (galingale) (optional)	inches long and ½ inch thick
2 macadamia or kemiri nuts, ground	

1. Chop the onion and garlic. Heat the oil in a casserole, and sauté the onion and garlic, ginger, turmeric, chilies, daun salam or bay leaf, laos (if you are using it), and nuts. Cook gently for 3 minutes.

2. Add the vinegar and sugar. Bring to a boil, reduce heat, and simmer for 5 minutes.

3. Toss in the whole shallots, green beans, carrots, cauliflower, and cucumber. Mix thoroughly, and cover pan. Cook gently for 10 minutes. Check, and continue cooking, if necessary, until vegetables are crisp-tender. Remove from heat, and cool. Refrigerate overnight before serving.

Nutrients for 1 serving.

Calories: 57
Exchanges: 1½ vegetable; ½ fat

g	mg
carbohydrate: 8	potassium: 231
protein: 1	sodium: 14
fat: 3	cholesterol: 0
fiber: 2	

Baunjaun Bauranee
(Afghan Eggplant with Chaka and Mint)

Eggplant in peppery tomato sauce topped with Yogurt Chaka and fresh mint offers exciting flavors.

For 4 servings

1 pound eggplant	½ cup fresh tomato, chopped,
1 tablespoon unsaturated	or tomato sauce
vegetable oil	Freshly ground pepper
1 medium onion, finely	4 tablespoons Afghan Yogurt
chopped	Chaka (page 28)
¼ cup green bell pepper	2 tablespoons fresh mint,
Few dashes cayenne	chopped

1. Peel, and cut off stem end of eggplant. Slice crosswise into ⅜-inch circles.

2. Heat a nonstick skillet, and coat with 1 teaspoon oil. Brown the eggplant quickly on both sides, adding 1 teaspoon oil as needed. Keep eggplant warm on a platter.

3. Heat remaining oil in the skillet, and sauté the onion. Add the bell pepper and cayenne. Cook for a few minutes, and then stir in the tomato or tomato sauce and ¼ cup water. Bring to a boil.

4. Slip the eggplant slices into the sauce. Simmer gently until eggplant is tender, and the sauce thickens. Season with ground pepper.

5. To serve: Spoon ½ tablespoon of the Yogurt Chaka on 1 plate and spread out. Arrange one-fourth of the eggplant on the Yogurt Chaka. Spoon ½ tablespoon of the Yogurt Chaka over the eggplant. Top with one-fourth of the sauce from the skillet. Sprinkle with fresh mint. Repeat for the 4 servings. Serve warm or cold.

Nutrients for 1 serving without the Afghan Yogurt Chaka.

Calories: 72
Exchanges: 1½ vegetable; 1 fat

g	mg
carbohydrate: 9	potassium: 336
protein: 1	sodium: 8
fat: 4	cholesterol: 0
fiber: 3	

**Nutrients for 1 serving with
the Afghan Yogurt Chaka.**

Calories: 84
Exchanges: 2 vegetable; 1 fat

g	mg
carbohydrate: 11	potassium: 414
protein: 2	sodium: 93
fat: 4	cholesterol: 1
fiber: 3	

Dutch Apple Rings

Apple rings, sautéed until golden, are fun to make and simply delicious. Serve with red cabbage, game, or pork.

For 4 servings

2 small tart apples   **2 teaspoons unsalted
margarine or butter**

1. Wash, and dry the apples. Core but do not pare them. Slice crosswise into ½-inch rings.
2. In a heavy skillet, heat the margarine or butter, and very gently sauté the apple slices on both sides until golden. Divide into 4 servings. Serve warm.

Nutrients for 1 serving (½ apple).

Calories: 48
Exchanges: ½ fruit; ½ fat

g	mg
carbohydrate: 8	potassium: 61
protein: negligible	sodium: negligible
fat: 2	cholesterol: 0
fiber: 1	

Moussaka for Vegetable Lovers

You'll cook this low-calorie version of moussaka again and again for family and friends. It is easy to assemble and bake. Remember to make the spicy Eggplant Kima filling (replacing the usual meat layer) in advance (pages 148–49).

For 9 or 12 servings

2 pounds eggplant
3 tablespoons unsalted margarine or butter
4 tablespoons all-purpose flour
2 cups low-fat (1%) milk, scalded
1 tablespoon Parmesan or other grated cheese
1 egg, separated
1 tablespoon olive or vegetable oil
2 tablespoons dried bread crumbs

1 large potato, peeled and thinly sliced
1 large zucchini, scraped and sliced ¼ inch thick
2 tablespoons fresh parsley, chopped
2 tablespoons fresh dill, chopped
1 tablespoon dried oregano
2 garlic cloves, minced
Freshly ground pepper
2 cups Eggplant Kima (pages 148–49)

1. Using a scraper, partially peel the eggplant by removing strips lengthwise about every inch. Slice the eggplant either way in ¼-inch slices. Place on a pan, and broil on both sides until the eggplant steams. Set aside while preparing the sauce.

2. To make the white sauce: In a saucepan, melt the margarine or butter, and heat until it begins to bubble. Quickly stir in the flour. Lower the heat, and cook, stirring constantly, for 2 minutes. Avoid browning the flour. Remove from heat, and gradually add the milk. Stir until completely dissolved. Return to heat, and stir until the sauce thickens and boils. Season with half the cheese. Remove from heat, and cool thoroughly. Then stir the egg yolk into the sauce.

3. To assemble the moussaka: Very lightly oil a 10-inch square baking pan (to make 9 servings) or a 9x12x3-inch pan (for 12 servings). Sprinkle 1 tablespoon bread crumbs on the bottom (to absorb liquids released when baking). Layer half the eggplant, potato, and zucchini, strewing half the herbs, oil, and seasonings between the layers. (Parsley and dill are good with the potato, and oregano, crushed in your palms, and garlic are good with the eggplant.)

4. Mix the egg white into the Eggplant Kima. Spread over the vegetables.

5. Complete the layering, and spread the remaining vegetables and seasonings over the eggplant filling.

6. Top with the white sauce, remaining bread crumbs, and cheese.

7. Bake at 350°F for 45 to 50 minutes until golden and bubbly. Rest on a rack for 10 minutes before slicing. Cut moussaka in the 10-inch pan into 9 squares; cut moussaka in the larger pan into 12 pieces.

Nutrients for 1 serving moussaka
with Eggplant Kima in
9 × 12 × 3-inch pan (12 servings).

Calories: 98
Exchanges: ½ starch/bread; 1½ vegetable; ½ fat

g	mg
carbohydrate: 12	potassium: 311
protein: 3	sodium: 54
fat: 4.5	cholesterol: 25
fiber: 2	

Nutrients for 1 serving moussaka with
Eggplant Kima in 10-inch pan (9 servings).

Calories: 130
Exchanges: ½ starch/bread; ½ skim milk; 1 fat

g	mg
carbohydrate: 16	potassium: 415
protein: 4	sodium: 72
fat: 6	cholesterol: 33
fiber: 3	

Eggplant Kima

The idea for this recipe originated in Greece. For centuries during fasting periods before taking Holy Communion, all foods of animal origin are avoided among strict Orthodox Christians. Unique vegetarian dishes naturally evolved to vary the menus, especially during the 40-day lenten period preceding Easter. These inventive vegetarian dishes are called *sarakostiana* (from *sarakosti* or 40 days), and as a group constitute the best in Hellenic vegetable fare.

Eggplant kima is typical of this creativity in the kitchen. Kima means "ground" or "very finely chopped" from the Turkish *kiyma*, a word used throughout the Middle East and in India with different spellings (keema to kameh) to describe ground mixtures, originally made with meat. Over the years, the term became generic for any ground mixture. Interestingly, eggplant kima *looks* like ground meat and is used as a substitute in many dishes. It is delectable, but don't expect it to taste exactly like meat. Have fun seasoning and using the kima. Use eggplant kima to stuff mushrooms, baby zucchini, red and green bell peppers, as a spread for cucumbers and other vegetables, for canapés and in other dishes, including Moussaka for Vegetable Lovers (pages 146–47).

For 2 cups

1½ pounds eggplant	1 teaspoon each ground
2 tablespoons olive or	cinnamon, ground allspice,
unsaturated vegetable oil	grated orange rind, more to
2–3 garlic cloves, crushed	taste
Generous pinches fresh	Pinch salt (optional) and
parsley, dried oregano, and	freshly ground pepper
thyme	

1. Peel the eggplant, cut off the stem, and slice the eggplant in large chunks. Then chop eggplant into pieces larger than ground meat. A food processor or blender will do the job, but don't reduce the eggplant to mush. You should have about 3 cups.

2. In a skillet, heat 1 teaspoon of the oil and drop the chopped eggplant in the oil. Cook and stir over medium heat until the eggplant begins to steam. Keep stirring and adding only small amounts of oil to cook the eggplant until tender. (Eggplant is always starving for oil, so don't be carried away.) Stir in the garlic, and lower the heat.

3. Season the eggplant generously and judiciously with spices and herbs to suit your taste. Taste, and enhance the seasonings. Cool the eggplant. There will be about 2 cups.

4. If you can refrigerate the eggplant for at least 1 night before using it, the flavors will blend delightfully.

Nutrients for ½ cup.

Calories: 45
Exchanges: 1 vegetable; ½ fat

g	mg
carbohydrate: 4	potassium: 125
protein: negligible	sodium: 29
fat: 3.5	cholesterol: 0
fiber: 1	

Snake Gourd

Lovely light green and smooth, this mild gourd just happens to have a scary name because it is sinewy and long (15 inches to 6 feet, but usually shorter than a loaf of French bread). You'll find it in Asian and Italian markets. You may want to try it in a curry; substitute snake gourd for the okra and potatoes in Okra Curry, Bombay Style, pages 128–29.

For 4 servings

1 pound snake gourd

Scrub, and lightly scrape the gourd. Cut into ½-inch cubes. Steam or boil for 5 minutes. Drain and drop into soups, stews, or curries.

Nutrients for ½ cup.

Calories: 39
Exchanges: 1½ vegetable

g	mg
carbohydrate: 9	potassium: 445
protein: 2	sodium: 1
fat: negligible	cholesterol: 0
fiber: negligible	

Ärter (Swedish Peas)

This recipe is great fun when you want an informal dish at your table. Plan about 10 pea pods for a ¼-cup serving, quite filling as a side dish. Great as a first course for a convivial atmosphere! Incidentally, a Swedish woman I know is not familiar with this custom of serving peas.

For 4 servings

1 pound fresh peas in pods
Pinch salt (optional)

4 teaspoons unsalted margarine or butter, melted (optional)

1. Thoroughly wash pea pods but do not shell. To steam: Place peas on a steamer, and steam for about 12 minutes until pods soften. To boil: Cover with boiling water, and add a pinch of salt, if you wish. Boil for 8 to 10 minutes or only until pea pods are soft but not breaking open.

2. Drain the hot pea pods. While still hot, divide among 6 warm plates, and bring to table. If you are using melted margarine, spoon it into tiny dipping dishes (like those used by the Chinese and Japanese).

3. To eat: One at a time, dip end of pod in the margarine, put the pod in your mouth, and pull it out while keeping the peas behind your teeth! Discard the pods. Enjoy the peas.

Nutrients for 1 serving peas.

Calories: 80
Exchange: 1 starch/bread (add 1 fat, if using margarine)

g	mg
carbohydrate: 14	potassium: 222
protein: 1	sodium: 1
fat: negligible	cholesterol: 0
fiber: 1	

Potato Curry

The dish is perfect for your Mexican, Thai, Indian, African, Korean, and other friends who love highly seasoned foods. I first tasted it in India wrapped inside a fresh dosa (pancake). It's also good with fish and chapati.

For 4 servings

3 medium potatoes
Pinch salt
½ cup green peas, cooked, or
  any leftover cooked
  vegetable
2 teaspoons vegetable oil or
  Ghee (page 7)
2 shallots or 1 small onion
1 garlic clove, chopped
1 teaspoon fresh ginger, cut
  into fine strips

3 green chilies, finely slivered
½ teaspoon black sesame seeds
1 teaspoon ground coriander
½ teaspoon ground turmeric
1 teaspoon cumin seed
¼ teaspoon ground red pepper
  or flakes
1 tablespoon (10) unsalted
  peanuts, ground (optional)

1. Wash the potatoes, and cook in their jackets in lightly salted water. Peel, and dice potatoes. Combine in a bowl with peas or any chopped vegetable you like.

2. To make the curry: In a saucepan, heat the oil or ghee. Toss in the seasonings (not the peanuts), and cook over low heat for 5 minutes, stirring almost constantly to avoid browning.

3. Add the diced potatoes and peas to the curry, and stir thoroughly. Cook over low heat for 10 minutes or until potatoes are tender. Taste, and adjust seasonings. Divide into 4 portions. Serve warm or at room temperature, garnished with the nuts if you wish.

Nutrients for 1 serving with peanuts.

Calories: 131
Exchanges: 1 starch/bread; 1 vegetable; ½ fat

g	mg
carbohydrate: 22	potassium: 369
protein: 3	sodium: 50
fat: 4	cholesterol: 0
fiber: 3	

Potato Kugel

Kugel is popular among many groups, especially Ashkenazim and Northern Europeans.

For 12 pieces

5 medium potatoes, grated
1 large onion, finely grated
1 carrot, grated
2 eggs, lightly beaten
4 tablespoons matzo meal or
  ½ matzo, ground

Pinch salt and freshly ground
  pepper
1 teaspoon unsaturated
  vegetable oil
Fresh parsley or dill, chopped,
  for garnish

1. Mix potatoes, onion, carrot, eggs, matzo, salt, and pepper in a bowl. Season to your taste.

2. Oil a 7x10x2-inch baking dish. Spread the mixed potatoes into the pan, and smooth the top. Bake at 375°F for about 45 minutes, until brown and crisp. Remove from oven, and cut into 12 pieces. Serve hot, garnished with fresh herbs.

Nutrients for 1 piece.

Calories: 12
Exchange: ½ starch/bread

g	mg
carbohydrate: 11	potassium: 191
protein: 2	sodium: 29
fat: 1	cholesterol: 46
fiber: 1	

Potato Knishes

Knishes are delicious right out of the oven. To cut down on cholesterol, use unsaturated oil instead of the usual chicken fat. These knishes are smaller than the normal size.

For 4 servings (2 knishes)

4 medium potatoes, cooked in jackets

1 teaspoon unsaturated vegetable oil or chicken fat

Pinch salt and freshly ground pepper

1 egg, lightly beaten in a flat bowl

1 tablespoon fresh parsley, finely minced

1. Peel the cooked potatoes, and mash in a bowl with the chicken fat or oil, salt, and pepper. Cool slightly, and add all but 1 tablespoon of the beaten egg (save for later). Stir in the parsley, and beat potatoes until smooth.

2. Dip your fingers in flour, and divide the mixture into 8 pieces. Shape into balls in your palms. Flatten to ¼-inch-thick rectangles. Set knishes on a baking pan. Brush remaining egg on the knishes. Bake at 400°F for 20 minutes or until nicely browned, raising temperature during the last 5 minutes, if necessary. Serve hot.

Nutrients for 1 serving (2 knishes).

Calories: 128
Exchanges: 1½ starch/bread

g	mg
carbohydrate: 23	potassium: 388
protein: 3.5	sodium: 49
fat: 3	cholesterol: 68
fiber: 2	

Chestnuts

Chestnuts! What is your first thought when you see chestnuts in the market? Roasting them on your hearth, most probably. Here's how—with or without an open fire, as roasted in Italy and Greece.

For 2½ cups roasted

1 pound (about 50 or 3¾ cups
unshelled) fresh chestnuts

1. Using a very small, sharp knife, slash an X only on the round side of the chestnuts, without cutting through the chestnuts.
2. To roast by an open fire: Spread chestnuts in a pan, and place in the ashes under the fire. Keep potholders and a mitt handy. Check chestnuts in 10 minutes, turning them over to roast evenly (use a mitt; they're hot). Continue roasting until the outer skin curls back. Peel one, and taste for tenderness. When they're done, peel while they're still warm, and serve immediately.
3. To roast in an oven: Spread chestnuts in a pan, and pour a half cup of water in the bottom (to hasten the roasting). Bake in a moderately hot oven for 8 to 10 minutes or until skin curls back. Peel one and taste. If they are ready, serve immediately. For chestnuts as a side dish, see Chestnut Puree (page 156).

Nutrients for 50 g (1.75 ounces).

Calories: 97
Exchanges: 1½ starch/bread

g	mg
carbohydrate: 21	potassium: 227
protein: 1	sodium: 3
fat: negligible	cholesterol: 0
fiber: negligible	

Chestnut Puree

It's delicious with game or veal or vegetable dishes.

For 2½ cups

1 pound fresh chestnuts
1½ cups water or White
Chicken Stock (page 98)

Pinch salt (optional) and
freshly ground white pepper
1 tablespoon unsalted
margarine (optional)

1. To roast chestnuts: See Chestnuts (page 155). Peel off the outer and inner brown skins. Place peeled chestnuts in a saucepan.

2. Add the water or stock, cover pan, and simmer for 15 minutes or until chestnuts are soft and the liquid absorbed, adding additional liquid, if necessary.

3. Drain chestnuts. Mash through a ricer or food mill into a bowl. Taste, and season with a pinch of salt only if necessary. Beat in some pepper and margarine (if you are using it). Serve warm.

Nutrients for ½ cup cooked in water
without any optional ingredients.

Calories: 94.5
Exchanges: 1½ starch/bread

g	mg
carbohydrate: 20	potassium: 441
protein: 1	sodium: 3
fat: negligible	cholesterol: 0
fiber: negligible	

Chinese Water Chestnut

With its crunchy texture, the aquatic water chestnut is a wonderful touch in a mixed vegetable and meat or fish recipe. The rhizomes resemble "horse's hoofs," as they are called by the Chinese. Water chestnuts are covered with a thin layer of blackish brown skin, but the flesh is crisp and snow-white.

If you are using fresh water chestnuts, peel and thinly slice them crosswise for soups, stews, and stir-fried dishes. Chop or sliver for dim sum or dumplings. If you are using canned, keep the unused water chestnuts in water in a covered container in the refrigerator, and change the water daily until you use them. Water chestnuts won't lose their crispness when stir-fried or cooked in soups.

Nutrients for 5 water chestnuts.

Calories: 69
Exchange: 1 starch/bread

g	mg
carbohydrate: 17	potassium: 436
protein: 1	sodium: 17.5
fat: negligible	cholesterol: 0
fiber: negligible	

Taro

Taro is a plant of the Pacific Islands, whose starchy rootstock is a popular food in many different countries. When cooked, taro is soft, sweetish, and slippery. Taro is variously called dasheen, elephant's ear, ñampi, arum lily, cocoyam, yautia, malanga, eddo, and kolokassi. Asiatic people steam, boil, or stew taro. Hawaiians make their poi from it (and are among the few groups who also stew taro leaves), and Cypriots braise taro with pork or chicken, celery, and tomatoes. The Chinese name, *wu tau* (black head), is a good description of the plant as you see it in specialty markets.

For 4 servings

4 taro corms
¼ cup chard, chopped
   (optional)

2 garlic cloves, crushed
   (optional)
Oyster or other favorite
   dipping sauce (optional)

1. Peel the taro, and soak in cold water until ready to cook.
2. To cook, boil in water to cover, or steam in a bamboo steamer. Taste taro, and decide if you'd like to serve taro plain as you would boiled potato.
3. If you want to season taro, drain, and cut into cubes while it is still hot. Combine with the chard and garlic. Heat a wok or skillet with just enough vegetable oil to coat bottom. Stir-fry taro mixture for 1 minute. Serve hot or cold, with dipping sauce if you wish.

**Nutrients for ½ cup without
any optional ingredients.**

Calories: 92
Exchanges: 1½ starch/bread

g	mg
carbohydrate: 22	potassium: 319
protein: 2	sodium: 10
fat: negligible	cholesterol: 0
fiber: negligible	

Spicy Stewed Pumpkin

Delicate pumpkin spiced with ginger, cinnamon, and cloves comes from Zentralinstitut für Diabetes in Karlsburg bei Greifswald, East Germany. The pumpkin or calabaza makes this recipe very high in vitamin A.

For 4 servings

¼ cup vinegar
1 small cinnamon stick
1 small piece fresh ginger

3–4 cloves
Noncaloric sweetener to taste
4 cups pumpkin or calabaza

1. In a saucepan, combine 1 cup water with the vinegar, cinnamon, ginger, cloves, and sweetener. Boil for a few minutes.
2. Meanwhile, peel, seed, and cube the pumpkin (save the seeds to roast for a snack, page 181). Drop the pumpkin cubes into the saucepan with spices. Cook gently until fork-tender, stirring frequently. Divide into 4 equal servings. Serve warm or cold.

Nutrients for 1 serving.

Calories: 63
Exchange: 1 starch/bread

g	mg
carbohydrate: 16	potassium: 391
protein: 2	sodium: 9
fat: negligible	cholesterol: 0
fiber: 3	

Humita
(Argentinean Fresh Corn Cakes)

When fresh corn is in season, surprise your friends with these spicy cakes wrapped in husk leaves (a popular method of cooking throughout South and Central America) and spiced with cinnamon and hot pepper. This sensational recipe is from Ana Maria Malerba, nutritionist of the Liga Argentina de Proteccion al Diabético.

For 6 servings

1 medium onion
1 large bell pepper
1 large tomato
1 teaspoon corn oil
1 teaspoon cayenne pepper or paprika
Pinch salt and freshly ground black pepper

6 ears fresh corn (each about 6 ounces), including corn husks
¾ cup low-fat (1%) milk
1 teaspoon ground cinnamon
1 teaspoon liquid sweetener (optional)

1. Finely chop the onion, bell pepper, and tomato. Sauté in the oil, and season with cayenne or paprika, a pinch of salt, and black pepper.

2. Grate the corn off the cobs, and reserve the husks. In a bowl, combine the corn with the milk, cinnamon, and sweetener (if you are using it). Mix with the sautéed vegetables. Remove from the heat, and beat to complete the filling.

3. Take 2 fresh leaves of the corn husks, and arrange them in opposite directions, overlapping in the middle. Place 2 tablespoons of the filling in the middle. Fold the husk leaves to enclose the filling. Bind with string.

4. Place the corn cakes in a casserole with lots of water to cover. Cover the casserole, and cook over low heat for 2 hours.

5. Drain, and divide equally into 6 servings. Arrange on a warm platter or individual plates. Cut the string but do not unwrap. Serve warm in the husk wrapping.

Yard-Long Beans

You'll often find these long and slender green legumes in Italian and East Indian markets. The Chinese call them *dao kok* and horn bean. Greengrocers usually call them "yard" beans, but they are really only from 15 to 18 inches long. Whatever the name, they are delicious as a side dish or in soups and stews.

For 4 servings

**¾ pound yard-long beans (a
  subspecies of cowpeas)**

1. Wash the beans, and pinch off the ends. Cut beans in bite-size pieces.
2. Steam for 15 minutes until crisp-tender. Or, if you prefer, steam for 7 minutes. Divide into 4 portions. Serve hot.

Quibebe (Brazilian Pumpkin or Calabaza Stew)

Peppery pumpkin—this taste treat is from Brazil, where I learned how to make this unusual stew. You'll like it. Pumpkin and calabaza are very high in vitamin A.

For 3 servings

1 teaspoon unsaturated vegetable oil

1–2 dried malagueta peppers or 1–2 teaspoons cayenne pepper

1 large onion, chopped

1 fresh or canned tomato, chopped

1 pound pumpkin or calabaza, peeled and cubed

1 sprig fresh parsley, chopped

2 cups White Chicken Stock (page 98) or water

Fresh coriander or parsley for garnish

1. Heat the oil in a casserole or saucepan, and sauté the peppers, onion, and tomato until soft, about 3 minutes.

2. Add the pumpkin and parsley, stirring to mix thoroughly for a few minutes.

3. Pour in enough stock or water to cover the pumpkin. Cook until pumpkin is just tender. Divide into 3 servings. Serve warm or chilled, garnished with fresh coriander or parsley.

Nutrients for 1 serving.

Calories: 76
Exchange: 1 starch/bread

g	mg
carbohydrate: 15	potassium: 409
protein: 2	sodium: 13
fat: 2	cholesterol: 0
fiber: 4	

Cranberry Beans

Fresh white cranberry beans with ruby red speckles on the pods cook much more quickly than dried ones. Don't buy the beans with darkened or brownish pods because they are not fresh. Use them as you would any bean—drop in boiling broth for a soup or stew, or braise them in a little olive oil and make a tomato sauce.

For 3 servings

½ pound (28–30) cranberry
   beans in pods

1. Peel the pods; you should have about 1 cup beans.
2. In a saucepan or steamer, steam the beans until tender, about 25 minutes. You can expect the red speckles to fade when cooked, even with the freshest cranberry beans. Divide into 3 portions. Serve hot.

Nutrients for ⅓ cup.

Calories: 80
Exchange: 1 starch/bread

g	mg
carbohydrate: 14	potassium: 228
protein: 5.5	sodium: negligible
fat: negligible	cholesterol: 0
fiber: negligible	

Vegetable Niramish, Bangladesh Style

When you are eager for a new way to cook almost any vegetable, this recipe is for you. It was contributed by Shane Ara Kabir, assistant director of diet and nutrition at the Bangladesh Institute of Research and Rehabilitation in Diabetes, Endocrine and Metabolic Disorders.

For 1 serving

1 cup cauliflower, cabbage,
   green papaya, eggplant,
   green beans, radish, carrot,
   bottle gourd, or snake gourd
¼ teaspoon ground turmeric
Pinch salt

½ cup onion, chopped
1 teaspoon vegetable oil
¼ teaspoon cumin seed
1 teaspoon fresh coriander,
   chopped

1. Select any vegetable or combination of vegetables you wish, and cut into cubes.

2. In a saucepan, mix the vegetables with the turmeric, pinch of salt, and all but 1 teaspoon of the onion. Add ½ cup water. Cover pan, and cook for a few minutes until soft.

3. In a skillet, heat the oil, and add the cumin. Add the reserved onion, and stir until brown. Add the vegetables, and stir constantly for 1 to 2 minutes. Stir in the coriander. Serve hot.

Nutrients for 1 serving.

Calories: 81
Exchanges: 2½ vegetable; ½ fat

g	mg
carbohydrate: 12	potassium: 559
protein: 3	sodium: 123
fat: 3	cholesterol: 0
fiber: 5	

GRAINS, LEGUMES, NUTS, AND SEEDS

One meal without rice
mars domestic happiness
for a week.

JAPANESE PROVERB

Kolyva (Whole Wheat and Fruits)

Munchy, crunchy kolyva has been an unusual food of the Hellenes for centuries—served in little bags to parishioners following memorial services in Orthodox churches. Pomegranate adds to the beauty and ancient qualities of the dish.

Kolyva preparation had been a mystery to me as a child. I saw or tasted it only in church and associated kolyva with religion. It was *very* difficult for me to overcome this attitude and learn how to cook it and to serve it in a secular setting. Now I know it is easy to cook. Children and adults love to munch on kolyva as a snack or dessert. Use the cooked kolyva within 3 days or so, and always store in the refrigerator. You can store *dry* whole wheat kernels indefinitely in a covered jar.

Makes 18 servings

1 cup and 2 tablespoons unpeeled whole wheat kernels	¼ cup fresh basil, minced, or 1 tablespoon dried basil, crushed
Pinch salt	1 teaspoon ground cinnamon
½ cup walnuts, chopped	1 medium pomegranate (optional)
6 tablespoons golden currants	Noncaloric sweetener (optional)
½ cup sesame seeds, toasted	9 almond halves for garnish (optional)
¼ cup fresh parsley, minced	

1. Wash the wheat kernels in a large saucepan. Cover with water, and add a pinch of salt. Boil over medium heat until tender, about 1½ hours, adding water and stirring to prevent sticking. (Cooking time can be considerably shortened by soaking the wheat the evening before as you would soak beans, or by bringing the water to a boil and soaking for an hour or so.)

2. When the kernels are just beginning to break open, drain thoroughly. (I usually drop the kernels into a clean pillowcase and roll up to absorb all the excess liquid, but it isn't necessary. This much can be done a day in advance. Refrigerate until ready to mix kolyva.)

3. Combine the kernels in a large bowl with the walnuts, currants, sesame seeds, parsley, basil, and cinnamon. If you have a pomegranate on hand, cut it open and scoop the seeds into the bowl. Mix and taste.

4. You may not need to sweeten kolyva—the currants and basil are natural sweeteners.

5. Scoop the mixture into a crystal or china bowl, and smoothly mound the top. Garnish with almonds around the sides and middle. Refrigerate until ready to serve. Serve cold.

**Nutrients for ⅓ cup with 1 almond half
and pomegranate.**

Calories: 84
Exchanges: ½ starch/bread; ½ fruit; 1 fat

g	mg
carbohydrate: 11.5	potassium: 108
protein: 2	sodium: 7
fat: 4	cholesterol: 0
fiber: 1	

Nasi Kuning
(Indonesian Yellow Coconut Rice)

Rich with coconut calories—this recipe should be saved for a very important day.

For 9 servings

1 cup Coconut Milk (pages 30–31)
1 cup white long-grain rice
¼ teaspoon ground turmeric
½ teaspoon white or black peppercorns, tied in a cheesecloth bag

2 daun salam or bay leaves (optional)
Pinch salt

1. In a saucepan or casserole, slowly bring the coconut milk to a boil. Stir in the rice, turmeric, peppercorns in a bag, and daun salam or bay leaves (if you are using them), and salt. Lower the heat, and cover pan tightly. Cook for about 5 minutes. Then turn off heat, and leave the pan covered for about 10 minutes until the coconut milk is absorbed.

2. Remove the cheesecloth bag and daun salam or bay leaves (if you are using them).

3. Place rice in a steamer. Steam for about 30 minutes until tender. Divide into 9 servings. Serve hot. Garnish with sliced cucumber and celery leaves.

Nutrients for 1 serving (⅓ cup).

Calories: 142
Exchanges: 1 starch/bread; 1½ fat

g	mg
carbohydrate: 18	potassium: NA
protein: 2	sodium: NA
fat: 7	cholesterol: NA
fiber: negligible	

Steamed Rice

Hot, tender rice is the pivotal food of many menus. If you don't have an electric rice cooker (my favorite way), try this easy method.

For 3 cups cooked rice (9 servings)

1 cup long-grain rice

1. In a saucepan, cover rice with cold water. Pour off the water. Repeat until water clears slightly but not entirely.
2. Add 1½ cups cold water, and bring to a boil. Boil briskly for 2 minutes until water boils down.
3. Cover pan tightly. Lower the heat to minimum, and cook undisturbed for 15 minutes. Remove from heat, remove cover, drape dry towel over the top, and cover again for 5 minutes. Fluff rice with fork, and serve hot.
4. To steam or reheat rice: Place cooked rice in a steamer or strainer over boiling water. Cover steamer, and steam for 5 to 8 minutes until hot. Use for Deysel (page 275) and other dishes.

Nutrients for ⅓ cup.

Calories: 75
Exchange: 1 starch/bread

g	mg
carbohydrate: 16.5	potassium: 19
protein: 1	sodium: 1
fat: negligible	cholesterol: 0
fiber: negligible	

Spanish Rice

Leftover rice, spicy with cloves and chile, makes a quick and delicious supper or lunch dish. Each serving contains 51 mg vitamin C in addition to nutrients listed below.

For 4 servings

1 tablespoon olive or other
    unsaturated oil
1 cup onion, sliced
2 fresh or canned tomatoes,
    chopped, including some
    juice
1 medium green bell pepper,
    seeded and chopped

2–3 whole cloves
1 small bay leaf
1 hot green chile, seeded and
    chopped (optional)
1½ cups cooked rice
Pinch salt and freshly ground
    pepper

1. In a saucepan, heat the oil, and sauté the onion until soft.

2. Stir in the tomatoes, pepper, cloves, bay leaf, and chile (if you are using it). Simmer for 15 minutes. Remove the cloves and bay leaf.

3. Add the rice, and mix well. Heat thoroughly until all the flavors blend. Taste, and season the rice with a pinch of salt and lots of pepper. Divide into 4 portions. Serve hot.

Nutrients for 1 serving.

Calories: 148
Exchanges: 1½ starch/bread; ½ vegetable; ½ fat

g	mg
carbohydrate: 26	potassium: 324
protein: 3	sodium: 10.5
fat: 4	cholesterol: 0
fiber: 3	

Wild Rice

Who doesn't like crunchy, nutty wild rice? Although it is not a true grain, wild rice, a plant of Minnesota, can be as versatile as the real thing in casseroles or as a side dish. I love it plain.

For 8 servings

1 cup wild rice   **Pinch salt (optional)**

1. Place the wild rice in a colander, and rinse it thoroughly under cold running water. (Remember that wild rice triples in bulk when cooked. Choose any method of cooking. If you have a rice cooker, cook wild rice as you would cook rice.)

2. To boil the rice in a saucepan: Pour a large quantity of water into the pan. Add a little salt (if you are using it), and bring to a boil. Stir in the wild rice, cover pan, and cook for 30 minutes until tender but not mushy. Drain thoroughly, and serve hot.

3. To steam the wild rice: Dampen a double cheesecloth or a towel, and place on a steamer. Spread the wild rice on the cheesecloth or towel. Cover the steamer, and steam for 40 minutes or until tender. Divide into 8 portions of ⅓ cup each. Serve hot.

Nutrients for 1 serving.

Calories: 70
Exchange: 1 starch/bread

g	mg
carbohydrate: 15	potassium: 44
protein: 3	sodium: 15
fat: negligible	cholesterol: 0
fiber: 1	

Vegetable Pilau

In India, pilau is a savory rice dish to which vegetables, raisins, nuts, and spices are added in interesting ways. You can use the idea often to mix seasonal vegetables and, of course, the inevitable leftovers. Surely, pilau is a spicier, more complex offspring of many rice dishes with similar names from Greece eastward.

For 8 servings

1 tablespoon unsaturated oil or Ghee (page 7)
1 large onion, chopped
1 bay leaf, crushed
¼ teaspoon ground cloves
¾ teaspoon ground cinnamon
1 teaspoon fresh ginger, minced
1¼ cups long-grain rice
½ teaspoon powdered saffron
½ cup potato, diced
½ cup carrots, diced
½ cup zucchini or squash, diced
1 small red bell pepper, diced
½ cup fresh peas
½ cup cauliflower, chopped
½ cup green beans, cut into short pieces
1 teaspoon salt (optional)
¼ cup raisins
2 tablespoons cashews, chopped

1. Heat the oil or Ghee in a casserole, and sauté the onion and bay leaf until the onion is translucent.

2. Stir in the cloves, cinnamon, and ginger. Continue cooking for about a minute.

3. Add the rice and saffron, stirring to coat the rice. Then add the 7 vegetables, and mix thoroughly.

4. Carefully pour 3 cups cold water into the casserole, and season with salt (if you are using it). Cover, and cook over low heat for 20 minutes until the rice is tender, and the liquid absorbed.

5. Gently mix the raisins and cashews into the pilau. Heat for 5 minutes. Divide into 8 servings. Serve hot.

Nutrients for 1 serving (about ¾ cup).

Calories: 179

Exchanges: 2 starch/bread; ½ vegetable

g	mg
carbohydrate: 34	potassium: 260
protein: 4	sodium: 49
fat: 3	cholesterol: 0
fiber: 3	

Bulgur

Crunchy cracked wheat can be cooked simply as rice or just soaked and stirred into a salad (Tabbouleh, page 110). Bulgur is especially delicious hot with cold plain yogurt.

For 4 servings

1⅓ cups medium or coarse bulgur
1 teaspoon corn oil (optional)

Pinch salt and freshly ground pepper

1. Toast bulgur gently in a saucepan with or without the oil just until color begins to deepen.
2. Add 2¼ cups water, salt, and pepper, and bring to a boil. Cover pan, lower heat to minimum, and cook gently for 15 minutes until all water is absorbed. Or you can bake in oven in a casserole. Divide into 4 servings. Serve hot or cold.

Nutrients for ½ cup without oil.

Calories: 75

Exchange: 1 starch/bread

g	mg
carbohydrate: 16	potassium: 49
protein: 2	sodium: 28
fat: negligible	cholesterol: 0
fiber: negligible	

Maltese Baked Rice

Marie-Louise Mifsud of the Diabetes Association of Malta offers this recipe and also a tip to make your casserole easy to clean.

For 10 servings

1 large onion, finely chopped
2 teaspoons olive oil
½ pound extra lean ground beef
¼ cup tomato puree
1 tablespoon tomato paste mixed with some water

Freshly ground pepper
¾ cup brown rice
3 ounces Parmesan cheese, grated
2 eggs, lightly beaten
Pinch powdered saffron

1. In a large skillet, sauté the onion in a little oil. Add the ground beef, press, and stir over medium heat until the meat is grainy.

2. When the beef loses its red color, add the tomato puree, tomato paste, and enough water to make a sauce. Simmer for 5 minutes. Remove from heat, and season lightly with pepper.

3. Add the rice, cheese, and eggs to the meat, stirring to mix thoroughly.

4. Dissolve the saffron in a tablespoon of cold water, and stir into the mixture.

5. Lightly oil a 2½-quart casserole, and wet it with cold water (this will prevent the food from sticking to the casserole). Scoop the meat and rice mixture into the casserole. Add water to about 1 inch above the food level. Cover casserole, and bake at 300°F for about 55 minutes, or until the liquid has been absorbed, and the rice is tender. Divide into 10 portions. Serve warm.

Nutrients for 1 serving.

Calories: 161
Exchanges: 1 starch/bread; 1 medium-fat meat

g	mg
carbohydrate: 17	potassium: 207
protein: 9	sodium: 100
fat: 6	cholesterol: 75
fiber: 2	

Bigilla
(Broad Beans, Malta Style)

"This is a typical country dish. It is very high in fiber since its main ingredient is dried beans. It can be served as a side salad with fish and meat," says Marie-Louise Mifsud of the Diabetes Association of Malta, who generously offers this recipe. Freeze small portions to have on hand for quick thawing.

For 12 servings

1 pound (2 cups) dried broad
    beans or lima beans
Pinch salt
1 head garlic (8–10 cloves),
    crushed
1 chile, seeded and chopped

3 sprigs fresh parsley, chopped
1 tablespoon fresh marjoram
    and mint, chopped
Freshly ground pepper
1 tablespoon olive or other
    unsaturated oil

1. Wash the beans, and soak overnight. When ready to cook, top up the water, and bring to a boil. Simmer until the beans are tender. If necessary, top again with water. Alternatively, these beans can be cooked in a pressure cooker.

2. When tender, turn the beans into a bowl, and mash roughly. Stir in the other ingredients, and mix well. Divide into 12 portions. Heat thoroughly. Serve warm.

Nutrients for 1 serving.

Calories: 117
Exchanges: 1 starch/bread; 1½ vegetable

g	mg
carbohydrate: 20	potassium: 472
protein: 6	sodium: 11
fat: 2	cholesterol: 0
fiber: 4	

Kasha (Cracked Buckwheat)

Kasha is the Russian word for porridge and has been popularized in the United States as a term for buckwheat groats, from which kasha was often made in Eastern Europe. This recipe, without the egg, was given to me many years ago by a Russian-Jewish woman. Serve it as a side dish with meat, fish, or vegetables.

For 4 servings

3.5 ounces (100 g) kasha
1 egg, lightly beaten (optional)
2 cups boiling water or White Chicken Stock (page 98)

Pinch salt (optional) and freshly ground white pepper

1. Heat a casserole, and spread the kasha on the bottom, with or without the egg; if using egg, mix thoroughly until the kasha grains are coated with egg. Cook over medium heat, stirring constantly, until the groats are dry and separated.

2. Carefully stir in the boiling water or stock. (The liquid should cover about an inch above the kasha.) Season lightly with pepper, and avoid the salt, since kasha contains sodium.

3. Cook over a low burner. Or bake at 350°F for about 25 minutes or until the liquid has been absorbed. Remove from heat, and drape with a towel for a few minutes. Divide into 4 portions. Serve warm.

Nutrients for 1 serving without egg.

Calories: 87
Exchanges: 1½ starch/bread

g	mg
carbohydrate: 20	potassium: 40
protein: 2	sodium: 84
fat: negligible	cholesterol: 0
fiber: NA	

Polenta

Bright yellow polenta makes a hearty side dish plain or a main dish layered with meat sauce. Italian families usually have at least one polenta enthusiast, who stirs the polenta with a special stick (a sanded broom handle will do).

For 9 servings

Pinch salt
1 tablespoon corn oil
1 cup polenta (coarse yellow cornmeal)

2 cups Homemade Tomato Sauce (page 19) or favorite sauce (optional)

1. Pour 5½ cups water in a large pot, and bring to a boil. Stir in the salt and oil.

2. When water is boiling briskly, *very gradually* add the polenta, stirring constantly. Wait until water boils again before sprinkling in more polenta. Keep adding and stirring to avoid lumping.

3. Cook, and stir almost constantly until the polenta thickens enough to make the stirrer stand straight without holding it. Dump the polenta onto a board or platter. Spread into a 1-inch-high rectangle (or any shape you like). Cool slightly, and cut into 9 squares. Serve warm, with or without sauce.

Nutrients for 1 square polenta without sauce.

Calories: 107
Exchanges: 1 starch/bread; ½ fat

g	mg
carbohydrate: 18	potassium: 28
protein: 2	sodium: 18
fat: 3	cholesterol: 0
fiber: 2	

Pansit Bihon or Lug-Lug
(Filipino Dried Rice Thread)

These very fine threads look like snow-white vermicelli. Unlike Chinese "cellophane" noodles that are made of beans, *pansit bihon* is usually a rice product. Japanese and Chinese versions can be substituted for the Filipino types. They are all available dry in plastic bags and have a long shelf life.

For 4 servings

3.5 ounces pansit bihon or lug-
lug (about 2 cups loosely
packed dry noodles)

1. Use either method to soften the noodles: Place in a sieve. Bring water to boil in a large pot. Dip the sieve with noodles into the boiling water for a minute. Lift sieve with the softened noodles, and pour onto a plate. Continue until all noodles are softened.

2. Another method: Place noodles in a bowl, and pour boiling water over them. Soak for a few minutes—or longer, if you get busy (it won't hurt the noodles to soak longer). Drain.

3. If you are planning to eat the noodles with chopsticks, or to stuff them into rolls, as in Vietnamese Cha Gio (pages 249–51), leave them long; if you are planning to use them in soup, chop them to fit into a spoon. Divide into 6 portions. Serve cold or warm.

Nutrients for ⅓ cup.

Calories: 58.5
Exchange: 1 starch/bread

g	mg
carbohydrate: 14	potassium: 2
protein: 1	sodium: 2
fat: negligible	cholesterol: 0
fiber: negligible	

Cooked and Roasted Soybeans

I know a chic, active woman who travels constantly in her consulting work. She carries these munchy crunchies as an ideal, nutritious snack. Soybeans are easy to prepare and store.

For about 6 cups toasted soybeans

2 cups soybeans

1. Rinse soybeans under cold water. To cook, use one of these methods: Soak soybeans overnight in cold water; or, if you start the same day you plan to cook, cover the soybeans with water, bring to a boil, and soak, covered, for an hour or so. After either method, boil the soaked soybeans for an hour. Test one of the soybeans to see if skins are loose, and if they are tender. If not, continue boiling for 20 or 30 minutes longer until you can easily rub off the skins.

2. Cool the soybeans by running cold water into the pot. Rub between your palms to loosen the skins. Discard skins as they rise to the surface. Continue until soybeans are all peeled. Rinse, and spread soybeans to dry on a kitchen towel.

3. To roast (and toast): Spread soybeans on a flat baking dish. Roast at 325°F for 45 minutes to an hour, depending on how brown you like them. Stir frequently, and taste occasionally to see how crispy they are. For really dry soybeans, you can turn off the oven, and leave them overnight to dry. (After roasting, soybeans will shrink to about half the uncooked size.) When cool, store in airtight container to preserve crispness. Use roasted soybeans in granola, mixed with dried fruit, and in salads and casseroles for variety.

Nutrients for 2 tablespoons.

Calories: 58
Exchanges: ½ starch/bread; ½ lean meat

g	mg
carbohydrate: 5	potassium: 243
protein: 5	sodium: 1
fat: 3	cholesterol: 0
fiber: 2.5	

Pasta e Fagioli
(Pasta and Beans, Italian Style)

Dean Martin celebrates this glorious "Pasta Fasul" dish when he sings the song, "That's Amore." That may be the familiar way to pronounce it, but the recipe is another story. Find any native of Italy, and you'll learn his unique way to cook this staple dish. Substitute any type of dried beans (white or red, large or small) or pasta (noodles or tiny pasta). But the seasoning has to be your own!

For 10 servings

½ pound (1 cup) navy, kidney, or broad beans
2 tablespoons olive oil
1–2 bay leaves
3 garlic cloves, chopped
1 large onion or 3 green onions, chopped
1 large stalk celery, chopped
½ carrot, chopped
4 fresh ripe or canned tomatoes, chopped

Herbs: 2 tablespoons fresh basil, chopped; 1 large pinch dried oregano, crushed; 2 sprigs fresh parsley, chopped
Freshly ground white pepper
½ pound medium spinach noodles
Parmesan cheese, grated (optional)

1. Soak the beans overnight. Next day, pour off the water, and cover with cold water to a depth of 2 inches above the beans. Bring to a boil, and skim off the foam.

2. Add 1 tablespoon of the oil, the bay leaves, garlic, onion, celery, carrot, and tomatoes. Cook until the beans are tender, about 1½ hours.

3. Season with the remaining oil, the herbs, and some pepper. (The beans should be thick, and some liquid should remain.)

4. Cook the noodles in lightly salted water until al dente; then drain.

5. Stir noodles into the beans. Taste, and adjust seasonings. Serve hot (with cheese or plain), accompanied by a crisp green salad.

Pumpkin Seed

Wherever you find pumpkins or calabaza (the West Indian variety), you find pumpkin-seed aficionados. Mediterranean and Caribbean people especially like to munch on them, and you will, too. Roast pumpkin seeds after Halloween. Seeds last a long time in jars. And cook the pumpkin, too. Try Spicy Stewed Pumpkin (page 159).

For about 2 cups

1 pumpkin   **Salt**

1. Cut the pumpkin in half, using a sharp knife. Remove the fibers and seeds. (Use the pumpkin to cook a recipe from this book.) Place the seeds in cold water with some salt for a few hours. Gradually separate the seeds, and discard the fibers. Spread the seeds on a towel to dry, preferably by a sunny window.

2. Transfer seeds to a baking tray. Roast at 300°F for 1 hour or until crispy, shaking pan frequently to mix. Cool thoroughly, and then store in a covered jar.

Vegetable Kichuri

Shane Ara Kabir of the Bangladesh Institute of Research and Rehabilitation generously shares this famous vegetable dish with you. A kichuri (also spelled khichari) is sometimes made with fish, hence the English dish kedgeree.

For 4 servings

3 tablespoons long-grain rice
4 tablespoons mung beans
  (mung dal)
2 teaspoons unsaturated
  vegetable oil
½ teaspoon cumin seed
2 tablespoons onion, chopped
1 bay leaf

1 small potato, peeled and
  diced
½ teaspoon fresh ginger,
  minced
¼ teaspoon garlic, crushed
2 tablespoons fresh peas,
  shelled
½ cup cauliflower, chopped

1. In a small bowl, wash together the rice and mung beans.

2. In a saucepan, heat the oil. Drop the cumin into the oil. Stir in the onion and bay leaf. Cook, stirring, until light brown.

3. Add the mixed rice and beans, the potato, ginger, garlic, peas, and cauliflower. Cook, and stir for 2 minutes.

4. Pour in enough hot water to make a sauce, and stir until the liquid boils. Lower heat, and simmer for 20 minutes until tender. Remove the bay leaf. Divide kichuri into 4 portions. Serve hot.

Nutrients for 1 serving.

Calories: 103
Exchanges: ½ starch/bread; 1½ vegetable; ½ fat

g	mg
carbohydrate: 17.5	potassium: 232
protein: 4	sodium: 11
fat: 3	cholesterol: 0
fiber: 4	

Boiled Lentils à la Bangladesh

Shane Ara Kabir of the Bangladesh Institute of Research and Rehabilitation reveals this easy yet imaginative recipe. Use any kind of dal or lentils you like.

For 2 servings

¼ cup lentils
½ teaspoon fresh ginger, sliced
1 teaspoon onion, chopped
Pinch salt
½ green chile, seeded and
   chopped

1 small tomato, chopped
   (optional)
1 teaspoon corn oil
1 teaspoon garlic, crushed

1. Rinse the lentils in a saucepan. Add 4 cups cold water, the ginger, and onion. Cook until lentils are soft, about 40 to 45 minutes.

2. Grind the lentils in a blender. Stir in a little salt, the chile, and tomato (if you are using it). Pour back into the saucepan, and bring to a boil.

3. In a skillet, heat the oil, and sauté the garlic. Add the lentils, and stir thoroughly. Divide into 2 portions. Serve hot.

Nutrients for 1 serving.

Calories: 115
Exchanges: 1 starch/bread; ½ vegetable; ½ fat

g	mg
carbohydrate: 16	potassium: 324
protein: 7	sodium: 59.5
fat: 3	cholesterol: 0
fiber: 4.5	

Curried Dal

Served as a soup or side dish with other curries, this spicy dal is a staple food of India. You'll find it fragrant to cook and versatile to serve.

For 4 servings

½ cup channa dal (split bengal gram or Indian chick-peas)
Salt
2 teaspoons corn oil
1 heaping teaspoon cumin seed
¾ teaspoon ground turmeric
½ teaspoon cayenne

1 teaspoon fresh ginger, minced
1 teaspoon ground coriander
½ teaspoon yellow mustard seed
5 cloves
1 small cinnamon stick

1. Wash the dal in a saucepan. Cover dal with cold water, and bring to a boil over medium heat. Cover the pan, and soak for at least an hour. (You can eliminate this step by soaking dal overnight in advance.)

2. When ready to cook, bring to a boil, add a pinch of salt, and cook until dal is very soft, and most of the water has been absorbed. While it's cooking, add small amounts of water, if necessary, and stir frequently. The dal should be thick. Whirl in the blender, if you want a smoother dal. You should have about 1½ cups. (This much can be done a day in advance and stored in the refrigerator until ready to cook.)

3. To spice the dal: Heat the oil in a skillet. Add the spices, and stir them over low heat for a few minutes until the mustard seed begins to pop. Remove skillet from heat.

4. Stand back, and carefully add a spoonful of the dal to the spices (it will spatter). Gradually add all the dal. Continue cooking to make a thick mixture, stirring frequently. Remove the cinnamon stick and cloves. Divide into 4 portions. Serve hot.

Nutrients for 1 serving.

Calories: 157
Exchanges: 1½ starch/bread; ½ fat

g	mg
carbohydrate: 23	potassium: 299
protein: 8	sodium: 36
fat: 4	cholesterol: 0
fiber: 6	

Cypriot Haricot Beans Soleas

"Cypriots in the villages tend to eat a lot of beans and pulses [legumes] and not as much meat as their urban counterparts," says nutritionist Moira Beaton, who works with Dr. C. Theophanides at his Diabetic Clinic in Paphos. "Soleas is a district in Cyprus, famous for beans, where this recipe is said to have originated." Use Great Northern beans as a very good substitute if you do not find Cypriot beans. This is an excellent recipe to freeze in small portions.

For 12 servings

1 pound (2 cups) Great Northern beans
1 medium onion or 3 green onions, finely chopped
2 medium stalks celery with leaves, chopped
2 large tomatoes, chopped
1 tablespoon tomato paste
2 medium carrots, scraped and sliced
Pinch salt and freshly ground pepper
1 tablespoon fresh parsley, chopped

1. Wash the beans, cover with cold water, and soak overnight. Next day, drain, and place beans in unsalted, cold water in a large saucepan. Bring to a boil, drain again, and cover with fresh, unsalted water.

2. Bring beans to a boil, cover, and simmer for 30 minutes. Add the onion, celery, tomatoes, tomato paste, and carrots. Boil for about 30 minutes longer or until tender.

3. Season with salt, pepper, and parsley. Simmer for 5 minutes. Divide into 12 portions. Serve hot with fresh green onions.

Nutrients for 1 serving.

Calories: 127
Exchanges: 1 starch/bread; 2 vegetable

g	mg
carbohydrate: 24	potassium: 726.5
protein: 8	sodium: 44
fat: negligible	cholesterol: 0
fiber: 6.5	

Ful Madamis (Egyptian Beans)

Hot and hearty Ful Madamis is the national breakfast dish in Egypt. Vendors sell the beans to workers on their way to work. And with a touch of lemon juice and herbs, the dish is hard to resist anytime, anywhere. Dried or canned ful (to cut down preparation time) are available at Middle Eastern shops.

For 4 servings

1 cup dried ful or substitute
  red kidney beans
1 small onion, chopped
1 tablespoon olive oil
Juice of ½–1 lemon
1 teaspoon dried oregano

Pinch salt and freshly ground
  pepper
Fresh parsley, chopped, for
  garnish (optional)
Lemon wedges for garnish
  (optional)

1. Wash the beans, and place in a pot. Cover with enough cold water to immerse beans. Soak overnight.

2. Next day, pour off the water, and cover with fresh water. Bring to a boil, skim off the foam, and add the onion. Cover pot, and simmer for 2 to 3 hours, stirring frequently and adding water only if necessary, until fork-tender. (All liquid should be absorbed; if not, cook uncovered until no liquid remains in the beans, about 3 minutes.)

3. In a large bowl, whisk the oil and lemon juice. Rub the oregano between your palms into the dressing, and season with salt and pepper. Gently stir the ful into the dressing until it is coated, mashing beans slightly with a fork. Taste, and adjust seasonings. Divide into 4 portions. Serve hot, and garnish, if you wish, with parsley and lemon wedges for guests to squeeze into the ful.

Nutrients for 1 serving.

Calories: 116
Exchanges: 1 starch/bread; ½ vegetable; ½ fat

g	mg
carbohydrate: 16	potassium: 295
protein: 5.5	sodium: 33
fat: 4	cholesterol: 0
fiber: 4	

Garbanzos Salteados
(Spanish Sautéed Chick-Peas)

Hungry for spicy Spanish chick-peas in 30 minutes? This quick version of the famous dish is from S. Betancourt of the Embassy of Spain Commercial Office in New York.

For 4 servings

1 medium onion, minced
1 garlic clove, minced
1 tablespoon Spanish olive oil
1 (1 pound) can garbanzos (chick-peas), drained
1 medium tomato, peeled and chopped
2 tablespoons fresh parsley, minced
2 ounces chorizo (Spanish sausage) or ham, chopped
Freshly ground pepper

1. In a casserole, sauté the onion and garlic in the oil until soft.
2. Add the remaining ingredients, seasoning to please your taste. Simmer for 10 minutes. Serve hot or cold.

Nutrients for 1 serving.

Calories: 135
Exchanges: 1 starch/bread; ½ medium-fat meat; ½ fat

g	mg
carbohydrate: 15	potassium: 322
protein: 6	sodium: 164
fat: 6	cholesterol: 9
fiber: 4	

Vadas

Savory vadas, although *not* sweet, are like doughnuts in three ways: They have a hole in the middle; they are fun to make; and youngsters clamor to eat them. Serve them as a snack or with curries and chutney or with a fresh green salad. Be sure to shake off excess oil, and keep the oil hot or the fat exchange will be higher.

For 12 vadas

½ cup urad dal or any lentils
1 large onion, minced
1 garlic clove, crushed
2 fresh green chilies, seeded
   and chopped

1 small piece fresh ginger,
   chopped
Pinch salt
Corn oil for frying

1. Wash the dal in a bowl. Cover with cold water, and soak overnight or for at least 3 hours.

2. Drain, and grind dal into a thick paste, using a food processor or blender. Add the onion, garlic, chilies, ginger, and a pinch of salt. Mix until smooth.

3. To shape the vadas: Very lightly flour a sheet of waxed paper. Divide the dal paste into 12 pieces. Flatten each piece into a circle.

4. Heat the oil in a deep fryer as you would to fry potatoes. To fry: Lift each vada, and shape it in your palms. Push through the middle with your finger to make a hole. Drop 3 or 4 vadas into the hot oil. Turn to brown on both sides. *Remove from oil and shake off excess;* drain on paper towels. Divide into 6 portions—2 vadas for each serving. Serve hot.

Nutrients for 2 vadas.

Calories: 116
Exchanges: ½ starch/bread; 1½ vegetable; 1 fat

g	mg
carbohydrate: 13	potassium: 264
protein: 5	sodium: 22
fat: 5	cholesterol: 0
fiber: 3	

Fresh Peanuts

It's hard to believe that the peanut (groundnut) is a native of South America. It is now an important crop in all the tropics and subtropics and widely produced in China, India, Nigeria, Senegal, and Gambia. It's even more difficult to accept how much we miss by not eating *fresh* peanuts more frequently. Peanuts are easy to cook and are a good vegetable protein source without sodium or cholesterol. This recipe serves as an introduction for you to try them when you can find them in Chinese and other Asian markets, especially. Boil, steam, or roast them, and then use them in any recipe—sauce, soup, salad, casserole—that calls for peanuts.

For about ½ cup

½ pound raw peanuts (78–80)
  in shells

1. Wash peanuts, and place in a saucepan. Cover with cold water, and cook for 15 minutes. Shell and taste one; if they taste raw, continue cooking for 5 minutes.

2. Drain, and shell the peanuts; there will be about 150 medium (½ pound) peanuts. Spread on a towel to dry thoroughly. Store in the refrigerator. Eat as snacks, sprinkled in salads, combined with soybeans and grains to complement the proteins. Use within 3 or 4 days.

Nutrients for 50 g (slightly less than 1 ounce).

Calories: 142
Exchanges: 3 fat

g	mg
carbohydrate: 4	potassium: 168.5
protein: 6.5	sodium: 1
fat: 12	cholesterol: 0
fiber: negligible	

Hopping John

This famous Southern dish pops up on Caribbean tables—often with coconut milk. A simpler recipe is offered here by Jill Kempe of the Bermuda Diabetic Association. If you serve it as a side dish, divide into 8 portions; for a main dish, divide into 4 portions.

For 4 or 8 servings

½ cup black-eye peas (common cowpeas)	1 large Bermuda or Spanish onion
2–3 sprigs fresh thyme	½ cup long-grain rice
2 slices bacon, diced	Salt and freshly ground pepper

1. Pick over and wash the peas in a saucepan. Cover, and soak overnight. Or bring to a boil, remove from heat, cover pan, and soak the peas for an hour or so to cut down on the cooking time.

2. Boil the peas with 1 sprig thyme until the peas split.

3. In a skillet, fry the bacon and onion until brown. Add to the peas. Stir in the rice and enough water, if necessary, to cook the rice. Cover pan tightly, and simmer over low heat for about 20 minutes, until the rice is tender.

4. Season lightly with salt and pepper and more thyme. Divide into 4 or 8 portions. Serve hot.

Nutrients for 1 serving as a side dish (8 servings).

Calories: 89

Exchanges: 1 starch/bread; ½ vegetable

g	mg
carbohydrate: 16	potassium: 195
protein: 4	sodium: 30
fat: 1	cholesterol: 1
fiber: 4.5	

Nutrients for 1 serving as a main dish (4 servings).

Calories: 178

Exchanges: 2 starch/bread; ½ vegetable

g	mg
carbohydrate: 32.5	potassium: 390
protein: 8	sodium: 61
fat: 2	cholesterol: 3
fiber: 9	

Spiced Dal Snack

Children in India munch this nutritious snack after school. Season the dal with your favorite seasonings. You may use tur dal (split pigeon peas known as red gram or arhar dal in India) instead of the channa. Dal Snack can be fried in hot oil following step 2, but the fat content will increase. Roasting is simpler.

For 3 cups (about 48 tablespoons)

1 cup channa dal (split bengal gram or Indian chick-peas)
Large pinch salt

1–2 teaspoons ground cumin, more to taste
1–2 teaspoons chili powder or cayenne pepper

1. Wash the dal in a saucepan. Cover with 4 cups water. Add the salt, and bring to a boil. Skim off any foam on the surface. Remove from heat. Season liberally with spices you like. Cover, and soak for a few hours.

2. Drain thoroughly. Spread dal on a towel to dry. Place dal in a bowl. Taste, and sprinkle with more spices, if you like.

3. To roast, spread dal on a flat pan. Roast at 250°F for 30 minutes. Taste, and continue roasting until they are as crisp as you like them. Remove from oven, and cool. When thoroughly cool, store in a covered container.

Nutrients for 2 tablespoons.

Calories: 38
Exchange: ½ starch/bread

g	mg
carbohydrate: 6	potassium: 83
protein: 2	sodium: 12
fat: negligible	cholesterol: 0
fiber: 2	

FISH AND SHELLFISH

Taste is in variety.
CHILEAN PROVERB

Chinese Sautéed Shrimps

We tasted this dish among the most savory ones at the Hotel Beijing in China. Assemble all your ingredients. Then the preparation is quick. Save some extra time for a beautiful presentation with garnishes.

For 4 servings

1 pound baby shrimps, cleaned, with tail shells left on

1 egg white

1 teaspoon cornstarch

Pinch salt

2 teaspoons peanut oil

1 cup bamboo shoots, sliced diagonally

4 medium mushrooms, sliced diagonally

1 leek (white part only), cut into ½-inch pieces

2 tablespoons rice wine

1 tablespoon light soy sauce

Pinch sugar (optional)

½ tablespoon rice wine vinegar

¼ teaspoon sesame oil

Cucumber fans for garnish (optional)

Green bell pepper for garnish (optional)

1. In a bowl, mix the shrimps, egg white, cornstarch, and a pinch of salt.

2. Heat 1 teaspoon of the oil in a wok or skillet. Drop the shrimps into the oil, and sauté quickly. Transfer to a strainer.

3. Pour 1 teaspoon of the oil into the wok, and when it is hot, stir-fry the bamboo shoots, mushrooms, and leek. Stir the shrimps into the vegetables.

4. Sprinkle with the wine, soy sauce, and a speck of sugar (if you are using it). Stir-fry for a minute to heat thoroughly.

5. Drizzle with a little vinegar and a few drops of sesame oil. Divide into 4 portions, and transfer to heated plates. Garnish with cucumber fans and green pepper rings. Serve immediately.

Nutrients for 1 serving without soy sauce (check the label for soy nutrients).

Calories: 137
Exchanges: 1½ lean meat; 2 vegetable

g	mg
carbohydrate: 8	potassium: 351
protein: 18	sodium: 167
fat: 3	cholesterol: 129
fiber: 2	

Qaqqocc Mimli
(Tuna-Stuffed Artichokes)

This popular Maltese dish is contributed by Marie-Louise Mifsud of the Diabetes Association of Malta.

For 4 servings

4 globe artichokes
Juice of ½ lemon
3 garlic cloves, crushed
1 sprig fresh parsley, chopped

1 olive, pitted and chopped
1 cup tuna (packed in water)
Freshly ground pepper
2 teaspoons olive oil

1. Remove stalks and choke from the artichokes, and discard the small outer leaves. Soak the artichokes in water mixed with the lemon juice.

2. To make the stuffing: In a small bowl, mix all remaining ingredients except the pepper and oil, and mash well. Fill each artichoke by pushing the stuffing between the leaves.

3. Stand the artichokes upright in a casserole just large enough to hold them. Season lightly with pepper. Drizzle ½ teaspoon oil over each artichoke, and pour about 2 cups water into the casserole. Cover the casserole. Simmer artichokes for about 45 minutes, or until a leaf can be removed. Serve warm.

Nutrients for 1 stuffed artichoke.

Calories: 139
Exchanges: 1½ lean meat; 2½ vegetable

g	mg
carbohydrate: 14	potassium: 459
protein: 16	sodium: 499
fat: 3	cholesterol: 29
fiber: 5	

Seemannsspiesschen
(Seaman's Kebabs)

Dotted with onion and apple, these kebabs are delicious. The recipe comes from Dr. P. Dieterle of the Deutsche Diabetes-Gesellschaft in Munich. Try this combination.

For 2 servings

4 ounces fish fillet (nonoily type) or shellfish
1 teaspoon vinegar or lemon juice
2 small onions, peeled

1 small apple, cored
1 small or ½ large green bell pepper, seeded
2 teaspoons corn oil
Pinch salt

1. Cut the fillet in 1-inch squares. Place in a small bowl, and sprinkle with the vinegar or lemon juice.

2. Slice the onion, apple, and pepper in ½-inch squares.

3. Mix the fillet, onion, apple, and pepper in a bowl. Sprinkle with oil and salt.

4. Divide the ingredients in half. Alternating the varieties, skewer the foods on 2 wooden or metal skewers. Charcoal-broil or broil in the oven until seafood is tender. Serve hot.

Nutrients for 1 serving.

Calories: 186

Exchanges: 1½ lean meat; 2½ vegetable; 1 fat

g	mg
carbohydrate: 11	potassium: 443
protein: 15	sodium: 132
fat: 9	cholesterol: 34
fiber: 2	

Steamed Fish and Vegetables

Seasonal fish and local vegetables are a natural combination. Here's a wholesome Mediterranean dish from the Randazzo brothers, owners of the three-generation Randazzo's Fish Market, Bronx, New York.

For 5 servings

½ tablespoon each olive oil
  and unsalted margarine
5 baby carrots, scrubbed
5 very small new potatoes,
  scrubbed
5 small yellow or white onions
1 cup turnip chunks
2 pinches salt
Freshly ground pepper
¾ pound white cabbage, cut
  into 5 pieces

10 ounces lean fish fillets or
  steaks (hake, pollack,
  redfish, rockfish, pike,
  perch, etc.)
2 tablespoons fresh parsley,
  chopped, more for garnish
1 tablespoon fresh rosemary,
  chopped
5 small lemon wedges

1. In a casserole large enough to hold the fish and vegetables, heat together the oil and margarine. Drop in the carrots, potatoes, onions, and turnips, and shake the pan slightly to mix. Cover, and steam the vegetables over medium heat for a few minutes.

2. Uncover, and pour in enough water to half cover the vegetables. Season very lightly with a pinch of salt and pepper. Cook for 15 minutes until potatoes are almost tender.

3. Meanwhile, drop the cabbage into boiling water with a pinch of salt, and cook for 15 minutes until tender; drain.

4. Lay the fish fillets or steaks over the vegetables in the casserole. Sprinkle the parsley and rosemary over the food. Arrange the cabbage over the top. Cover casserole, and continue cooking for 15 minutes or until potatoes are fork-tender and the fish flakes.

5. To serve, divide fish and vegetables into 5 portions, and serve on warm plates. Garnish with parsley and lemon wedges.

Portuguese Grilled Sardines

Portugal, on the easternmost edge of the Iberian Peninsula, is blessed with abundant seafood from the Atlantic Ocean. Naturally, fish is a staple food, especially fresh sardines. "This is the most popular fish dish in Portugal," says Manuel Machado Sá Marques, director of assistance services, Associaçâo dos Diabéticos de Portugal. "It is served from April till October. The sardines must be raw and not canned, and should be 15 cm [6 inches] long. They are best if grilled on a barbecue. The sardines are served with boiled potatoes, and tomato, onion, and sweet pepper salad, dressed with olive oil." If 6-inch sardines are not available, grill smaller ones. Weigh your portion *after* grilling to determine the exchanges and calories.

For 4 servings

**10 ounces fresh sardines with
  heads, cleaned**

Wash sardines, and pat dry. Place on a grill, and cook on each side until the flesh is tender. Serve warm.

Marinated Fish Fillets

Here's a typical Mediterranean seafood dish. Marinate the fish an hour or the evening before you plan to serve it.

For 4 servings

10 ounces fish fillets, washed
  and dried
2–3 bay leaves
1 tablespoon olive oil
1 tablespoon dry white wine
2 onions, sliced into rings
3 tomatoes, peeled and
  chopped

Pinch sugar (optional)
Pinch salt and freshly ground
  pepper
2 garlic cloves, crushed with
  skin on
Fresh parsley for garnish

1. Cut the fillets into 4 equal portions. In a casserole, spread the fillets, and tuck bay leaves between the slices. Drizzle with ½ tablespoon of the oil and 1 tablespoon wine. Marinate for 1 hour.

2. Meanwhile, heat the remaining oil in a nonstick saucepan, and sauté the onions until soft. Add the tomatoes, a pinch of sugar, if you wish, and a little salt and pepper. Simmer for 5 minutes.

3. Pour the tomato sauce over the marinated fish. Drop the crushed garlic on top.

4. Bake at 350°F for 20 minutes until the fish flakes easily. Remove garlic before serving. Divide in warm plates with 1 portion fish and sauce on each. Delicious with steamed rice. Serve warm, garnished with parsley.

Nutrients for 1 serving.

Calories: 158
Exchanges: 2 lean meat; 1 vegetable; ½ fat

g	mg
carbohydrate: 6	potassium: 491
protein: 15	sodium: 112
fat: 8	cholesterol: 34
fiber: 1	

Haitian Crab and Okra

For a Caribbean-style lunch, how about this zesty dish mellowed with coconut milk? The recipe is from a native of Haiti.

For 4 servings

1 teaspoon unsalted margarine
1 medium onion, finely chopped
2 garlic cloves, minced
1½ cups okra, sliced, or spinach, chopped

4 tablespoons Coconut Milk (pages 30–31)
2 cups White Fish Stock (page 100) or water
Hot pepper sauce
8 ounces steamed crab meat

1. Heat the margarine in a casserole, and sauté the onion and garlic until soft. Stir in the okra, and mix thoroughly.

2. Pour in the coconut milk and stock or water. Bring to a boil, and season with pepper sauce. Simmer for about 10 minutes until okra is fork-tender.

3. Mix the crab meat into the sauce. Heat thoroughly. Taste, and enhance the seasonings. Divide into 4 portions. Serve warm with fluffy rice.

Nutrients for 1 serving.

Calories: 129
Exchanges: 1 lean meat; 1⅕ vegetable; ¾ fat

g	mg
carbohydrate: 8	potassium: 459
protein: 11	sodium: 70
fat: 6	cholesterol: 57
fiber: 3	

Crab Enchiladas

Crab meat tucked into tortillas, topped with salsa and cheese, emerges from your oven, and the appetizing aroma fills your kitchen.

Since the typical garnishes always add calories, nutrients are given for the crab enchiladas with and without the garnishes, so that you can choose.

For 6 enchiladas

6 corn tortillas
1–2 teaspoons corn oil
9 ounces crab meat
6 tablespoons onion, minced
1½ cups fresh tomato sauce or canned tomato sauce
2 ounces jack cheese, shredded

6 tablespoons diet sour cream (optional garnish)
3 olives, rinsed, pitted, and sliced in half (optional garnish)
6 slices avocado (optional garnish)
6 slices fresh tomato (optional garnish)

1. In a skillet, heat the tortillas in 1 teaspoon of the oil, turning tortillas until soft. Add the second teaspoon oil, if it's necessary.

2. In the middle of each tortilla, place 1½ tablespoons crab meat, 1 tablespoon onion, and a little tomato sauce. Roll each enchilada, and place in a casserole.

3. Cover with the remaining sauce, and sprinkle with the cheese. Bake at 400°F for about 10 minutes, or until hot, and cheese melts.

4. If you wish, garnish each enchilada with 1 tablespoon sour cream, ½ olive, a slice of avocado and tomato. Serve immediately.

Nutrients for 1 enchilada without garnishes.

Calories: 169

Exchanges: ½ starch/bread; 1 lean meat; 2 vegetable; ½ fat

g	mg
carbohydrate: 16	potassium: 220
protein: 12	sodium: 108.5
fat: 6.5	cholesterol: 52
fiber: 2	

Nutrients for garnishes (1 tablespoon sour cream, ½ olive, slice avocado, slice tomato).

Calories: 83

Exchanges: 1 vegetable; 1½ fat

g	mg
carbohydrate: 6	potassium: 264
protein: 2	sodium: 54.5
fat: 7	cholesterol: 0
fiber: 1	

Stockfish in Wine Sauce, Monaco Style

Among the traditional recipes sent to me by the late Princess Grace of Monaco is this one. The instructions note: "If stockfish is dry, soak in cold water for 4 to 5 days, changing water 3 or 4 times a day. This recipe can be used for codfish; but codfish should be left in cold water for only 12 hours."

For 8 servings

1 pound stockfish, codfish, or any nonoily fish
2 tablespoons olive oil
2–3 bay leaves
1 tablespoon fresh rosemary, chopped, or 1 teaspoon dried rosemary, crumbled
1 tablespoon fresh thyme, chopped, or 1 teaspoon dried thyme, crumbled
1 medium onion, minced
1 garlic clove, minced
½ cup white wine
2 tomatoes, sliced, or 2 tablespoons tomato puree
8 small potatoes, peeled
8 black or green olives
Salt and freshly ground pepper
Fresh parsley for garnish

1. Cut the stockfish into 8 pieces.
2. Brown fish in the oil in a shallow pan or casserole.
3. Add the bay leaves, rosemary, and thyme. Sprinkle in the onion and garlic. Cook for a few minutes.
4. Pour in the wine, and simmer for 5 minutes.
5. Add the tomatoes or tomato puree, the potatoes, olives, and almost enough water to cover the fish and vegetables. Season with salt and pepper. Simmer until the potatoes are tender. If the fish reaches the tender stage before the potatoes, remove it and keep it warm. Divide into 8 portions with 1 piece fish, potato, and tomato with sauce for each serving. Top with the parsley. Serve hot.

Nutrients for 1 serving.

Calories: 156
Exchanges: ½ starch/bread; 1½ lean meat; ½ vegetable; ½ fat

g	mg
carbohydrate: 8	potassium: 399
protein: 12	sodium: 118
fat: 7	cholesterol: 25
fiber: 1	

Fish Dopeyaja

Any kind of fish can be curried. Here's a mellow recipe from Bangladesh, offered by Shane Ara Kabir of the Bangladesh Institute of Research and Rehabilitation.

For 4 servings

½ teaspoon ground turmeric
½ teaspoon chili powder
½ teaspoon garlic, crushed
1 tablespoon corn oil
½ cup onion, sliced

8 ounces fish of any kind, cut
　　into 4 slices
Pinch salt
1 tomato, cubed
1 tablespoon fresh coriander
　　leaves, chopped

1. Mix the turmeric, chili powder, and garlic with just enough water to make a paste.

2. Heat the oil in a saucepan or casserole. Sauté half the sliced onion until light brown. Stir in the spice paste, and cook for 30 seconds. Add the fish to the pan with the remaining sliced onion, a pinch of salt, and ½ cup water. Shake the pan to mix. Add the tomato and coriander. Simmer over low heat until fish is tender. Divide into 4 portions. Serve fish hot with steamed rice or chapati.

Nutrients for 1 serving.

Calories: 143
Exchanges: 2 lean meat; ½ vegetable; ½ fat

g	mg
carbohydrate: 3	potassium: 386
protein: 15	sodium: 106.5
fat: 8	cholesterol: 34
fiber: negligible	

Spicy Calamari in Wine Sauce

Calamari (squid) is very popular among Mediterranean and Asiatic people and here's why: It is not only delicious, but also high in protein (only 84 calories and less than a gram of fat in 100 grams or 3½ ounces).

If you dislike cleaning this sea mollusk, you can buy calamari already cleaned. It costs more than the unprepared variety, however.

For 6 servings

1 pound calamari, cleaned at your fish shop, or uncleaned
1 tablespoon olive or other unsaturated oil
2 onions, chopped
2 garlic cloves, chopped
1 small bay leaf, crushed
¼ cup dry white wine

2 cups fresh tomatoes, chopped, or 1 cup tomato puree
1 tablespoon tomato paste
½ cinnamon stick
3 whole cloves
Freshly ground pepper

1. To clean the calamari: Separate the sac from the tentacles by pulling them apart. Discard the translucent support by pulling it out. Cut the innards to separate from the tentacles. You can save a few ink sacs before discarding the innards (to add flavor and color to the sauce). Cut off the eye portion of the tentacles, and squeeze out the round cartilage inside and discard it. Now rub the bodies and pull off the outer skin. Wash the sacs and tentacles; drain. Cut the sacs into rings or strips. Chop the tentacles, if you wish. (You can do this much hours in advance or the night before; if so, squeeze some lemon juice over the calamari, cover, and refrigerate.)

2. Heat the oil in a casserole or saucepan, and sauté the onions and garlic until soft. Add the bay leaf and the wine, and cook for a few minutes until the alcohol evaporates. Drop the calamari into the casserole, and sauté over medium heat for 2 minutes.

3. Add the tomatoes and tomato paste with enough water to make a fairly thick sauce. Stir in the spices. Simmer for 25 minutes until tender. Discard cinnamon stick and cloves. Divide into 6 portions. Serve warm with hot rice, noodles, or other pasta with a crisp salad on the side.

Nutrients for 1 serving
(2 ounces calamari plus sauce).

Calories: 97
Exchanges: 1 lean meat; ½ fruit; ⅕ fat

g	mg
carbohydrate: 7	potassium: 228.5 (wine sauce only)
protein: 9	sodium: 33.5 (wine sauce only)
fat: 3	cholesterol: negligible
fiber: 1.5	

Lenguado Monte de Oro
(Sole Mountain of Gold)

When you need a tasty international recipe, try this one from Angela Vera, nutritionist with the Asociación de Diabeticos del Uruguay. Serve the fish with whole wheat bread and a seasonal salad or vegetable.

For 4 servings

8 ounces sole or flounder fillets	2 tablespoons all-purpose flour
1 egg white, lightly beaten	2 tablespoons corn oil
Pinch salt	Juice of 1 lemon

1. In a flat bowl, dip the fillets in the egg white. In another bowl, mix the salt and the flour. Then dip fillets in the mixture.

2. Heat the oil in a nonstick skillet. When hot, brown the fillets on both sides. Drain on paper towels, and place on a warm platter. Splash with the lemon juice. Divide into 4 portions. Serve warm.

Nutrients for 1 serving.

Calories: 195
Exchanges: ½ starch/bread; 2 lean meat; 1 fat

g	mg
carbohydrate: 6	potassium: 329
protein: 16	sodium: 117.5
fat: 12	cholesterol: 34
fiber: negligible	

Paella

Paella is the quintessential rice casserole—a colorful contribution of Spain. With the saffron-flavored rice base, a diverse assemblage of vegetables and seasonings, seafood, poultry, and meats are transformed into a beautiful and savory culinary apogee. Paella is named for the *paella*, a wide, two-handled metal or earthenware pan in which the dish is cooked and served. By partially cooking major ingredients before combining them with the rice, you can have them ready in advance to cut down on last-minute preparation time. Baking paella in the oven, covered, ensures more even cooking than over a burner, which concentrates the heat on only about 8 inches of the 16-inch paella pan. (A paella pan doesn't have a cover, but a 16-inch pizza pan or aluminum foil will do.) You may vary the seafood (substitute calamari, fish segments, mussels, or prawns for the lobster, shrimps, and clams), the poultry (rabbit or chicken segments), the meat (smoked sausage, bacon, or pork for the chorizo), or vegetables. For a superb blending of flavors, save all cooking liquids from clams and vegetables to use when baking the paella. Olé!

For 10 servings

2 teaspoons plus 1 tablespoon olive oil
1 chicken breast (6 ounces), boned and cut in 1-inch pieces
Freshly ground pepper
8 ounces shrimps, cleaned with tails on
1 cup fresh or frozen artichoke hearts, sliced in half
2 ounces chorizo (Spanish-style sausage), thinly sliced
20 live clams, soaked for 30 minutes in lightly salted water (to remove sand)
2 sprigs parsley
2 sprigs thyme
1 bay leaf
Small piece celery

½ cup dry white wine
2 or 3 garlic cloves, minced
1 large onion, minced
½ green or red bell pepper, diced
1½ cups long-grain or Spanish rice
2 pinches salt (optional)
½ teaspoon saffron
½ cup fresh or canned plum tomatoes, chopped
2–2½ cups White Chicken Stock (page 98)
1 cup fresh or frozen peas
3 lobster tails (6 ounces lobster), steamed
Fresh parsley for garnish
1 pimiento, sliced into long strips (optional)

1. In a paella pan or wide casserole, heat 1 teaspoon of the oil and sauté the chicken until lightly browned. Grind pepper over the top. Lift chicken with a slotted spoon and keep warm.

2. Drop the shrimps into the hot pan, and stir-fry only until the color turns pink. Remove the shrimps and add to the chicken.

3. Heat the second teaspoon of oil and sauté the artichoke hearts over medium heat until lightly browned. Add enough water to cover pan bottom, cover, and steam gently for 10 minutes. Transfer artichokes to another plate and reserve the liquid.

4. Brown the chorizo slices in the paella pan and cook for 4 to 5 minutes. Drain the chorizo on paper towels, and squeeze out all excess fat. Discard all fat from the paella pan and wipe clean.

5. To prepare the clams: Drain the clams and discard the soaking water and sand. Scrub the shells and rinse. To steam: In a saucepan, combine parsley, thyme, bay leaf, celery, and wine with the clams. Cover, and steam for 8 minutes until clam shells open. Strain over a bowl and reserve the clam stock for the paella. Reserve the clams in their shells.

6. To prepare rice: Coat the bottom of the paella pan with the tablespoon olive oil and sauté the garlic, onion, and bell pepper until softened. Stir in the rice and cook for 2 minutes over very low heat, stirring constantly. Mix the saffron (you don't need salt). Add the tomatoes and cook for 1 or 2 minutes. Stir in enough of the stock to almost cover the rice and bring to a boil over the burner (to cut down the baking time).

7. Stir the peas and artichokes into the rice. Tuck in the chorizo slices. Pour the reserved clam and vegetable liquids and chicken stock over the rice. Cover, and bake at 350°F for 10 minutes. Uncover (there should still be remaining liquid; if not, add more stock or water); then arrange the chicken, shrimps, clams, and lobster tails attractively on top. Cover, and continue baking until rice is tender, and all ingredients are hot and savory, about 10 to 15 minutes. Remove from oven. Sprinkle with parsley and garnish with pimiento slices, if you like. With a damp paper towel, clean off side of paella pan, if necessary. Serve immediately in the pan.

Nutrients for 1 serving.

Calories: 217
Exchanges: ½ starch/bread; 2 lean meat; 2½ vegetable

g	mg
carbohydrate: 22	potassium: 328
protein: 20	sodium: 189
fat: 5	cholesterol: 80
fiber: 2	

Escabeche (Jamaican Tangy Fish)

From the Spanish word for pickle or pickled fish, escabeche (also called escovitch) is prized throughout the Caribbean.

Marinate the fish a day in advance to allow the flavors to develop. Escabeche is usually fried, but I've adapted the recipe for grilling to cut down on fat and calories.

For 6 servings

1 pound nonoily fresh fish, cleaned
½ large lime or small lemon
Freshly grated black pepper
2 tablespoons olive or other vegetable oil
¼ cup vinegar
1 large onion, finely chopped

2 garlic cloves, chopped
1 red chile, chopped (optional), or cayenne pepper
1 bay leaf, crushed
5–6 allspice seeds, crushed
Pinch salt (optional)
Fresh thyme leaves

1. Wash, and dry the fish. On a plate, sprinkle the fish inside and out with plenty of lime or lemon juice. Grate black pepper over it and in the cavity. Set aside while making the marinade.

2. In a small saucepan, mix the oil, vinegar, onion, garlic, chile or cayenne, bay leaf, and allspice. Beat lightly with a fork to make a spicy marinade. Taste, and season with salt, if you like, and add more seasonings. Bring to a boil, and remove from the heat. Cover marinade, and keep it hot.

3. Grill or bake the fish in a flat baking dish or casserole until the flesh turns white and flaky (don't overcook or it will toughen).

4. Immediately pour the hot marinade over the fish to cover on all sides. Cool to room temperature. Cover, and refrigerate. Divide into 6 equal portions. Serve cold, garnished with thyme.

Nutrients for 1 serving.

Calories: 160
Exchanges: 2 lean meat; 1 vegetable; ½ fat

g	mg
carbohydrate: 6	potassium: 414
protein: 15	sodium: 98
fat: 9	cholesterol: 34
fiber: 2	

Sushi

CHOOSING SUSHI AND
JAPANESE DISHES IN RESTAURANTS

Sushi bars have sprung up in most American cities, tempting us with beautifully prepared specialties. Dr. Kempei Matsuoka, chief of endocrinology and metabolism, Saisekai Central Hospital, Tokyo, divulges nutrition tips for you when eating out. They appear in *Medical Treatment with Food for Diabetes* by Tadayoshi Takai and Kayoko Asami.

"When eating out, sushi is a good choice from a menu. Sushi provides quality proteins from fish. Fish is also good for the control of cholesterol." Popular types of seafood and fish for sushi include tuna, calamari (squid), octopus, sea bass, shellfish, including shrimp, bright orange roe, and other very fresh seafood.

Nori seaweed is another nutritious component of sushi. Wrapped around vinegared rice and a fish filling, nori holds the filling compactly. It is then sliced across into cylinders and served with the fish. Other accompaniments include very thin egg omelet, sliced into strips or triangles, shredded fresh ginger, horseradish, and dipping sauce.

The Japanese experts add, "Americans and Europeans like meat, but too much meat isn't good for diabetes. Tofu is excellent for diabetes."

A warning when lunching or dining at a restaurant: "Count how much fat you are getting. Be careful when you eat tempura, because it is fried. Also be careful when you choose rice with cooked eel, deep-fried pork sandwiches, and hot dogs!"

The Japanese physicians offer sound advice: "If you cannot control your food when eating out, carry your lunch from home to your office, school, or wherever you visit."

SUSHI AT HOME

Should you like sushi at home, use these suggestions as a guide:

Nutrients for 2 ounces raw shrimps.

Calories: 52
Exchange: 1 lean meat

g	mg
carbohydrate: negligible	potassium: 126
protein: 11	sodium: 80
fat: negligible	cholesterol: 86
fiber: 0	

(continued)

Nutrients for 1 ounce fresh nonoily fish.

Calories: 49
Exchange: 1 lean meat

g	mg
carbohydrate: 0	potassium: 150
protein: 7	sodium: 38
fat: 2	cholesterol: 17
fiber: 0	

Nutrients for 2 ounces tofu (bean curd).

Calories: 43
Exchange: ½ medium-fat meat

g	mg
carbohydrate: 1	potassium: 25
protein: 5	sodium: 4
fat: 2.5	cholesterol: 0
fiber: 0	

Nutrients for ½ cup bamboo shoots.

Calories: 13
Exchange: ½ vegetable

g	mg
carbohydrate: 2	potassium: 52
protein: 1	sodium: 4.5
fat: negligible	cholesterol: 0
fiber: 0	

Nutrients for nori seaweed (soaked and drained).

Exchange: ½ cup = 1 vegetable

Nutrients for daikon radish curls

Exchange: 1 cup = 1 vegetable

MEATS,
POULTRY,
AND GAME

**When man has raw meat,
he looks for fire.**

JAMAICAN PROVERB

Blinde Vinken
(Blind Finches or Veal Birds)

Tender veal cutlets rolled around herb stuffing are called Blind Finches by the Dutch. Follow the same tradition. Serve Blinde Vinken with rice and peas.

For 4 servings

4 veal cutlets (1½ ounces each), sliced ½ inch thick
1 small onion, minced
1 slice white bread
2 tablespoons low-fat (1%) milk
Dried or fresh sage and savory
Pinch salt and freshly ground pepper

½ tablespoon unsalted margarine
½ cup plain low-fat yogurt
Nutmeg
4 slices toast
2 tablespoons fresh parsley, chopped

1. Pound each cutlet to ¼-inch thickness. Set aside while making the stuffing.

2. Place the onion in a bowl. Moisten the bread with the milk, adding a few drops more, if necessary. Add to the onion. Season the stuffing with sage, savory, salt, and pepper.

3. Divide the stuffing equally into 4 parts. Place each part on a cutlet. Roll up, and tie with string.

4. In a casserole or skillet, heat the margarine, and sauté each cutlet on all sides. Pour ½ cup water and the yogurt into the casserole. Stir the sauce to mix. Grate nutmeg over the top. Cover, and simmer for 30 minutes or until tender, turning every 10 minutes or so. Remove the string.

5. To serve, place each cutlet on a slice of toast. Strain the sauce directly over the veal. Sprinkle with parsley and serve immediately.

**Nutrients for 1 Veal Bird,
1 slice toast, and sauce.**

Calories: 254
Exchanges: 1 starch/bread; 2 medium-fat meat; 1 vegetable

g	mg
carbohydrate: 21	potassium: 439
protein: 20	sodium: 260
fat: 11	cholesterol: 35
fiber: 1	

Roast Beef, Maltese Style

This Maltese specialty, cooked with potatoes and onions, from Marie-Louise Mifsud of the Diabetes Association of Malta, may not be like your standard roast beef. It's a homey, hearty dish!

For 10 servings

2½ pounds lean beef roast
2 pounds potatoes, halved or
  quartered
4 medium or 3 large onions,
  sliced

Pinches salt and freshly
  ground pepper
2 garlic cloves, crushed
2 cups White Beef Stock
  (page 99) or water
Fresh parsley for garnish

1. Wash, and dry the beef.
2. Rinse the inside of a roasting pan or casserole with cold water. Spread a layer of potatoes and onions in the pan or casserole. Sprinkle with salt and pepper.
3. Lay the meat on top. Cover with more potatoes and onions.
4. Season very lightly with salt and pepper. Spread the crushed garlic over the potatoes. Add the stock or water to the pan.
5. Roast at 350°F, allowing 20 minutes per pound plus an additional 20 minutes, or until you reach your favorite degree of doneness. Baste the meat from time to time. If it is done before the potatoes, remove the roast, and keep warm until the potatoes are cooked.
6. Surround the roast with the potatoes and onions. Slice the beef, and divide into 10 servings. Serve warm, garnished with parsley.

**Nutrients for 1 serving (2 ounces beef,
vegetables, and sauce).**

Calories: 223
Exchanges: ½ starch/bread; 1½ medium-fat meat; 2½ vegetable

g	mg
carbohydrate: 20	potassium: 561
protein: 18	sodium: 61
fat: 8	cholesterol: 46
fiber: 3	

Japanese Style Meat
and Dipping Sauce

How about a dish of succulent meat slices prepared in seconds and served with a tangy dipping sauce? The recipe is now yours—from Akiyo Tsukahara of Tokyo and Osaka. You'll have fun cooking this with your friends. The sauce and beef nutrients are listed separately for your mixing and matching convenience.

For 6 servings

¼ cup low-sodium soy sauce
¼ cup lemon juice
½ cup white radish (daikon),
    finely grated

6 very thin slices beef from
    tenderloin (12 ounces)
1 tablespoon unsalted
    margarine or butter

1. Make the dipping sauce in advance. In a bowl, mix the soy sauce, lemon juice, and radish.

2. When ready to serve, briefly sauté the beef in the margarine or butter. Serve 1 slice beef on each plate with the dipping sauce in small bowls on the side.

Nutrients for 1 tablespoon dipping sauce.

Calories: 4
Exchange: free

g	mg
carbohydrate: negligible	potassium: 28
protein: negligible	sodium: 152
fat: 0	cholesterol: 0
fiber: negligible	

Nutrients for 1 slice beef.

Calories: 135
Exchanges: 2 medium-fat meat

g	mg
carbohydrate: 0	potassium: 238
protein: 16	sodium: 36
fat: 7	cholesterol: 48
fiber: 0	

Zrazy (Polish Meat Rolls)

Ingrid Bolski, a native of Poland, hopes you'll like her favorite dish. She suggests serving it with kasha and red cabbage.

For 8 servings

4 slices, each about 8 inches long (1 pound) lean beef, thinly sliced

2 medium sour pickles, chopped

1 large onion, chopped

6 tablespoons fresh parsley, chopped, more for garnish

2 cups mushrooms, sliced

2 slices bacon

½ cup dry wine

1 cup White Beef Stock (page 99) or water

1. Using a mallet or board, flatten each beef slice.

2. Divide the pickles, onion, and parsley into 4 equal parts. Sprinkle across each slice of beef.

3. Divide the mushrooms in half, and reserve half for later. Divide the other half into 4 portions, and sprinkle each portion on the beef slices.

4. In a casserole, fry the bacon until crisp. Crumble the bacon, and divide evenly over the 4 slices. Pour off all but 1 tablespoon of the bacon fat. Keep the casserole warm.

5. Tightly roll up the beef slices. Tie with string, or seal with skewers.

6. Heat the casserole with the bacon fat. When the fat is very hot, add meat rolls, and brown them over medium-high heat, turning constantly.

7. Lower the heat, and add the wine (it will sizzle). Cook gently until the alcohol evaporates.

8. Add the remaining mushrooms and almost enough stock to cover the rolls. Cover the casserole, and simmer over low heat until fork-tender, about 60 minutes. Or bake at 350°F. Uncover during the last 15 minutes to thicken the sauce. Remove string or skewers from rolls, and slice each in half to make 8 servings. Sprinkle with fresh parsley. Serve hot.

Nutrients for 1 serving (½ meat roll).

Calories: 174

Exchanges: 1½ medium-fat meat; 2 vegetable

g	mg
carbohydrate: 5	potassium: 440
protein: 20	sodium: 293
fat: 7	cholesterol: 55
fiber: 2.5	

Souvlaki apo Arni
(Hellenic Lamb Souvlaki)

Lamb has been a favorite dish of Hellenes since ancient times, but other meats (lean veal or pork) are substituted in various seasons with delicious results. Enjoy this recipe, which appeared in an article I wrote for *Diabetes Forecast*.

For 8 servings

1 lean leg of lamb, cut in walnut-size cubes (1 pound net after boning and cooking)
1 tablespoon olive oil
2 tablespoons lemon juice
2 tablespoons dry red wine (optional)
½ teaspoon each of dried thyme, oregano, and rosemary

1 bay leaf, crushed
2 garlic cloves, crushed
Pinch salt and freshly ground pepper
8 small bay leaves
1 firm tomato, cut in eighths
1 crisp green bell pepper, cubed
Dried oregano and lemon wedges for garnish

1. Wash and dry the lamb cubes. Place in a bowl.

2. To make the marinade: In a small bowl, mix the oil, lemon juice, wine, herbs, garlic, a pinch of salt, and a few grindings of pepper. Pour the marinade over the meat, and mix well. Cover the bowl, and marinate in the refrigerator for at least 3 hours or (preferably) overnight.

3. Thread the meat on long skewers, alternating bay leaves with tomato and pepper slices. Reserve the marinade.

4. Grill over hot coals or broil 6 inches from the heat. Brush with the marinade, and turn frequently to cook evenly. Crush oregano over the top. Divide into 8 portions. Serve hot with lemon wedges.

Nutrients for 1 serving with
wine and lemon garnish.

Calories: 121
Exchanges: 1½ medium-fat meat; ½ vegetable

g	mg
carbohydrate: 2	potassium: 248
protein: 16	sodium: 53
fat: 5	cholesterol: 54
fiber: negligible	

Sate Manis
(Indonesian Shish Kebab)

The fabulous sate dishes of Indonesia, introduced by the Moslems, are usually lamb cubes skewered and grilled. An Indonesian cook in New York urges you to try this spicy dish. Marinate in advance, and serve with rice and vegetables.

For 4 servings

½ pound sirloin steak cut ½ inch thick
½ teaspoon ground coriander
1 garlic clove, crushed
1 teaspoon brown sugar

1 tablespoon low-sodium soy sauce
½ tablespoon lemon juice
Freshly ground pepper

1. Cut steak into 8 cubes. Place in a bowl. Add all remaining ingredients, and mix with the steak. Marinate in the refrigerator.

2. Thread the cubes on skewers. (If you are using bamboo skewers, soak for 5 minutes before using to avoid burning.)

3. Broil over hot charcoal, turning frequently until cooked rare or medium rare, as you like it. Divide into 4 portions. Serve hot.

Nutrients for 1 serving (2 cubes).

Calories: 144
Exchanges: 2 medium-fat meat

g	mg
carbohydrate: 2	potassium: 239
protein: 16	sodium: 193
fat: 8	cholesterol: 46
fiber: 0	

Teka Kebab
(Afghan Broiled Kebabs)

More kebabs! Tenderize these in yogurt and spices. Great for a summer barbecue party.

For 6 servings

1 cup plain low-fat yogurt	Freshly ground black pepper
Pinch salt	3 garlic cloves, crushed
½ teaspoon ground red pepper or cayenne	12 ounces lean lamb (from the leg) or beef, cut into 12 cubes

1. In a large bowl, mix the yogurt with the spices and garlic. Dip the meat into the yogurt. Cover, and marinate at room temperature for 2 hours or in the refrigerator from 6 hours to overnight.

2. When ready to broil, drain the meat, and reserve the marinade. Thread the meat on skewers. Broil or charcoal-broil evenly on all sides, brushing with yogurt marinade. Divide into 6 servings. Serve hot with Naun (pages 262–63) or chapati.

Nutrients for 1 serving (2 kebabs).

Calories: 130
Exchanges: 1½ medium-fat meat; 1 vegetable

g	mg
carbohydrate: 3	potassium: 260.5
protein: 18	sodium: 81
fat: 5	cholesterol: 56
fiber: 0	

Kibbe bi Saniyeh
(Moroccan Baked Specialty)

Meaty kibbe, a flat meatloaf—with bulgur to lighten it and cinnamon and pepper to spice it—is a Moroccan specialty. Kibbe is perfect for a picnic with lots of raw vegetables and pita bread, climaxed with fruit.

For 12 servings

For kibbe:

¾ pound lean ground lamb

Pinch salt

1 teaspoon black peppercorns, coarsely ground

½ teaspoon ground cinnamon

1 small onion, chopped

1 cup bulgur (cracked wheat), soaked in boiling water to cover for 15 minutes and drained

For filling:

½ pound lean ground lamb or beef

1 onion, minced

3 tablespoons pine nuts

Pinch salt

¼ teaspoon black peppercorns, coarsely crushed

2 tablespoons dried bread crumbs for sprinkling

Fresh parsley and tomato slices for garnishes (optional)

1. To make the kibbe: In a bowl, mix the ground lamb, a pinch of salt, pepper, cinnamon, and the onion. Knead well, and then run mixture twice through the meat grinder, or mix in a processor. Add the soaked bulgur, and knead thoroughly again. The mixture should be very moist, or it will dry out when baking. Add water by the tablespoonful, if needed. Set aside the kibbe while making the filling.

2. For the filling, crumble the ground lamb or beef into a warm nonstick skillet. Mash with a fork over medium heat until raw color changes, stirring in ¼ cup water as you stir. Add the onion, and cook, and stir until the onion softens. Skim off fat from the meat. Stir in the pine nuts, a speck of salt, and the pepper.

3. To layer and bake: Wet the inside of a 9x12x3-inch baking dish and shake out excess water (this prevents the food from sticking). Divide the kibbe in half. Spread one-half in the bottom of the dish. Over the kibbe spread the filling, smoothing out evenly. Top with the remaining half of the kibbe. Sprinkle top with bread crumbs.

4. Using a sharp knife, score the kibbe from top to bottom into diamonds or squares. First, cut lengthwise into 3 even sections. Then cut 4 times diagonally or straight across the first slashes to make 12 diamonds. Bake at 350°F for 30 minutes until tender. Serve warm or cold, garnished with fresh parsley and tomato slices, if you wish.

Nutrients for 1 serving.

Calories: 144
Exchanges: 1 medium-fat meat; 2⅕ vegetable

g	mg
carbohydrate: 11	potassium: 212
protein: 15	sodium: 56.5
fat: 5	cholesterol: 43
fiber: negligible	

Sephardic Lamb Pita

An interesting phenomenon among various cultures is how favorite ground meats and grains are used in everyday dishes. Compare this recipe, for example, to the Moroccan specialty, Kibbe bi Saniyeh (pages 222–23). This version is a flat meat loaf sandwiched between two layers of soaked matzoth. It is an easy Sephardic dish from a family in Greece. You can cut this pita in tiny squares to serve on crackers as appetizers. Or slice it into larger squares, as suggested here, and serve it as a substantial entrée.

For 9 servings

2 matzoth, finely ground
  (½ cup)
1 cup White Chicken Stock
  (page 98) or water
1 pound ground lean lamb or
  veal
2 garlic cloves, crushed
Handful fresh mint, chopped

Pinch salt and freshly ground
  black pepper
1 egg white
1 ripe tomato, thinly sliced
  (optional)
Fresh oregano or parsley,
  chopped, for garnish

(continued)

1. Heat a skillet, and spread the ground matzoth to toast gently, shaking the pan constantly. Remove from heat. Pour the stock or water over the matzoth, and soak.

2. Meanwhile, mix the meat in a bowl with the garlic, mint, salt, pepper, and egg white. Knead thoroughly.

3. To layer the pita, spread half the soaked matzoth in a 7x11x2-inch baking dish. Cover with the lamb mixture. Top with the remaining soaked matzoth, and smooth the surface.

4. Bake at 350°F for 30 minutes, or until golden brown and the sides shrink slightly. Remove from oven. Cool slightly before cutting into 9 squares. Serve warm with a tomato slice on top and sprinkled with fresh oregano or parsley.

Nutrients for 1 square with tomato garnish.

Calories: 121

Exchanges: 1 medium-fat meat; 2 vegetable

g	mg
carbohydrate: 6.5	potassium: 217
protein: 15	sodium: 90
fat: 3.5	cholesterol: 45
fiber: negligible	

Zürcher Geschnetzeltes
(Pork in Wine, Zurich Style)

Thanks are due to Myrtha Frick, Swiss nutritionist and columnist for the *Swiss Diabetes-Journal*, for suggesting this typical Swiss dish.

For 8 servings

16 ounces lean pork
1 tablespoon unsaturated oil or margarine
5 small onions, chopped
Pinch salt (optional) and freshly ground white pepper
Herbs: 1 bay leaf, 1 sprig fresh parsley, and 1 sprig thyme, rosemary, or sage

1 small cucumber, peeled, seeded, and diced
1 cup White Chicken Stock (page 98) or water
½ cup dry red wine
½ cup diet sour cream
1 small bunch fresh dill, chopped

1. Slice pork into 16 cubes.

2. Heat the oil or margarine in a casserole. Sauté the pork for 2 to 3 minutes until browned, stirring constantly.

3. Add the onions and continue cooking for another minute. Season very lightly with a pinch of salt (if you are using it) and pepper.

4. Tie the herbs together with a string, and add to the casserole. Stir in the cucumber, and mix well. Pour the stock over the food. Cover the casserole, and simmer for 20 to 25 minutes or until the pork is thoroughly cooked.

5. Add the wine, and cook, uncovered, for a few minutes until the alcohol evaporates. Remove the herbs.

6. Gradually add the sour cream, stirring until thoroughly heated. Divide into 8 portions. Sprinkle with fresh dill and serve hot.

Nutrients for 2 pork cubes and sauce.

Calories: 158
Exchanges: 1½ medium-fat meat; 1½ vegetable

g	mg
carbohydrate: 6	potassium: 421
protein: 18	sodium: 77
fat: 6	cholesterol: 52
fiber: 1	

Afelia
(Cypriot Coriander-Spiced Pork)

Moira Beaton, who works with Dr. C. Theophanides in his Diabetic Clinic in Paphos, Cyprus, suggests this popular dish, adding, "Serve afelia with boiled or baked potatoes and vegetables."

For 6 servings

12 ounces (¾ pound) lean pork
   (from the loin), cut in
   12 cubes
1 tablespoon coriander seed,
   crushed with a rolling pin

4 tablespoons dry red wine
1 teaspoon corn or olive oil
Pinch salt and freshly ground
   pepper

1. Wash, and dry the pork. Rub the coriander over the pork. Place pork in a glass bowl. Pour in the wine, cover, and refrigerate overnight or at least 3 hours.

2. When ready to cook, drain the pork, and reserve the marinade.

3. Heat the oil in a casserole, and sear the meat until just lightly browned. Add the reserved marinade and barely enough water to cover. Season to your taste with salt and pepper. Simmer gently for 45 minutes to 1 hour, or until the meat is tender, and the sauce is reduced. Divide into 6 servings. Serve hot.

Nutrients for 1 serving (2 pork cubes and sauce).

Calories: 158
Exchanges: 2 medium-fat meat

g	mg
carbohydrate: negligible	potassium: 232
protein: 15.5	sodium: 59
fat: 9	cholesterol: 51
fiber: 0	

Chicken Korma

Truly an exotic chicken curry to remember! It comes from Shane Ara Kabir of the Bangladesh Institute of Research and Rehabilitation. She cautions to be sure to use kewra (keora) *water* for flavoring. If you happen to have kewra *essence* (a very concentrated flavoring), dip a skewer into the essence and stir into the food. That's all you'll need. You'll find kewra water in specialty shops stocking foods of India and Pakistan.

For 2 servings

½ teaspoon garlic, crushed
1 tablespoon ground ginger
1 cup onion, finely chopped
1 cardamom seed
1 stick cinnamon
2 tablespoons plain low-fat
  yogurt or cottage cheese

Pinch salt
1 teaspoon corn oil or Ghee
  (page 7)
2 pieces chicken (4 ounces),
  skin discarded
½ teaspoon lemon juice
½ teaspoon kewra water (see
  note above)

1. In a saucepan or casserole, mix the garlic, ginger, onion, cardamom, cinnamon, yogurt or cheese, a little salt, and oil or ghee. Add ½ cup water to make a sauce.

2. Drop the chicken into the sauce, and cover the pan. Simmer over moderate heat for about 10 minutes. Lower the heat, and continue cooking for about 20 minutes until chicken is tender.

3. Stir in the lemon juice and kewra water, and keep the pan over very low heat for a few minutes until the oil separates out. Serve hot with porota or rice.

Nutrients for 1 serving.

Calories: 170
Exchanges: 2½ lean meat; 1½ vegetable

g	mg
carbohydrate: 8	potassium: 338
protein: 18	sodium: 123
fat: 7	cholesterol: 51
fiber: 2	

Kota Lemonato (Lemony Chicken)

Here's another terrific recipe from Moira Beaton, nutritionist in Cyprus. Lemony Chicken immediately became a favorite in my home the first time I cooked it.

For 8 servings

8 chicken segments (1½
  pounds)
½ cup fresh lemon juice
2 cups White Chicken Stock
  (page 98) or water

1 tablespoon all-purpose flour
Pinch salt and freshly ground
  white pepper

1. Place the chicken in a casserole. Add the lemon juice and stock or water. Bake uncovered at 350°F for 30 minutes. Baste frequently with the stock. Check for doneness, and continue baking for 30 minutes or until the chicken is tender.

2. Arrange chicken on a warm platter and keep warm.

3. Strain sauce through a cheesecloth or sieve directly into a saucepan. Skim off and discard all fat from the surface.

4. Dissolve the flour in a little cold water. Stir into the sauce. Cook over medium heat, stirring with a whisk until thick and smooth enough to pour. Taste, and adjust the seasoning. Add more lemon juice, if you like, and a pinch of salt and pepper. Pour over the chicken. Serve warm with fresh vegetables.

Nutrients for 1 serving (2 ounces chicken).

Calories: 144
Exchanges: 2½ lean meat

g	mg
carbohydrate: 2	potassium: 146
protein: 16	sodium: 63
fat: 8	cholesterol: 50
fiber: 0	

Hawaiian Chicken Luau

Here's a party dish with a gingery scent and a tropical dash of coconut. Taro tops, originally used in this recipe, are available in Hawaii, but you can substitute spinach or your favorite leafy green vegetable. Garnish it with flowers. This recipe is high in vitamin A.

For 10 servings

1 chicken (2 pounds)
1-inch piece fresh ginger, grated
3–4 garlic cloves, crushed
2 pinches salt and freshly ground white pepper

2 pounds fresh spinach or 2 packages frozen spinach or other leafy greens
1 cup Coconut Milk (pages 30–31)

1. Wash chicken, and place in soup pot with water just to cover. Gradually bring to the boil, and skim off foam and fat rising to surface. Simmer for 10 minutes, and degrease again.

2. Season chicken with ginger, garlic, a little salt, and pepper. Cover, and simmer for 40 minutes or until chicken is just tender. Strain over a bowl. Save broth for soup.

3. Separate chicken meat, and discard skin and bones. Shred chicken. (Up to this point you can prepare in advance and store the chicken, covered, in refrigerator. Reheat before serving.)

4. Wash, trim, and steam fresh spinach or thaw and steam frozen spinach until just tender. Mix with coconut milk, and heat thoroughly.

5. Divide chicken and spinach into 10 portions. Place chicken on plates with spinach on top. Serve warm.

Nutrients for 1 serving.

Calories: 193.5
Exchanges: 2 lean meat; 1 vegetable; 1½ fat

g	mg
carbohydrate: 3.5	potassium: 407 (chicken)
protein: 20.5	NA (coconut)
fat: 11	sodium: 114 (chicken)
fiber: 1	NA (coconut)
	cholesterol: 55 (chicken)
	NA (coconut)

Venison or Game Stew, German Style

When venison is in season, marinate it in buttermilk. Simmer the game with spices and wine. Then enjoy the creation. This recipe comes from Dr. P. Dieterle of the German Diabetes Association in Munich.

For 8 servings

1 pound venison or other game	2 teaspoons corn oil
2 cups low-fat buttermilk	1 medium onion, minced
Spices: 5–6 whole coriander, 2	2 tablespoons cream cheese
bay leaves, 2–3 peppercorns,	1 tablespoon lemon juice
2–3 red pepper seeds	2 tablespoons dry red wine

1. Place the venison in a bowl. Pour the buttermilk over the venison, and marinate, covered, in the refrigerator, for 3 to 4 days; turn frequently.

2. Wash, and dry the venison. Partially grind the spices, and rub into the venison with the oil and onion.

3. Place the venison in a casserole with 2 cups water, and roast at 350°F or until tender, or simmer over low heat for about 50 minutes, basting frequently.

4. Transfer game to a warm platter. Add the cream cheese, lemon juice, and wine to the sauce, and stir until cheese melts. Strain, and pour over the game. Divide into 8 servings. Serve warm with vegetables.

**Nutrients for 1 serving
(2 ounces venison and sauce).**

Calories: 130
Exchanges: 2 lean meat; 1 vegetable

g	mg
carbohydrate: 3	potassium: 288
protein: 18	sodium: 85
fat: 4	cholesterol: 15
fiber: negligible	

Tripes à la Vaudoise
(Swiss-Style Tripe)

Nutritionist Myrtha Frick of the *Swiss Diabetes-Journal* lauds this quick recipe. Use it when you plan a Swiss meal. This recipe is high in vitamin A.

For 4 servings

9 ounces beef tripe
2 small carrots
3 ripe tomatoes
2 teaspoons corn oil
1 small onion, minced

1 cup White Chicken Stock
 (page 98) or water
Pinch salt and freshly ground
 pepper
Ground cumin to taste

1. Cut the tripe into strips, the carrots into slices, and the tomatoes into dice.

2. In a casserole, heat the oil, and sauté the onion until soft. Add the tripe, carrots, and tomatoes. After about 2 minutes, add the stock.

3. Season with salt, pepper, and cumin to taste. Cover casserole, and simmer for 1 hour or until tender. Add more stock, if necessary. Divide into 4 equal servings. Serve warm.

Nutrients for 1 serving.

Calories: 127
Exchanges: 1 medium-fat meat; 1 vegetable; ½ fat

g	mg
carbohydrate: 7	potassium: 231
protein: 15	sodium: 102
fat: 5	cholesterol: NA
fiber: 2	

Sausages and Cannellini Beans, Tuscan Style

A quick and delicious recipe such as this one has to come from a native of Tuscany and a superb cook, and that's Louis Loffredo. You can cook cannellini beans at home or use canned when you are in a hurry.

For 6 servings

6 ounces fresh Italian fennel sausage

3 garlic cloves, crushed

2 cups peeled fresh or canned tomatoes, chopped

2 cups cooked fresh or canned cannellini beans (white kidney beans), drained

Fresh fennel leaves, chopped

1. Slice the sausage into 6 pieces (the smaller the slices, the quicker the cooking). Gently brown the sausage on both sides in a casserole. (To reduce cooking time, begin cooking sausage in a small amount of water, turning sausage until water evaporates.) When nice and brown on all sides and cooked thoroughly, drain sausage on paper towel.

2. Pour off the fat, and leave only a coating on the casserole. Heat the casserole gently, and sauté the garlic for 1 minute. Stir in the tomatoes, and simmer for 10 minutes or so. Tuck the sausage into the sauce. Mix in the beans. Cover, and simmer for 30 minutes or bake at 350°F until boiling hot. Divide into 6 portions. Serve hot, garnished with fennel. It's excellent with crisp cucumber salad.

Nutrients for 1 serving
(1 ounce sausage and ⅓ cup beans).

Calories: 181
Exchanges: ½ starch/bread; 1 medium-fat meat; 2 vegetable; 2 fat

g	mg
carbohydrate: 17	potassium: 457
protein: 11.5	sodium: 269.5
fat: 8	cholesterol: 22
fiber: 4	

CASSEROLES, STUFFED, AND ROLLED SPECIALTIES

When the food tastes best, stop eating.
SLOVAKIAN PROVERB

Cocido, Mexican Style

Cocido as a noun means "a cooked dish" and is found in various forms wherever Spanish-speaking people live, throughout Central America and the Caribbean islands. A cocido is the homiest, friendliest type of dish to cook and vary to suit your needs as the seasons change. Versatile for a family gathering or a party. This recipe is high in vitamin A.

For 8 servings

¾ pound beef shank or chuck,
   cut in chunks
2 ripe tomatoes, chopped
2 garlic cloves, chopped
1 onion, chopped
Pinch salt

8 peppercorns
2 cups green beans, sliced
2 carrots, sliced
3 medium zucchini, sliced
3 ears corn

1. Make a broth: Wash the beef, and place it in a soup pot with 8 cups water. Bring to a boil, and skim off the foam and any fat rising to the surface. Add the tomatoes, garlic, onion, and a little salt, and the peppercorns. Simmer until meat is tender.

2. Strain the broth directly into another pan. Degrease. Trim off all fat from the beef. Cut beef into bite-size cubes, and keep warm.

3. Add the beans to the broth, and simmer until half done. Then stir in the carrots and zucchini. Cook for 5 minutes.

4. Cut the corn in 1-inch pieces. (Put the corn on a cutting board, position a cleaver or other sharp knife wherever you want to slice the ear; then whack the blunt edge of the cleaver with a mallet or smaller board.) Add the corn to the cocido with water, if needed (the cocido should be soupy). Simmer until the corn is tender, about 7 minutes. Add the meat cubes, and heat to the boiling point. Taste and enhance the seasonings to your pleasure. Ladle into 8 bowls. Serve hot with Mexican Salsa Picante (page 17) or plain.

Nutrients for 1 serving without salsa.

Calories: 187

Exchanges: ½ starch/bread; 1½ medium-fat meat; 1½ vegetable

g	mg
carbohydrate: 17	potassium: 570
protein: 16	sodium: 67
fat: 7	cholesterol: 45
fiber: 6	

Bakmi Goreng (Indonesian Noodle-Meat-Vegetable Dish)

Indonesia blends the culinary influences of Indians, Chinese, Arabs, and Dutch. When in an Indonesian mood, you can toss together these ingredients for a quick trip in your own home. The recipe, reflecting the Chinese influence, is from an Indonesian woman. Leftovers are fine.

For 4 servings

3 ounces thin egg noodles
1 teaspoon unsalted margarine
2 green onions, chopped
1 garlic clove, chopped
1 cup cabbage, shredded
½ stalk celery, chopped
½ cup cooked chicken or
   meat, finely diced

½ cup cooked shrimps,
   chopped
2 teaspoons low-sodium light
   soy sauce
Freshly ground white pepper
1 tablespoon Fried Onion
   Flakes (page 5) for garnish
   (optional)

1. Cook the noodles in boiling water until al dente. Drain, and rinse with cold water. Drain thoroughly, and set aside until ready to mix.

2. Heat the margarine in a nonstick skillet, and sauté the onion and garlic until golden. Add the cabbage, celery, chicken or meat, shrimps, and enough water to provide some sauce. Simmer for 7 minutes until the vegetables, chicken, and shrimps are hot. Season with soy sauce and pepper to suit your taste. Mix in the noodles, and heat thoroughly. Sprinkle with onion flakes (if you are using them). Divide into 4 servings. Serve hot.

Nutrients for 1 serving.

Calories: 177
Exchanges: ½ starch/bread; 1½ lean meat; 2½ vegetable

g	mg
carbohydrate: 19	potassium: 322
protein: 18	sodium: 181
fat: 3	cholesterol: 87
fiber: 2	

Ajies Rellenos con Carne
(Baked Stuffed Peppers with Meat)

Now you have Uruguay's version of the famed *chiles rellenos* of Mexico. The recipe is from Angela Vera, a nutritionist in Uruguay. *Aji* is the Spanish word for chile and capsicum peppers, and they are prized in South and Central America, where they originated.

For 8 servings

8 long or bell peppers
4 ounces small sausages, peeled
3 ounces cooked chicken breast, sliced in lozenge shapes
1 cup cooked beef or other meat, chopped

½ onion, grated
2 teaspoons grated cheese
¼ cup soft bread crumbs
Low-fat milk to soak bread
1 cup cooked fresh or canned green peas
1 egg, lightly beaten
Nutmeg, pinch salt, and freshly ground pepper

1. To peel and clean the peppers: Using tongs, turn peppers over an open flame or place 2 inches under a broiler. Let the skin blister but not burn. Place peppers in a damp towel or plastic bag for 15 minutes to release moisture, and soften. Peel off the skins. Slash only one side of each pepper, but don't cut off either end. Remove core with seeds and veins. Rinse, and dry the peppers. Set aside while making the filling.

2. For the filling, mix the sausages, chicken, meat, onion, and cheese. Soak the bread in milk and squeeze. Then add the peas to the filling.

3. Bind with the egg. Season with nutmeg, salt, and pepper to make a tasty filling.

4. Stuff the peppers with the filling. Sprinkle a baking pan or casserole with water. Line up the peppers in the pan. Cover with oiled baking paper to prevent the filling from drying out. Bake at 350°F for 30 minutes. Remove the paper, and check for doneness. Continue baking uncovered for 10 minutes. Serve warm.

Nutrients for 1 stuffed pepper.

Calories: 128

Exchanges: ½ starch/bread; 1 lean meat; ⅕ vegetable; ½ fat

g	mg
carbohydrate: 10	potassium: 308
protein: 9	sodium: 219
fat: 6	cholesterol: 57
fiber: 4	

Patlijan Karni Yarek
(Armenian Stuffed Eggplant)

You can begin this spicy Armenian eggplant dish a day in advance. It will be devoured quickly. No wonder it is a famous dish.

For 4 servings

½ pound ground lean lamb or beef

2 medium onions, finely sliced

1 small green bell pepper, seeded and chopped

Pinch salt and freshly ground white pepper

1–1½ teaspoons ground allspice

2 garlic cloves, crushed

½ cup fresh or canned plum tomatoes with juice

½ cup fresh parsley, chopped

2 medium eggplants (1 pound each)

1 tablespoon unsalted margarine, melted

1 tablespoon tomato paste diluted in ½ cup water

1 fresh ripe tomato, cut in 4 slices

1. In a skillet, mash and stir the lamb or beef with a fork until the raw color disappears, adding ¼ cup water as you stir. Skim off all fat.

2. Add the onions and green pepper, mixing well. Cook for about 5 minutes. Season lightly with salt, pepper, and liberally with allspice. Then stir in the garlic, tomatoes, and half the parsley. (This filling can be made a day in advance, and stored in the refrigerator.)

(continued)

3. Using a sharp knife, cut eggplants in half lengthwise. Sprinkle eggplants lightly with salt, and invert over a rack. Let drain for 20 minutes. Rinse thoroughly to remove all salt. Dry the eggplants.

4. Place eggplants on a baking dish and brush with the margarine. Bake at 425°F for 10 minutes until light brown. Cool slightly.

5. To stuff: Slash eggplant halves across the middle to make a cavity in each. Divide filling among the slices, and stuff into the cavity. (You may prefer to make 2 slashes, and divide the filling.)

6. Arrange eggplants in a baking pan or casserole. Pour the diluted tomato paste into the pan. Dot each eggplant slice with a tomato slice. Bake at 350°F for 30 minutes or until tender. Serve hot, garnished with remaining fresh parsley.

Nutrients for ½ stuffed eggplant.

Calories: 196
Exchanges: 1½ medium-fat meat; 3⅕ vegetable

g	mg
carbohydrate: 17	potassium: 779
protein: 18	sodium: 112
fat: 7	cholesterol: 51
fiber: 5	

Noodle Casserole with Chicken

Speckled with vegetables and noodles and spiced with pepper—here's a tasty chicken casserole for lunch or dinner from Zentralinstitut für Diabetes. The carrots make the recipe high in vitamin A.

For 8 servings

1 chicken breast (½ pound after boning)	1 cup carrot, chopped
1 medium onion, chopped	1 cup kohlrabi, chopped (optional)
Pinch salt	1 large stalk celery, chopped
4–5 peppercorns	1 cup cauliflower, chopped
Bouquet garni: 1 carrot, 1 stalk celery, 1 parsley root, and 1 bay leaf	4 ounces noodles
	Fresh parsley for garnish

1. In a soup pot, cover the chicken with cold water, and bring to a boil. Skim off the foam and fat. Add the onion and a little salt and peppercorns. Tie together the bouquet garni, and slip into the stew. Simmer gently until chicken is tender, about 15 minutes. Transfer chicken to a warm bowl, and set aside to cool slightly. Strain the broth directly into a casserole.

2. Bring the broth to a boil, and stir in the chopped carrot, kohlrabi (if you are using it), and celery. Simmer for about 10 minutes, and add the cauliflower and noodles. Add enough water to cook the noodles and vegetables. Continue cooking until noodles are tender.

3. Meanwhile, remove chicken from the bones, and discard the bones. Shred the chicken, and add to the casserole. Season to your taste. Divide into 8 servings. Sprinkle with parsley. Serve warm.

Nutrients for 1 serving.

Calories: 105

Exchanges: 1 lean meat; 2 vegetable

g	mg
carbohydrate: 11	potassium: 262
protein: 11	sodium: 75
fat: 1	cholesterol: 33
fiber: 2	

Locro (Argentinean Corn-Vegetable-Beef Casserole and Piquant Sauce)

The zest of South American music is in this corn stew—specked with sweet potato, chorizo, and squash, splashed with beans and beef, zingy with red pepper. Ana Maria Malerba, nutritionist with the Liga Argentina de Proteccion al Diabético in Buenos Aires, sends a piquant sauce recipe to serve with her very special recipe of locro—a national dish.

For 10 servings

1 cup dried white corn kernels
Pinch salt
1 pound lean beef, cubed
1 slice bacon
Pork bones (optional)
1 cup cooked or canned green beans

2 ounces chorizo (Spanish sausage), grilled and sliced
1 sweet potato, cubed
2 cups cabbage, sliced in julienne strips
½ pound squash, cubed

For sauce:

2 tablespoons corn oil
1 large onion, sliced in julienne strips

Ground red pepper, paprika or cayenne

1. Wash the dried corn. Place in a saucepan, and pour 2¼ quarts cold water over the corn. Soak overnight. The next day, boil corn until nearly cooked. Season lightly with salt.

2. Slice the beef into small cubes and the bacon in the same size squares. Add beef, bacon, pork bones (if you are using them), beans, and chorizo slices. Simmer for about 40 minutes until beef is tender.

3. Add the sweet potato, cabbage, and squash. Continue cooking until all ingredients are tender. If the sauce is all absorbed, stir in more water. Divide into 10 servings. Serve hot.

4. To make the piquant sauce: Heat the oil in a skillet, and sauté the onion until translucent but not brown. Add 1 cup water, and simmer for 5 minutes. Season with red pepper to make a spicy sauce. Serve in a small bowl as an accompaniment to locro.

Nutrients for 1 serving without sauce.

Calories: 203

Exchanges: ½ starch/bread; 1½ medium-fat meat; 2 vegetable

g	mg
carbohydrate: 18	potassium: 438
protein: 17	sodium: 283
fat: 8	cholesterol: 45 ·
fiber: 8	

Nutrients for 1 tablespoon piquant sauce.

Calories: 35

Exchanges: ½ vegetable; ½ fat

g	mg
carbohydrate: 2	potassium: 48
protein: negligible	sodium: 2
fat: 3	cholesterol: 0
fiber: negligible	

Bermuda Pawpaw Montespan

The versatile tropical vegetable/fruit we know as papaya is called pawpaw in many Caribbean islands. And how imaginatively it is used! Bermuda Pawpaw Montespan, a layered dish with papaya, beef, cheese, and tomato, is typical. I adapted the recipe, offered by Jill Kempe of the Bermuda Diabetic Association. Each serving contains 55 mg of vitamin C.

For 4 servings

2 cups green papayas, cooked and mashed

2 ripe fresh or canned tomatoes, thinly sliced

¼ pound extra lean ground beef

2 medium onions, finely chopped

3 tablespoons grated cheese

1 tablespoon bread crumbs

1. Choose a small casserole that will allow space for layers. Rinse casserole with cold water to make cleanup easier. Divide the papayas into 3 parts. Spread one-third in the bottom of the casserole. Cover with half the tomato slices.

2. In a small skillet, heat the oil, and sauté the beef and onions. Spread half of the beef and onions over the tomatoes and papayas in the casserole. Sprinkle with 1 tablespoon of the cheese.

3. Continue layering: 1 portion papayas, remaining tomatoes, remaining beef and onions, 1 tablespoon cheese, remaining papayas on top. Finally, sprinkle with the bread crumbs and remaining tablespoon cheese.

4. Place the baking dish into a larger one. Pour hot water in the outer pan. Bake at 350°F for 35 to 40 minutes until firm and the top golden. Cut into 4 squares. Serve hot.

Nutrients for 1 square.

Calories: 150

Exchanges: 1 medium-fat meat; 1½ vegetable; ½ fruit

g	mg
carbohydrate: 14	potassium: 467
protein: 10	sodium: 112
fat: 6	cholesterol: 27
fiber: 3	

Hungarian Goulash

Spicy with paprika and pepper, goulash is perfect on a wintry day. Make it in advance, and heat before you serve. This recipe is from Ed Weiss, owner of Paprikas Weiss Hungarian shop in New York. I've adapted from chicken fat to unsaturated oil and reduced the amount of beef, but the flavors are still Hungarian!

For 6 servings

1 teaspoon corn or other unsaturated oil

3 onions, chopped

1 small green bell pepper, seeded and chopped

1 tablespoon paprika, preferably Hungarian, more to taste

½ pound lean beef, cut in 1-inch cubes

1 tablespoon tomato paste

1 cup White Beef Stock (page 99) or water

Salt and freshly ground pepper

6 tablespoons plain low-fat yogurt or diet sour cream for garnish

1. Heat the oil gently in a heavy saucepan, and sauté the onions until soft and transparent. Stir in the bell pepper and paprika, and cook over low heat until the pepper softens.

2. Add the beef, and brown on all sides over medium heat, stirring constantly. Cover pan, lower heat, and steam beef for 10 minutes.

3. Stir in the tomato paste and stock or water. (If you prefer a soupy goulash, add enough stock or water to make 6 or 7 cups of liquid.) Season lightly with salt and generously with pepper. Simmer over low heat or bake at 325°F until tender, about 1 hour. Taste, and season with more paprika if you like. Divide on 6 plates or bowls. Serve hot, topped with a heaping tablespoon of yogurt or diet sour cream for each serving.

Nutrients for 1 serving.

Calories: 126

Exchanges: 1 medium-fat meat; 2 vegetable

g	mg
carbohydrate: 8	potassium: 394.5
protein: 13	sodium: 97
fat: 4.5	cholesterol: 31
fiber: 2	

Tunisian Chicken Couscous

"Tunisian red, Moroccan white," says Rasika Mezmi, diplomat at the Tunisian Mission in New York, explaining the major difference between the couscous of her country and the Moroccan version. To make it red, she says, stir a dash of the hot sauce Harissa (page 16) into the dish. Couscous can be cooked with fish, poultry, or lamb, with a variety of vegetables.

For 10 servings

1 cup chick-peas, soaked in water overnight	2 cups baby green beans, trimmed and sliced
1½ pounds chicken, segmented	1 teaspoon Harissa
2 large onions, minced	1 teaspoon ground coriander
½ tablespoon corn or olive oil	1 cup couscous (cracked wheat)
2 medium carrots, scraped and sliced	1 teaspoon ground cinnamon

1. When you are ready to cook, pour off the soaking water, and cover the chick-peas with fresh water. Boil until tender, about 1½ hours. Drain, and rub off the skins. Rinse, and drain.

2. In bottom of a couscoussière or casserole, sauté the chicken with onions in the oil, turning to brown on all sides. Add the carrots, green beans, Harissa, and coriander with almost enough water to cover the food. Cover, and simmer while preparing the couscous.

3. In a warm skillet, toast the couscous over very low heat for a few minutes, shaking constantly. Turn couscous into a bowl, and cover with boiling water. Soak for 15 minutes. Drain thoroughly, and drape on a clean napkin or cheesecloth over the top of the couscoussière. Set over the cooking chicken, cover, and continue simmering the chicken while the couscous steams on top.

4. Taste chicken, and adjust the seasonings. Divide into 10 portions. Scoop couscous into a warm bowl, and sprinkle with cinnamon. Stir with a fork. Divide couscous into 10 portions. Serve warm.

Nutrients for 1 serving chicken and couscous.

Calories: 185

Exchanges: 2 lean meat; 3 vegetable

g	mg
carbohydrate: 14	potassium: 385.5
protein: 20	sodium: 67
fat: 6	cholesterol: 50
fiber: 3.5	

Dolmeh Sib
(Persian Stuffed Apples)

Apples and a simple meat-lentil-cinnamon filling blend their flavors exquisitely in this recipe. Dolmeh (meaning "stuffed" from the Turkish *dolma*) is one Persian version of the many stuffed dishes of the Middle East. As you're enjoying this dish, think of the variety of mixtures stuffed in vegetables and fruits begun by the ancient Hellenes. They had stuffed everything from game birds to fig leaves!

For 4 servings

2 tablespoons yellow lentils	Freshly ground white or black
¼ pound lean ground beef	pepper
1 teaspoon unsalted margarine	4 large baking apples
1 small onion, minced	1 teaspoon lemon juice
½ teaspoon ground cinnamon	1 tablespoon vinegar

1. Soak the lentils in water overnight, the evening before you plan to serve. If you forget, cover lentils with water in a saucepan; bring to a boil, and cook them while making the filling.

2. Whiten the beef by mashing it in a saucepan with ½ cup water over medium heat until the raw color changes, and the meat is grainy. (This is an effective method of cooking ground meat without fat; it will release liquid, including fat.) Pour off all fat. Remove from heat, and place meat in a bowl.

3. In a small pan, heat the margarine and sauté the onion for 2 minutes. Add to the meat in the bowl.

4. To mix the filling: Drain the lentils, and add them to the meat and onion. Season with cinnamon and pepper.

5. To prepare the apples: Wash and dry them. Cut off the stem tops, and save as "lids" for baking. Carefully remove the core without breaking through to the other end. Remove some of the apple pulp to make room for the filling.

6. Chop the apple pulp, and add about half to the filling. Squeeze as much juice as possible from the remaining pulp directly into the bowl with the margarine. Add the lemon juice and vinegar to that mixture, and set aside to baste the apples while baking.

7. Now taste the filling, and adjust seasonings. Stuff the apples with the filling. Cover with the apple "lids." Set apples in a casserole or pan. Pour in just enough water to cover the bottom. Bake at 350°F for 20 minutes.

8. Remove from oven, and uncover the apple "lids." Baste with the

vinegar marinade, and any juices in the pan. Cover again, and continue baking for 20 minutes or until apples are fork-tender. Serve warm with some of the pan sauce on each apple.

Nutrients for 1 stuffed apple.

Calories: 146

Exchanges: 1 starch/bread; ½ medium-fat meat; ½ fruit

g	mg
carbohydrate: 21	potassium: 277
protein: 7	sodium: 20
fat: 5	cholesterol: 19
fiber: 3	

Chinese Egg Roll

Egg rolls are now enjoyed by many people, not just the Chinese who invented them. If you only eat fried foods once in a while, let the choice be egg rolls. I've been varying this recipe with success for years. The only cardinal rule: Eat them freshly fried and piping hot.

For 24 egg rolls

¼ pound extra lean beef, ground or finely minced
Freshly ground black pepper
1 teaspoon light Chinese soy sauce
1 teaspoon fresh ginger, minced
2 garlic cloves, minced
3 teaspoons peanut oil
1 cup Chinese white (bok choy) or celery cabbage, shredded
1 cup fresh bean sprouts
1½ cups green onion, or 1 medium onion, finely chopped, or 3 Chinese chives *(gau tsoi)*, chopped
1 cup fresh mushrooms, chopped, or ¼ cup dried Chinese mushrooms, soaked in warm water, drained, and chopped
½ cup celery or Chinese celery *(kun tsoi)*
1 cup shrimps, cleaned and chopped
2 egg whites, lightly beaten
24 egg roll wrappers
5 cups corn or peanut oil for frying

1. To prepare the filling: First, in a bowl, marinate the beef with the pepper, soy sauce, ginger, and garlic for 15 minutes or longer. Heat 1 teaspoon of the peanut oil in a wok or skillet. When it is hot, drop the beef into the wok, and stir-fry for 1–2 minutes until the raw color changes. Lift the meat into a strainer to drain.

2. Continue with the vegetables: Heat another teaspoon of the oil in the wok. Stir-fry the bok choy, sprouts, 1 cup of the onion, mushrooms, and celery for a few minutes until they become limp. Transfer to another strainer, and drain thoroughly.

3. Finally for the filling, cook the shrimps and eggs: Heat the remaining teaspoon of peanut oil in the wok. Stir-fry the shrimps with the remaining onion over high heat just until the shrimps turn pink. Quickly add the eggs, and scramble together until fluffy. Remove from heat.

4. Using a slotted spoon, lift the shrimp-and-egg mixture, and combine with the beef, mixing thoroughly. Mix in the drained vegetables to complete the filling. Divide into 24 parts.

5. To stuff the egg rolls: Lay a wrapper before you with a point facing you. Place one part of the filling near the front point of the wrapper. Turn the wrapper point over the filling; then turn in the side points and tightly roll back to enclose the filling. Cover egg rolls as you work until all are stuffed.

6. To fry: Preferably in a wok, heat 5 cups frying oil to 350°F. Using tongs, slip a few egg rolls into the hot oil. Turn, and fry until brown, adjusting the temperature to maintain the heat. Shake off excess oil, and drain on paper towels. Keep hot in a heated oven until you have fried as many as you need for your meal. Serve hot.

Nutrients for 1 egg roll.

Calories: 174
Exchanges: 1 starch; ½ lean meat; 1 vegetable; 1 fat

g	mg
carbohydrate: 19	potassium: 141.5
protein: 7	sodium: 46
fat: 8	cholesterol: 42
fiber: 1.5	

Vietnamese Cha Gio

Cha Gio, as flaky and aromatic as Vietnamese rolls can be, are wrapped in lettuce with fresh mint and coriander. Dried fungus and mushrooms are available in Chinese, Japanese, and Korean food shops.

For 32 small Cha Gio

For rolls:

3½ ounces (2 cups) loosely packed dry bean thread
6 dried black fungus or Chinese mushrooms
¼ pound lean ground pork
½ pound fresh shrimps or crab meat, finely chopped
1 medium onion, finely minced
3 green onions, minced

1 carrot, slivered
Salt and freshly ground white pepper
Pinch sugar (optional)
16 whole or 32 halves or 64 quarters (10 ounces) round rice noodle wrappers (banh trang)
2 cups corn or peanut oil for frying

(continued)

For garnish:

1 head lettuce leaves, washed and thoroughly drained	Bunch fresh coriander
	Nuoc Mam Sauce (page 14)
Bunch fresh mint	(optional)

1. Soak bean thread in warm water for 30 minutes. Drain and squeeze to discard liquid; then coarsely chop the bean thread. Soak fungus the same way but reserve the liquid; chop the fungus.

2. To make the filling: In a large bowl, combine bean thread, fungus, pork, shrimps or crabmeat, onion, green onions, and carrot. Season lightly with a pinch of salt and pepper and a pinch of sugar, if you wish. Knead the filling. Add reserved fungus liquid, if necessary, for a moist but not runny filling.

3. Wrappers are available in full, half-, or quarter-circles, and can be used in any form. To prepare the wrappers: First, soften the wrappers. To soften, dip each wrapper quickly into a pie plate filled with water, or sprinkle dry wrappers lightly with water. Allow them to soften for a few minutes. Instructions are given for half-circle wrappers. If you are using full circles, cut 16 in half with kitchen shears or a knife; you should have 32 halves. If you are using quarter-circles, overlap two at the edge to make one half-circle out of two quarters.

4. To stuff, lay out a half (or 2 quarters). Spread 1 tablespoon filling on one short side. Fold wrapper back over filling, turn sides in lengthwise, and roll up tightly to make a small roll. Place on a plate, cover with a dampened towel, and continue stuffing the Cha Gio. (This much can be done in advance; keep refrigerated or frozen until you are ready to fry.)

5. To fry, in a wok or deep fryer, heat 2 cups oil to 350°F (a small piece of bread will turn brown). Slip 2 or 3 Cha Gio into the oil, and turn them to brown on all sides. Shake off all excess oil. Drain on paper towels, and keep hot until all are fried.

6. To serve, arrange a platter with the garnishes. Guests wrap each Cha Gio in a lettuce leaf with mint and coriander tucked inside. Pour 1 tablespoon Nuoc Mam into a dipping saucer for each guest. Serve immediately. Dip into sauce as you enjoy the Cha Gio.

Nutrients for 1 Cha Gio with garnishes but without Nuoc Mam Sauce.

Calories: 55
Exchanges: ½ starch/bread; ½ fat

g	mg
carbohydrate: 6	potassium: 68.5
protein: 3	sodium: 18
fat: 2.5	cholesterol: 14
fiber: negligible	

Filo (Phyllo, Fillo)

Filo pastry dough is as fine and supple as a fresh leaf. The word derives from the Greek word *fyllon* (leaf). I think of filo as dough-leaves to turn, twist, roll, or stuff into beautiful, delicious dishes. Another word in Greek, *filos*, means "friend." So think of this filo pastry dough as both *leaf* and *friend*.

Fresh filo should be *white*, supple, and moist. Look carefully at the filo inside the sealed plastic. If you see any flakiness, flecked with brown, and filo appears coarse and very dry, don't buy it. If you should accidentally buy such a product, take it back. Find the best available filo for the best results.

Filo is much lower in calories than doughs with eggs and butter. You can use less of it to do the job. Filo contains no cholesterol, since it is made of vegetable ingredients. You can also control the size and shape of your dish; for example, use the filo leaves for pies and layered dishes in full size (12x17 to 14x18 inches), or cut the leaves into halves, thirds, or quarters for turnovers or tarts. These are the major reasons for substituting filo for heavier pastry doughs in Argentinean Empanadas (pages 256–57) and Vegetable Samosa (pages 254–55). Filo also enables you to freeze your stuffed dishes in advance, with confidence, for it puffs up impressively when reheated.

On the other hand, filo certainly has to be handled carefully to avoid drying out as you work. But *if you keep the unbaked filo covered* with waxed paper and a dampened kitchen towel, and only work with one exposed leaf at a time, you will easily master the technique. Filo will be flakier if sprinkled with warm margarine or butter, but I have used it with practically none to cut down on calories. The notable exception is when

(continued)

you layer filo leaves; then you need to sprinkle or lightly brush margarine on each leaf (you can use a fingertip to avoid losing so much margarine on the brush). But when rolling triangles, you can get fine results by brushing only the tops with margarine.

The usual ingredients of filo, according to the labels, are flour, cornstarch, water, vegetable oil, salt or sodium propionate, and potassium sorbate to maintain freshness. A computer analysis from the USDA data base of ingredients used by Athens Food Company, Cleveland, Ohio, was conducted at a local university nutrition department. The results indicated the following breakdown: For 1 ounce (1½ leaves of the 22 in the package): 90 calories; 19 g carbohydrate; 3 g protein; ¼ g fat. From these 1½ leaves you can make 6 small triangles or 4 larger ones, depending on whether you cut each filo leaf into thirds or quarters. Athens Food Company produces filo under the following labels: Alpha, Apollo, Athens, Krinos. Another company, Fantis Foods, Inc., New York, produces filo under the Fantis label. The package does not yet have a nutritional breakdown but, according to a company spokesperson, Fantis is planning to label the package soon.

Spanakopitakia (Spinach Triangles)

Rolling fillings in flexible coverings intrigued cooks in ancient Greece when cheese fillings were stuffed in fig leaves and called *Thrion. Fine* dough began in the Middle East and naturally swept westward with enthusiasts. Wonderful fun to stuff and pleasant to eat! Spinach is a traditional filling. Substitute any vegetable you like. Just drain it well before stuffing.

For 24 spinach triangles

1 tablespoon olive or corn oil	2 tablespoons fresh dill or
1 cup green onions or onion,	mint, chopped
chopped	1 tablespoon fresh parsley,
2 cups cooked and chopped	chopped
spinach, chard, or other	8 leaves filo pastry dough
vegetables	2 tablespoons unsalted
1 egg white	margarine, melted and
1 cup low-fat cottage cheese	warmed

1. In a saucepan, heat the oil, and sauté the onions until soft. Stir in the spinach, and mix well. Drain, and cool slightly.

2. Add the egg white, cheese, dill or mint, and parsley. Drain thoroughly. Mix the filling. Divide into 24 parts.

3. Lay the filo leaves flat. With a sharp knife, cut across the width, dividing the leaves into thirds; you will have 24 strips. Pile them up, and cover with waxed paper and a dampened towel. (You can make smaller triangles by cutting the filo lengthwise into 4 strips. They are trickier to stuff, but quite dainty as appetizers.)

4. To stuff: Lay 1 filo strip with a short end near you. Very lightly spread margarine on the filo strip. Place 1 part of the filling an inch from the end. Fold filo back over filling; turn sides in ⅛ inch. Fold filo back, flag style, all the way to top end to form a triangle; handle lightly. Brush both sides with margarine, and set on baking sheet (or place separately in a plastic bag, if you are planning to freeze the triangles to bake another time; avoid squeezing them together). Continue until all are stuffed.

5. Bake at 350°F for 15 minutes or until golden and puffy. Serve piping hot.

Nutrients for 1 spinach triangle.

Calories: 42
Exchanges: 1 vegetable; ½ fat

g	mg
carbohydrate: 4	potassium: 91 (NA for filo)
protein: 2.5	sodium: 51 (NA for filo)
fat: 2	cholesterol: 1
fiber: negligible	
(NA for filo)	

Vegetable Samosa

Samosas are India's popular savories, increasingly available in specialty shops, ready to cook. Have fun cooking your own. Make the filling a day in advance to cut down preparation time. I have substituted filo pastry leaves for the usual dough to simplify preparation and reduce calories. The nutrient equivalents for filo are as estimated for Filo (pages 251–52).

For 20 samosas

For filling:

1 tablespoon green chilies, minced

2 garlic cloves, chopped

1 inch fresh ginger, chopped

½ teaspoon ground turmeric

¼ teaspoon ground coriander

¼ teaspoon cumin seed

2 teaspoons unsaturated vegetable oil

1 medium onion, chopped

½ cup fresh or frozen green peas

1 medium carrot, diced

1 medium potato (6 ounces), diced

Juice of 1 small lime or lemon

2 sprigs fresh coriander, chopped

5 leaves filo pastry dough

4 teaspoons unsalted margarine, melted and warmed

1. Grind together the chilies, garlic, ginger, turmeric, coriander, and cumin to make a paste.

2. To make the filling: In a saucepan, heat the oil, and sauté the onion until soft. Add the spice paste, and stir over low heat for 1 minute. Stir in the peas, carrot, and potato. Mix well, and cover the pan. Allow to steam for a few minutes. Add ½ cup water, and stir the bottom and spices thoroughly. Cover, and simmer for about 15 minutes until potatoes and peas are tender, and the liquid is absorbed. If the filling is watery, drain it.

3. Stir the lime or lemon juice and coriander into the filling, and set aside to cool. (Refrigerate, if you are making samosas the next day.)

4. To stuff the samosas: Lay the 5 filo leaves in a flat pile before you. Cut straight down the length into quarters (you'll have 20 long strips). Cover the strips with waxed paper and a damp kitchen towel, and only work with 1 strip at a time.

5. Place 1 tablespoon filling 1 inch from the edge of the filo strip near you. Turn lengthwise edges slightly in toward the middle to make smooth edges. Fold filo edge near you back over the filling, then fold back, moving right and left, flag style, to make a compact triangle. Lightly brush top on both sides with margarine, and set on baking sheet. Keep covered with waxed paper or plastic wrap. Continue stuffing until all are stuffed.

6. Bake at 350°F for 12 to 15 minutes until golden, puffy, and crisp. Serve hot.

Nutrients for 1 samosa filling without filo.

Calories: 24

Exchange: 1 vegetable

g	mg
carbohydrate: 3	potassium: 57
protein: negligible	sodium: 7
fat: 1	cholesterol: 0
fiber: negligible	

Nutrients for 1 samosa and 1 strip filo.

Calories: 37.5

Exchanges: 1½ vegetable

g	mg
carbohydrate: 4	potassium: NA for filo
protein: negligible	sodium: NA for filo
fat: 1	cholesterol: 0
fiber: negligible	

Argentinean Empanada

Empanada tarts with spicy fillings are specialties in South America. They have even become street snacks in New York. These baked versions, stuffed with seasoned meat and olive, are the gift of Ana Maria Malerba of the Liga Argentina de Proteccion al Diabético. Your friends will relish the flavors. I replaced the usual dough (which uses butter, eggs, and milk) with filo to cut down on cholesterol and calories.

For 12 empanadas

For filling:

1 teaspoon corn oil
1 medium onion (¼ pound), chopped
6 green onions (¼ pound), white and green parts chopped separately
½ pound extra lean ground beef or other meat
1 tablespoon sweet red pepper or paprika
½ teaspoon chili powder
1 teaspoon oregano, crumbled
1 teaspoon ground cumin
Pinch salt
1 hard-cooked egg, chopped
4 large pitted green olives, rinsed and chopped

4 leaves filo pastry dough
2 tablespoons unsalted margarine, melted and warmed

1. To make the filling: Heat the oil in a skillet, and sauté the onion and the white part of the green onions until soft.

2. In another skillet or casserole, whiten the meat by pouring about ½ cup boiling water over it. Stir over medium heat until meat loses its red color, and grains are separated. Combine the meat and onion away from the heat. Season meat with the sweet red pepper or paprika, chili powder, oregano, cumin, and a little salt.

3. In a small bowl, combine the egg, olives, and green part of the onion. Add to the meat mixture, mix thoroughly, and cool.

4. To stuff the empanadas: Lay the leaves in a flat pile. Cut straight across the width, dividing them into thirds. You will have 12 strips. Keep covered with waxed paper and a damp kitchen towel while working. Follow directions for stuffing and baking Vegetable Samosa (pages 254–55), steps 3, 4, and 5.

Nutrients for 1 empanada filling.

Calories: 74

Exchanges: ½ medium-fat meat; ½ vegetable; ½ fat

g	mg
carbohydrate: 2	potassium: 117
protein: 6	sodium: 39
fat: 5	cholesterol: 39
fiber: negligible	

Nutrients for 1 empanada filling and 1 strip filo.

Calories: 93

Exchanges: ½ medium-fat meat; 1½ vegetable; ½ fat

g	mg
carbohydrate: 5.5	potassium: 117 (NA for filo)
protein: 6	
fat: 5	sodium: 39 (NA for filo)
fiber: negligible	cholesterol: 39

Carbonada

With fresh vegetables and peaches, carbonada is an Argentinean specialty from Ana Maria Malerba of Liga Argentina de Proteccion al Diabético. It is a fun dish for a large party. The challenge is timing all ingredients as you add them. Carbonada is *the* favorite for many Argentineans.

For 10 servings

1 large onion, chopped
1 teaspoon corn oil
1 pound lean beef or other meat, cubed
3 ripe tomatoes, peeled and chopped
Pinch salt and freshly ground pepper
Dried oregano
1 bay leaf

2 sweet potatoes, cubed
½ pound potato, cubed
2–3 cups White Chicken Stock (page 98) or water
1 pound squash, cubed
2 ears corn, each cut crosswise into 5 wheels
½ cup white long-grain rice
2 medium peaches, sliced

1. In a nonstick casserole, sauté the onion in warm oil until golden. Add the meat, and brown for several minutes, stirring constantly. Cover the casserole, and allow the meat to steam over medium heat for 5 minutes. Skim off all fat.

2. Add the tomatoes. Season to your taste with salt, pepper, oregano, and bay leaf. Simmer for 10 minutes.

3. Mix in the sweet potatoes and potato with enough stock or water to cover the food. Simmer gently until potatoes are half done, about 15 minutes.

4. Add the squash, corn, and rice with more stock, if necessary. Continue cooking until meat, potatoes, and rice are tender, adding the peaches during the last 5 minutes. Carbonada should be very juicy. Remove bay leaf. Serve hot.

Nutrients for 1 serving.

Calories: 189
Exchanges: ½ starch/bread; 1 medium-fat meat; 3 vegetable

	g		mg
	carbohydrate: 22		potassium: 502
	protein: 15		sodium: 43
	fat: 5		cholesterol: 38
	fiber: 3		

BREADS

**First eat the black bread,
then the white.**
SWISS PROVERB

Cheese Muffins, New Zealand Style

Zesty cheese muffins are favorites of Murray V. F. Jones, national secretary of the New Zealand Diabetes Association. He generously suggests this recipe and hopes you add a large pinch of cayenne pepper.

For 12 muffins

1 cup all-purpose flour	1 cup Parmesan or other
2 teaspoons baking powder	grated cheese
½ teaspoon salt	1 egg, lightly beaten
Large pinch cayenne pepper	½ cup low-fat (½%) milk

1. Sift the flour, baking powder, salt, and cayenne into a bowl.

2. Stir in the cheese, egg, and only enough of the milk to make a wet batter. Do not overmix.

3. Lightly oil or spray 12 muffin tins. Drop batter into the tins. Bake at 400°F for 12 to 15 minutes until golden and puffed.

4. Remove muffins from tins. Serve warm or cold.

Nutrients for 1 muffin.

Calories: 83

Exchanges: ½ starch/bread; ½ medium-fat meat

g	mg
carbohydrate: 10	potassium: 41
protein: 5	sodium: 187
fat: 3	cholesterol: 28
fiber: negligible	

Whole Wheat Dosa

This dosa doesn't pretend to be the paper-thin wafer that emerges from a tandoori oven. Light brown, flecked with green coriander and chile with a hot aftertaste, it is a kind of griddle cake—a bit thicker than a crepe, thinner than an American-style pancake. And it's good!

For about 12 dosas

2 cups atta (whole wheat flour)
¼ teaspoon baking soda
Pinch salt (optional)
2 medium onions, finely
  chopped
3 fresh green chilies, seeded
  and chopped

1 small bunch fresh coriander,
  chopped
3–5 curry leaves (sweet neem)
Vegetable oil to wipe griddle
1 teaspoon unsalted margarine
  or ghee (page 7), melted

1. In a bowl, mix the atta, baking soda, and salt (if you are using it). Make a well in the middle.

2. To shorten preparation time, chop together the onions, chilies, coriander, and curry leaves in a food processor or blender. Drop the mixture into the flour well. Rinse out the bowl with ½ cup cold water, and pour it into the well. Fill the cup with water, and keep it by your bowl.

3. Mix the batter, preferably with your fingers to get the feel of it, and gradually add water to make a thin batter similar to a crepe batter. (Batter can be made in advance.)

4. Heat a griddle, and when it is hot, wipe with vegetable oil. (Bake one dosa at a time until you like the result.)

5. Pour a large spoonful of the batter onto the griddle. With the back of the spoon, spread the batter. Pour a few drops of the margarine or ghee around the batter (to avoid sticking). Turn to bake the other side. If the dosa is too thick, add 1 to 2 tablespoons water to the batter. Keep warm until all are baked. Serve warm with chutney.

Nutrients for 1 dosa.

Calories: 77
Exchange: 1 starch/bread

g	mg
carbohydrate: 16	potassium: 110
protein: 3	sodium: 28
fat: negligible	cholesterol: 0
fiber: 2	

Naun (Afghan Bread)

Serve Afghan bread hot from the oven, and you'll stop the show. The aromatic onion seeds give it a distinctive flavor. Be sure to buy onion seeds from a Middle Eastern shop. They are blacker, more irregular, and more aromatic than black sesame. Enjoy Afghan bread with any meal or snack. A Persian family enjoys it with feta and tea for breakfast. Make it the day before, and reheat a few slices at a time in a toaster oven.

For 1 large or 2 medium loaves (10 servings)

1 package active dry yeast
  (1 tablespoon)
½ teaspoon sugar
2½ cups atta (chapati) or whole
  wheat flour

½ cup all-purpose flour
Pinch salt
2 tablespoons black onion
  seeds

1. In a small bowl, dissolve yeast and sugar in ¼ cup lukewarm water. Cover, and allow to double in bulk.

2. In a large warmed bowl, mix the flours and a pinch of salt. Make a well in the flour, and add ⅔ cup warm water. Mix by hand or machine to make a soft dough, adding more water, if necessary. Knead until smooth.

3. Cover dough, and rest in a warm place until almost doubled in bulk, about 1 hour.

4. To make the traditional Afghan bread, your oven must be wide enough to accommodate a loaf 23 inches wide. If it is too narrow, divide the dough into 2 sections, and make 2 medium-width loaves. Knead each section, then let it rest for a few minutes.

5. Roll each section into a long flat loaf with rounded ends, tapering slightly in the middle (this is the traditional shape); each large loaf is about 7x23x⅛ inches, and the medium ones about 6x14 inches.

6. Dip your finger in cold water, and make three lengthwise grooves in each bread (or use a knife to score the top as made professionally; score lengthwise in ¼-inch slashes from tip to tip). Sprinkle liberally with onion seeds.

7. Cover a cookie sheet with heavy aluminum foil, and preheat in oven. Place the rolled loaves on the warm foil. Bake at 450°F for 6 to 8 minutes until the bread is just beginning to turn brown. If the bread is baked but not brown enough, place under the broiler to brown the top slightly. Divide into 10 servings. Serve hot with kebabs, soups, and other dishes.

Nutrients for 1 slice.

Calories: 127
Exchanges: 1½ starch/bread

g	mg
carbohydrate: 27	potassium: 131.5
protein: 5	sodium: 12
fat: negligible	cholesterol: 0
fiber: 3	

Porota (Paratha, Parata, Parota)

Flakier than chapati, porota is also flat, round, unleavened, and best when hot. In India it is usually brushed with ghee, but this version suggests using unsaturated fat instead. The recipe is yet another great contribution of nutritionist Shane Ara Kabir of Bangladesh. You can double the recipe to make 4 porotas.

For 2 (6-inch) porotas (4 servings)

1 cup atta (whole wheat flour) (100 g)	3 tablespoons cooking oil
¼ teaspoon salt	2 tablespoons all-purpose flour for rolling

1. In a bowl, combine atta, salt, and 1 teaspoon oil. Mix thoroughly by rubbing with your fingers.

2. Make a well in the flour mixture, and add about ¼ cup water. Mix to make a fairly stiff dough. If it is too stiff, wet your hands, and knead the dough to work water into it and soften.

3. Knead dough thoroughly. Divide the dough into 2 balls.

4. Sprinkle a little flour on a bread board. Roll out each ball into a thin, flat circle.

5. Brush each dough circle with 1 teaspoon oil. Sprinkle lightly with flour. Starting at end near you, roll up the dough into a rod. Hold one end, and firmly wind dough rod into a coil. Tuck the end firmly underneath.

6. Now roll out this coil into a 6-inch circle.

7. Heat a tava, heavy skillet, or griddle. Add 1 tablespoon oil, and fry the porota on both sides until brown and crisp. As you fry, lightly press the porota from both sides. Slice in half to make 4 servings. Serve hot with omelet, kebab, or cooked vegetable.

Nutrients for ½ porota.

Calories: 150
Exchanges: 1½ starch/bread; ½ fat

g	mg
carbohydrate: 25	potassium: 115.5
protein: 4.5	sodium: 49
fat: 4	cholesterol: 0
fiber: 3	

Scottish Oat Scones

Puffy, textured triangles—the British counterparts of biscuits—are easier than biscuits to mix and cut. In Scotland, oat is a prized grain for porridge, cakes, and scones. Oat scones are usually served for afternoon tea, but are also nice for breakfast and brunch.

For 16 scones

1½ cups all-purpose flour
1 cup old-fashioned rolled oats
Pinch salt
½ teaspoon baking soda
1 teaspoon cream of tartar
1 tablespoon sugar

4 tablespoons unsalted
   margarine, at room
   temperature
½ cup low-fat (½%) milk
2 eggs, lightly beaten

1. In a large bowl, lightly mix the flour, oats, salt, baking soda, cream of tartar, and sugar.

2. Using a pastry cutter or fork, cut in the margarine until the mixture resembles cornmeal.

3. Make a well in the middle, and add the milk and eggs. Quickly mix with a fork.

4. Divide the dough in half. Turn out on a floured board. Dip your fingers in flour, and lightly flatten each dough half into a ½-inch-thick circle. You'll have 2 large circles.

5. Using a knife, cut each circle in half. Cut each half again in half, and repeat, to make 8 triangles from each circle, or a total of 16 triangles.

6. Place triangles on a baking sheet. Bake at 400°F for 15 minutes or until golden chestnut and puffy. If not brown enough, move pan to highest oven shelf for 3 minutes. Serve hot.

Nutrients for 1 scone.

Calories: 107
Exchanges: 1 starch/bread; ½ fat

g	mg
carbohydrate: 14	potassium: 51
protein: 3	sodium: 45
fat: 4	cholesterol: 34
fiber: negligible	

English Wheat-Bran Bread

Of all the wonderful wheat and bran breads of England, this may be the quickest and chewiest recipe.

For 6½-inch round loaf (8 or 10 slices)

2 cups whole wheat flour	½ teaspoon salt
1 cup bran	1¼ cups buttermilk
1 teaspoon baking soda	1 tablespoon corn or other
1 teaspoon cream of tartar	unsaturated oil

1. In a large bowl, mix the flour, bran, baking soda, cream of tartar, and salt.

2. Make a well in the middle, and pour in the buttermilk and oil. Mix quickly with your fingers to make a fairly soft dough. Knead on a floured board.

3. Shape into a round loaf, slightly domed in the middle, about 6½ inches in diameter. Place in an oiled baking dish. With a knife, cut a cross on top, from one side of the loaf to the other (to prevent bread from cracking).

4. Bake at 450°F for 25 minutes. Lower heat to 400°F for 10 minutes longer, or until the bread sounds hollow when tapped with your knuckles. Cool on a rack at least 15 minutes before slicing. Cut into 8 to 10 slices. Serve warm or cold.

Nutrients for 1 slice (¹⁄₁₀ loaf).

Calories: 121
Exchanges: 1½ starch/bread

g	mg
carbohydrate: 23	potassium: 206
protein: 5	sodium: 173
fat: 2.5	cholesterol: 1
fiber: 4	

Nutrients for 1 slice (⅛ loaf).

Calories: 151
Exchanges: 2 starch/bread

g	mg
carbohydrate: 28	potassium: 257.5
protein: 6	sodium: 217
fat: 3	cholesterol: 1
fiber: 5	

Papadum

Crispy and spicy or crispy and plain, papadum is a flat, round, 7-inch wafer. Papadum or papad is usually made from lentils or from urad dal, a split lentil of India known as black gram, and is available in specialty shops catering to Indians and Pakistanis. (The trick is to buy the best of the many brands. Ask the shopkeeper which brand she or he prefers.) Papadums come in 250-g (8.75 ounces) packages with 20 to 22 in each package. If you weigh them at home, you can estimate the weight of each. Nutrients are given below for 3 weights. Papadums are delicious briefly baked (less fat) or fried and eaten plain with curries or sprinkled with condiments, as suggested below, as appetizers and snacks. Shredded coconut is another popular seasoning on top.

For 4 servings

8 papadums (plain or chile)
1 tablespoon fresh coriander
  or mint for garnish
  (optional)

2 tablespoons roasted unsalted
  peanuts, chopped, for
  garnish (optional)
Garam Masala (page 2) or chili
  powder (optional)

1. Separate the papadums from the package, and keep covered until ready to bake.

2. To bake: Place papadums on baking sheet. Bake at 325°F for 5 to 7 minutes until they bubble slightly, and begin to brown around the edges, and are crisp. Remove, and cool on a rack.

3. Serve plain or sprinkled with your favorite herb, peanuts, and spices suggested above or your own mixture.

Nutrients for 9-g papadum.

Calories: 26
Exchange: ⅓ starch/bread

g	mg
carbohydrate: 5	potassium: NA
protein: 2	sodium: NA
fat: negligible	cholesterol: 0
fiber: NA	

Nutrients for 11-g papadum.

Calories: 32

Exchange: ½ starch/bread

g	mg
carbohydrate: 6	potassium: NA
protein: 2	sodium: NA
fat: negligible	cholesterol: 0
fiber: NA	

Nutrients for 13-g papadum.

Calories: 37

Exchange: ½ starch/bread

g	mg
carbohydrate: 7	potassium: NA
protein: 2	sodium: NA
fat: negligible	cholesterol: 0
fiber: NA	

Breads of India

Flat, flaky, and usually made of atta (whole wheat flour), breads of India are popular in and out of the subcontinent. Indian people break off small pieces of the bread and use them as scoops to dip up curry and the many fascinating accompaniments in an Indian meal.

Nutrients of these breads are included for you to keep in mind when dining out at an Indian restaurant; they are reprinted with permission from *Common Indian Snacks and Nutritive Value* by Swaran Pasricha, et al. (1987). Calculations for potassium, sodium, cholesterol, and fiber are not available for breads below.

Nutrients for 1 dosa.

Calories: 181
Exchanges: 2 starch/bread; 1½ fat

g
carbohydrate: 23
protein: 4
fat: 8.5

Nutrients for 1 idli.

Calories: 79
Exchange: 1 starch/bread

g
carbohydrate: 17
protein: 3
fat: negligible

Nutrients for 1 porota (paratha).

Calories: 146
Exchanges: 1 starch/bread; 1½ fat

g
carbohydrate: 18.5
protein: 3
fat: 6

Nutrients for 1 phulka.

Calories: 73
Exchange: 1 starch/bread

g
carbohydrate: 15
protein: 2.5
fat: negligible

Nutrients for 1 puri.

Calories: 79
Exchanges: 1 starch/bread; ½ fat

g
carbohydrate: 10
protein: 2
fat: 3.5

Pita

Everyone knows *this* round flat bread with the pocket you can fill for a sandwich. It is now available everywhere you turn. Pita's fame spread westward from the Middle East via the fast-food circuit. And as you've probably guessed while leafing through this book, "pita" has many culinary meanings and flavors.

When ready to use, slice pita in half to expose the pocket, and fill with a portion of any salad in this book for sandwich, snack, picnic. . . .

Nutrients for ½ pita.

Calories: 60
Exchange: ¾ starch/bread

g	mg
carbohydrate: 11.5	potassium: 34
protein: 3.5	sodium: 167
fat: 0	cholesterol: 0
fiber: 1	

Chapati

Hot flat breads are wonderful with Indian meals, and chapati (chupatty) is probably the most popular. This unleavened staple of India has many names (*roti* is the Bengalese name) and it has a legendary history. Chapati was even used by mutineers against the British in 1857; it was broken into

(continued)

five or ten pieces by runners to relay messages—the month and day of the mutiny—according to John Masters in *Nightrunners of Bengal*.

Break off little pieces as you eat and dip into curry. You'll be complementing proteins in the wheat and dal (lentils). This recipe, without added fat, is sent by nutritionist Shane Ara Kabir of the Bangladesh Institute of Research and Rehabilitation. Nutrients for both a whole chapati and half are given below.

For 4 (7-inch) chapatis (4 or 8 servings)

1⅔ cups atta (whole wheat
    chapati flour) or other whole
    wheat flour

½ teaspoon salt
1 tablespoon all-purpose flour
    for rolling

1. Mix the atta and salt in a bowl. Make a well in the middle, and add ½ cup water. Mix to make a fairly stiff dough, adding water or all-purpose flour in teaspoonfuls, if necessary.

2. Knead thoroughly on a floured board. Cover with a towel, and rest for 30 minutes or 1 hour.

3. Divide dough into 4 parts. Roll each in your palms to make balls.

4. Flour a board, and roll each ball as flat and round as possible into 7-inch circles.

5. To bake, heat a tava (Indian curved bread griddle), iron skillet, or griddle. Bake chapati on both sides. "Serve hot with egg omelet or cooked vegetables," Shane suggests. For 8 servings, slice chapatis in half.

Nutrients for ½ chapati.

Calories: 87
Exchange: 1 starch/bread

g	mg
carbohydrate: 19	potassium: 93
protein: 3	sodium: 25
fat: negligible	cholesterol: 0
fiber: 2	

Nutrients for 1 chapati.

Calories: 175
Exchanges: 2⅕ starch/bread

g	mg
carbohydrate: 37	potassium: 186.5
protein: 7	sodium: 50
fat: 1	cholesterol: 0
fiber: 5	

DESSERTS
AND FRUITS

**If sweetness is excessive,
it is no longer sweetness.**
SWAHILI (BANTU) PROVERB

Yogurt and Fruit Dessert

For a quick snack or dessert, topped with apricots or strawberries, sprinkled with walnuts, yogurt soars to Olympian heights. You'll enjoy combining plain yogurt with your favorite seasonal fruits and various nuts. Experiment.

For 1 serving

1 cup plain low-fat yogurt
1 apricot or 6 strawberries,
    sliced, or 1 tablespoon
    dietetic apricot preserves

½ walnut, chopped

Scoop the yogurt into a glass dessert dish. Top with fresh fruit or preserves and the chopped walnut. Serve cold.

Nutrients for 1 serving.

Calories: 174
Exchanges: ½ fruit; 1 low-fat milk

g	mg
carbohydrate: 20	potassium: 645.5
protein: 13	sodium: 160
fat: 5	cholesterol: 14
fiber: negligible	

Deysel (Tibetan Yogurt Dessert)

Contrasting hot rice and cold yogurt, Deysel is a most unusual and appealing dessert. This version is inspired by the one served at a Tibetan restaurant in New York where I discovered it. Even the presentation is original, hence the careful instructions in step 2.

For 4 servings

1⅓ cups steamed (not mushy)
   long-grain rice
2 tablespoons raisins

1 teaspoon noncaloric
   sweetener (optional)
1 cup plain low-fat yogurt

1. Steam the rice, mixed with raisins, in a covered steamer or strainer over boiling water until hot, about 5 minutes.

2. Sweeten the rice, if you like, but it isn't necessary because raisins are sweet. Use 4 rice bowls to serve the Deysel. Divide rice equally into 4 portions, and spoon each *diagonally* to angle down one side of the bowl. Fluff rice with a fork (it shouldn't look flat on top). Drop 2 tablespoons yogurt on the other side of each bowl. Serve immediately.

Nutrients for 1 serving.

Calories: 125
Exchanges: 1½ starch/bread

g	mg
carbohydrate: 24	potassium: 213
protein: 4.5	sodium: 40
fat: 1	cholesterol: 4
fiber: negligible	

Mock Pavlova

You've probably heard the story of the famous Pavlova dessert, created for Pavlova when she visited New Zealand. Now here's a superb variation for you from Murray V. F. Jones of the New Zealand Diabetes Association. "Make sure eggs are fresh and at room temperature," he cautions. "Try kiwi fruit," he suggests, as a garnish. You'll need a piece of kitchen parchment.

For 4 servings

4 egg whites at room temperature	2 teaspoons cornstarch
Sweetener equivalent to 1 teaspoon	1 teaspoon vanilla extract
	1 teaspoon vinegar
Pinch salt	2 kiwis

1. In a bowl, beat the egg whites until foamy. Add the sweetener and salt, and continue beating. Beat in the cornstarch, vanilla, and vinegar until soft peaks form. Work quickly, and take care not to overbeat.

2. Rinse a piece of kitchen (greaseproof) parchment with water. Place on a baking pan.

3. Pile the egg white mixture onto the parchment in a 1½-inch-high circle. Bake at 250°F for 1 hour or until firm.

4. Remove from oven, and cool in the pan. Invert on a platter, and peel off the paper. Peel, and slice the kiwis crosswise into circles; leave some round or cut some in half. Arrange in an attractive design on the pavlova. Cut into 4 portions. Serve cold.

Nutrients for 1 serving.

Calories: 48

Exchanges: ½ lean meat; ½ fruit

g	mg
carbohydrate: 8	potassium: 196
protein: 4	sodium: 79
fat: negligible	cholesterol: 0
fiber: 1	

Kheer

An aromatic milk dessert of India has been simplified by Rekha Sharma, a dietitian with All India Institute of Medical Sciences. With her recipe in hand, you can make a bowl of kheer for yourself in a twinkling. And if a friend stops in, just double the recipe.

For 1 serving

1 cup low-fat milk
2 tablespoons Cream of Rice
   or Cream of Wheat

Essence for flavor (rose water,
   vanilla, grated orange rind,
   etc.)
Noncaloric sweetener

1. In a small saucepan, mix the milk and Cream of Rice or Wheat. Simmer until kheer thickens, stirring frequently to prevent lumping.
2. Flavor to please your taste. Serve hot or cold.

Nutrients for 1 serving.

Calories: 165
Exchanges: 1½ starch/bread; ⅕ low-fat milk

g	mg
carbohydrate: 26	potassium: 405
protein: 9	sodium: 124
fat: 3	cholesterol: 10
fiber: 1	

Fresh Cheese Gâteau

I remember with pleasure the leisurely coffee-and-cake customs throughout Europe. Here is a delicious cheesecake for you to serve with tea or coffee, offered by Zentralinstitut für Diabetes in East Germany.

For 20 servings

4 teaspoons unsalted
  margarine
6 eggs, separated
½ cup noncaloric granulated
  sweetener

6 cups low-fat cottage cheese
Rind of 1 lemon, grated
¾ cup fine semolina
2 teaspoons baking powder

1. In a bowl, cream the margarine. Gradually add the egg yolks, sweetener, cheese, lemon rind, and semolina mixed with the baking powder.

2. In another bowl, beat the egg whites until fluffy and stiff but still moist. Fold into the batter.

3. Turn into a buttered 9-inch rectangular baking pan. Bake at 350°F for 45 minutes until light and firm. Cool on a rack. Cut into 20 squares. Serve warm or cold.

Nutrients for 1 square.

Calories: 107
Exchanges: ½ medium-fat meat; ½ low-fat milk

g	mg
carbohydrate: 6	potassium: 89
protein: 12	sodium: 328
fat: 4	cholesterol: 88
fiber: negligible	

Crema Ghiacciata alla Vaniglia
(Frozen Vanilla Cream)

Perfumed with vanilla and kirsch, this dessert can be frozen in advance for a *rare* high-calorie treat! The recipe was developed for diabetic diets in Italy, suggested by Professor G. M. Molinatti in Torino. I adapted it to this form without the egg yolk.

For 4 servings

½ cup heavy cream
Powdered noncaloric
   sweetener

1 teaspoon vanilla extract
½ teaspoon kirsch or anisette

1. In a bowl, beat the cream until light and fluffy, gradually adding the sweetener.
2. Continuing to beat, add vanilla and kirsch or anisette. Pour or scoop into 4 parfait glasses or dessert cups. Serve immediately, or cover, and freeze until ready to serve.

Nutrients for 1 serving.

Calories: 104
Exchanges: 2⅕ fat

g	mg
carbohydrate: negligible	potassium: 22
protein: negligible	sodium: 12
fat: 11	cholesterol: 42
fiber: 0	

New Zealand Pikelets

Pikelets are miniature pancakes, topped with lemon honey (New Zealand name for lemon custard) and a dab of preserves or jelly. A plate of pikelets is a welcome treat anytime in New Zealand, but especially with afternoon tea, says Ingrid Banwell, who has enjoyed them since her childhood days. Whipped cream is often used as a topping instead of the lemon honey. If you are using lemon honey, make it in advance, and chill before serving.

For 28 pikelets

LEMON HONEY

Grated rind and juice of
  2 lemons
3 tablespoons unsalted
  margarine

2 eggs, lightly beaten
¾ cup granulated sugar
  replacement

MINIATURE PANCAKES

1 egg
1 tablespoon granulated sugar
  replacement
½ teaspoon unsalted
  margarine, melted

⅔ cup low-fat (1%) milk, more
  if necessary
1 cup all-purpose flour
½ teaspoon baking soda
Sugar-free dietetic strawberry
  or other preserves

1. To make the lemon honey: In top of a double boiler, mix the grated rind, lemon juice, margarine, and eggs. Stir with a wooden spoon over boiling water until thickened; do not allow custard to boil. Remove from heat, and cool slightly. Add the sugar replacement. Taste for flavor, adding more sweetener, if necessary. Cool. Refrigerate before serving.

2. To make the miniature pancakes: In a bowl, beat the egg with the sugar replacement. Stir in the margarine and milk.

3. Mix the flour and baking soda. Gradually add to the batter, stirring until smooth and fairly thick.

4. Heat a pancake griddle to 400°F. Drop by tablespoonfuls onto the hot griddle. When light brown on the bottom and bubbly, turn, and brown the other side.

5. Arrange on a serving plate. Drop lemon honey from a tablespoon onto the hot pancake. Add a dab of preserves in the middle. Serve immediately.

**Nutrients for 4 miniature pancakes
(without toppings).**

Calories: 95
Exchange: 1 starch/bread

g	mg
carbohydrate: 16	potassium: 64
protein: 4	sodium: 80.5
fat: 1.5	cholesterol: 40
fiber: negligible	

Nutrients for 1 tablespoon lemon honey.

Calories: 38
Exchange: ½ medium-fat meat

g	mg
carbohydrate: negligible	potassium: 22
protein: 1	sodium: 16
fat: 3	cholesterol: 55
fiber: 0	

Easy Carrot Halwa

Halwa—from the Arabic halwā—is another of the culinary terms that has acquired many meanings, flavors, and spellings among various cultures. Here's a quick and unfussy version of halwa—a dessert that can be based on semolina or tahini in the Middle East and Greece or on fruits, squashes, or vegetables in India. This recipe from dietitian Rekha Sharma of the All India Institute of Medical Sciences offers a choice of fresh or dry milk. Each serving is high in vitamin A.

For 2 servings

2 medium carrots   Noncaloric sweetener
½ cup low-fat (1%) milk or
½ ounce dry nonfat milk

(continued)

1. Scrape and grate the carrots. Place in a saucepan with just enough water to avoid burning the carrots. Cook over low heat until soft.

2. Add the fresh milk or dry milk with additional water; mix well. Simmer for 10 minutes.

3. Remove from heat, and sweeten to your taste. Serve hot.

Nutrients for 1 serving.

Calories: 43
Exchanges: 1½ vegetable

g	mg
carbohydrate: 7	potassium: 184
protein: 2	sodium: 57
fat: negligible	cholesterol: 3
fiber: 1	

Paludeh (Persian Fruit Delight)

How about a sparkling and refreshing fruit dessert for a hot day, topped with crushed ice? Choose any seasonal fruit you like. A long-stemmed glass heightens the impression of coolness.

For 4 servings

2 ripe peaches	Rose water (optional)
1 cup cantaloupe or melon	Crushed ice
Sweetener (optional)	

1. Peel the peaches, and slice into a bowl, saving all the juice with the slices. Scoop out cantaloupe or melon balls, and combine with the peaches.

2. Sweeten fruits only if necessary. If you like, sprinkle with rose water. Refrigerate for a few hours.

3. To serve, divide the fruit among 4 dessert dishes. Top each with crushed ice. Serve immediately.

Baked Quince, Balkan Style

Quince is so identified with preserves in many countries that in Portuguese, the word for quince is *marmelo*, from which *marmelada* (the confection of quinces) and *marmalade* certainly derive. This recipe is a less familiar but appealing and less calorific use of the fruit. Quince used to be eaten by newlyweds before they went to their nuptial bed.

For 2 servings

1 medium quince
Ground cinnamon

Noncaloric sweetener to taste

1. Using a sharp knife, cut off the quince stem end to make a lid. Remove the core without piercing the bottom.
2. Sprinkle with cinnamon and sugar replacement. Cover with the quince lid. Place in a small baking pan.
3. Pour 1 cup water into the pan. Bake uncovered at 400°F for 25 minutes.
4. Cut quinces in half. Serve warm or cold.

Moroccan Orange Dessert

With a hint of rose water and cinnamon, the ubiquitous orange becomes sublime. Persian people sprinkle rose water or ground cardamom on peaches. Spice your own favorite fruit.

For 4 servings

4 flavorful oranges or	**Ground cinnamon**
mandarin oranges	**Rose water**

1. Peel the oranges, remove membranes, and divide into segments. Drop the orange segments into a bowl. Sprinkle very lightly with cinnamon and rose water. Rest for 15 or 20 minutes until flavors are absorbed.

2. Divide the segments evenly into 4 parts. Arrange each group of segments decoratively on 4 dessert plates. Serve immediately.

Nutrients for 1 serving (1 orange).

Calories: 62

Exchange: 1 fruit

g	mg
carbohydrate: 15	potassium: 237
protein: 1	sodium: 0
fat: negligible	cholesterol: 0
fiber: 2	

Banana in Wine Sauce

The banana of prehistoric India is now grown, in its many sizes and varieties, throughout the tropics, and is available widely in temperate zones. Dessert bananas have a higher sugar content than cooking bananas, which include Plantain (page 297), and the very small, slender "lady's finger" banana is one of the sweetest, most delicious varieties. You are more likely to find it in Chinese markets than supermarkets. For all dessert bananas, cooks everywhere devise their own blend of flavorings for desserts, creams, puffs, banana flambé. . . . This version is aromatic with wine and orange without the brandy—and it is especially fun to cook in a chafing dish at the table when guests are watching.

For 4 servings

2 medium or 4 small bananas	1 medium orange
1 tablespoon unsalted margarine or butter	2 tablespoons sweet dessert wine (optional)

1. Peel the bananas, and slice in half lengthwise.
2. In a chafing dish or skillet, melt the margarine or butter. Slip the bananas in, sautéing on both sides without breaking the bananas.
3. Slice the orange, and squeeze half over the bananas. Shake the pan to mix. Then squeeze the other orange half over the bananas. When the bananas are soft and the sauce begins to thicken, pour the wine over the bananas (if you are using it). Cook until the alcohol evaporates. Using a spatula, transfer the bananas to plates, offering ½ banana with some sauce for each serving. Serve immediately.

Nutrients for ½ banana with wine.

Calories: 104
Exchanges: 1½ fruit; ½ fat

g	mg
carbohydrate: 18	potassium: 292
protein: negligible	sodium: 2
fat: 3	cholesterol: 0
fiber: 2	

Banana Dessert from India

Here's an idea from India, where bananas originated. Whip up this soft and flavorful treat for an occasion when everyone wants something special —deliciously special.

For 4 servings

3 ripe but firm bananas
4 teaspoons Ghee (page 7),
   melted

Granulated sugar replacement
   for sprinkling (optional)

1. Peel bananas, and cut across into 6 segments.
2. Heat a small skillet or saucepan. Heat the Ghee, and when it is almost smoking, slip 4 or 5 banana segments into the skillet. Lower heat, and fry, turning, until ruddy all around. Remove and drain on paper towels. Keep hot until finished frying.
3. Taste, before sprinkling lightly with sugar replacement (you may not need any). Divide into 4 portions. Serve immediately.

Nutrients for 1 serving (4 or 5 pieces).

Exchanges: 1⅓ fruit; ½ fat

g	mg
carbohydrate: 20	potassium: 340
protein: negligible	sodium: 42.5
fat: 4.5	cholesterol: 11
fiber: 2	

Easy Old-World Applesauce

Tart and sweet, crisp apples and soft apples blend lusciously for a simple applesauce treat.

For 8 servings

8 apples of different types	1 teaspoon grated orange zest
¼ teaspoon ground cloves	Noncaloric sweetener
½ teaspoon grated nutmeg	(optional)

1. Wash, and quarter the apples. Place in a saucepan with about 1 cup water. Cook until tender, stirring occasionally.

2. Push the apples through a food mill directly into a bowl. Sprinkle with cloves, nutmeg, and orange zest. Taste, and sweeten only if necessary. Adjust the spices, and refrigerate until ready to serve. Serve chilled.

Nutrients for ½ cup.

Calories: 62

Exchange: 1 fruit

g	mg
carbohydrate: 16	potassium: 122
protein: negligible	sodium: 1
fat: negligible	cholesterol: 0
fiber: 2	

Pomegranate

The fruit of mythology and legends and artists, pomegranate symbolizes fertility to the Chinese people (because of its many seeds) and to the Hellenes (because of the myth of Demeter and Persephone). The latter throw the pomegranate across the threshold on New Year's Day and predict a prosperous year if the seeds scatter.

The red acid-sweet fruit seeds are even more beautiful in grain dishes (see Kolyva, pages 166–67), or delicious eaten raw as a fruit, or squeezed (like oranges) for the juice. Traditionally grenadine syrup was made from pomegranate juice, in fact. You can store pomegranates for months; keep them in a dry place. The leathery skin will dry and almost shrivel, but the fruit inside the loculi stays moist.

For 2 servings

1 red or yellow pomegranate

To serve in a dessert, snack, or fruit bowl, use a very sharp knife, and slice the pomegranate crosswise. Scoop out the fruit seeds with a small spoon. Seeds can be chewed and eaten, or discarded after the fruit is enjoyed.

Nutrients for ½ pomegranate.

Calories: 52
Exchange: 1 fruit

g	mg
carbohydrate: 13	potassium: 200
protein: negligible	sodium: 2
fat: negligible	cholesterol: 0
fiber: 1	

Lichi (Lychee)

The succulent white pulp of the lichi, inside a hard red pod, is unforgettably delectable and full of flavor surprises. Originating in China, lichi is now grown in Florida (like the Taiwanese variety) and in other countries. The seed inside ranges from small tooth size in China to almost the entire fruit in others, so it makes an enormous difference which you buy. Enjoy fresh lichis with friends as served to us graciously by Rupert and Margaret Li in Hong Kong.

For 5–6 servings

1 pound (about 28) fresh lichis

1. Place lichis unpeeled in beautiful serving bowl. After dinner, bring the bowl to the table (the dining table or, if you prefer, the coffee table in your living room).
2. Give each guest a plate (for peels and seeds), and ask them to help themselves from the bowl. Peel lichis one at a time as you enjoy the fruit. (Keep count of how many you eat by the number of discarded seeds.)

Nutrients for 5 fresh lichis.

Calories: 29

Exchange: 1 fruit

g	mg
carbohydrate: 15	potassium: 8
protein: negligible	sodium: 1.5
fat: negligible	cholesterol: 0
fiber: negligible	

Kiwi Fruit

Kiwi fruit is a succulent enigma. Originating in China, where it is called a Chinese gooseberry, the kiwi traveled to New Zealand. It was first exported from there to the United States. New Zealanders always refer to it as kiwi *fruit* to differentiate it from their charming kiwi bird and their own nickname. Kiwi is now grown in the United States and also in Greece.

The dull fuzzy outer skin never prepares you for the appearance of the cut-open fruit—stunning green flesh and radiating design with tiny black edible seeds. Besides being rich in vitamin C (1 kiwi has 89 mg), kiwi juice can tenderize meats.

For 1 serving

1 ripe kiwi fruit (soft to touch)

1. To serve informally in the skin: Slice kiwi crosswise in half. Place on 4 dessert plates. Serve with a spoon.

2. To serve in a salad or with cereal, custard, or other dessert: Peel the skin with a sharp knife. Slice kiwi crosswise in circles (to garnish Mock Pavlova, page 276). Or cut again into half-moons or quarters. You may prefer to cut kiwi into cubes.

Nutrients for 1 kiwi.

Calories: 55
Exchange: 1 fruit

g	mg
carbohydrate: 13.5	potassium: 302
protein: negligible	sodium: 4
fat: negligible	cholesterol: 0
fiber: 2	

Mango

A native of India enjoyed since prehistoric times, the tropical mango is glorious as a delicate climax to a meal. It is also superb teamed with shrimp (as in the Philippines) and rice, raita, pilau, chutney, curry, halwa, biscuits, fritters, pie, and ice cream (as in India). Try this pleasant way of serving mango fresh.

For 4 servings

**2 mangoes, washed and dried
with peel left on**

1. To serve as you would a custard: Slice across the mango just off center to avoid cutting the seed. Turn over, and slice the other side. Now you have 2 mango portions in the original shells. Peel off the skin of the remaining fruit. Slice the mango flesh around the seed, and divide between the 2 mango cups. Place on dessert dishes. Serve at room temperature or chilled.

2. To serve cubes: Slice across the mango as described above. Then score crisscross fashion across the mango with the knife point. Bend the peel backward to create space between the cubes. Carefully cut off the cubes near the mango peel. Arrange mango cubes in dessert dishes.

3. Or just peel and eat it lustily (and drippingly) right off the seed (which is also juicy).

Nutrients for ½ mango.

Calories: 68
Exchange: 1 fruit

g	mg
carbohydrate: 18	potassium: 161
protein: negligible	sodium: 2
fat: negligible	cholesterol: 0
fiber: 1.5	

Persimmon (American)

Native to the southern United States (*Diospyros virgininia*), the native American persimmon is smaller than the more prolific Japanese variety. It varies in color from dark red to maroon.

Nutrients for 1 fruit (.9 ounce or 25 g).

Calories: 32

Exchange: ½ fruit

g	mg
carbohydrate: 8	potassium: 78
protein: negligible	sodium: 0
fat: negligible	cholesterol: 0
fiber: negligible	

Persimmon (Japanese)

The soft pulpy flesh is pleasantly sweet, and the size, smooth skin, and color reminiscent of the tomato. You'll see Chinese, Japanese, and other Asians carefully selecting these persimmons in fruit stands and markets. Take your cue from the experts. Originating in China (where it is known as the Chinese date plum), the Japanese persimmon is scientifically known as *Diospyros kaki*. Now widely cultivated with hundreds of known varieties, the persimmon is usually eaten raw and is available in autumn.

Nutrients for 1 fruit (5.5 ounces or 168 g).

Calories: 118

Exchanges: 2 fruit

g	mg
carbohydrate: 31	potassium: 270
protein: negligible	sodium: 3
fat: negligible	cholesterol: 0
fiber: 2	

Passion Fruit (Granadilla)

Originally native to Brazil, the passion fruit *(Passiflora)* now grows in all the tropics, in the Mediterranean area, and in Florida where it is available from July to December. The fruit can be pink, purple, or yellow-green, but it is best to eat when wrinkled and ripe. Squeeze the passion fruit juice into tea, punches, and shakes. You can add a small squeeze of lime for additional flavor. Passion fruit seeds are edible.

Nutrients for 3 fruits (.6 ounce or 18 g each).

Calories: 54

Exchange: 1 fruit

g	mg
carbohydrate: 13	potassium: 189
protein: 1	sodium: 15
fat: negligible	cholesterol: 0
fiber: 6	

Mamey

A tropical fruit of Central America, the mamey (also spelled mammey, mamie, etc.) is now grown in Florida and is enthusiastically promoted as a "gift from the Gods." When you taste it, you can understand why. The thick brown skin of the fruit, ranging from six to nine inches, contrasts sharply with the soft flesh, which varies in color from salmon to red. The flesh tastes like pumpkin custard. Use mamey in shakes or mixed with cold cereals and fruit salads.

Nutrients for 3.5 ounces (100 g).

Calories: 51

Exchange: 1 fruit

g	mg
carbohydrate: 12.5	potassium: 15
protein: negligible	sodium: 15
fat: negligible	cholesterol: 0
fiber: 1	

Carambola (Star Fruit)

High in vitamins A and C, the carambola, originally from Indonesia, is beautiful when sliced across to reveal the 5-pointed star. The skin is edible. The flavor can vary from sweet to acid. Combine in salads, stir-fry with vegetables, or use as a garnish.

Nutrients for 1 fruit (126 g).

Calories: 42
Exchange: less than 1 fruit

g	mg
carbohydrate: 10	potassium: negligible
protein: negligible	sodium: 2
fat: negligible	cholesterol: 0
fiber: 1	

Longan

A native of China related to the lichi, the longan can climax any meal with sweet succulence.

Nutrients for 3.5 ounces (100 g).

Calories: 60
Exchange: 1 fruit

g	mg
carbohydrate: 15	potassium: 266
protein: 1	sodium: 0
fat: negligible	cholesterol: 0
fiber: negligible	

Sapodilla (Naseberry)

The sapodilla, originally a native of Central America, is an egg-shaped berry from 2 to 5 inches long. It is best when very ripe. The seeds are not edible. The sap (chicle) is used to make chewing gum.

Nutrients for ½ fruit (3 ounces or 85 g).

Calories: 70

Exchanges: 1½ fruit

g	mg
carbohydrate: 17	potassium: 164
protein: negligible	sodium: 10
fat: negligible	cholesterol: 0
fiber: 1	

Sapote

White and black sapote both look like a large green tomato but belong to the persimmon family of fruits. Keep the sapote in a fruit bowl, not in the refrigerator. Serve sliced in half, with or without whipped topping, and eat with a spoon.

Nutrients for 3.5 ounces (100 g).

Calories: 134

Exchanges: 2 fruit

g	mg
carbohydrate: 34	potassium: 344
protein: 2	sodium: 10
fat: negligible	cholesterol: 0
fiber: 2	

Papaya

The tropical papaya (also known as pawpaw or papaw) is versatile as a fruit or vegetable, and teams well with other fruits in salads and shakes. Cook it with meat, and also use it as a meat tenderizer. Papaya is especially stunning served sliced in half with the black edible seeds shining.

Nutrients for ½ papaya (10.64 ounces or 304 g for whole papaya).

Calories: 53
Exchange: 1 fruit

g	mg
carbohydrate: 15	potassium: 390
protein: negligible	sodium: 4
fat: negligible	cholesterol: 0
fiber: 1	

Breadfruit

The breadfruit, a native of Southeast Asia, is now a very popular staple in the West Indies. The starchy breadfruit became famous in *Mutiny on the Bounty*, when Captain Bligh was commissioned to introduce it from Tahiti to Haiti. With its leathery green skin, it is unusual to see it in markets. It is often stored in water (to prevent overripening); it turns yellow when ripe. Before cooking, after peeling, soak in cold water for 30 minutes to refresh the breadfruit and remove the starchy sap. You'll find it from April to November.

Plantain

Plantain is a staple of East Africa and a favorite of Caribbeans and South and Central Americans, although it originated in India. It is considered a cooking banana, since it contains more starch than sugar and needs to be cooked. You can boil it in the skin before peeling. Puerto Ricans like it mashed plain or with a tomato sauce. Indonesians slice it thinly, sauté it in butter, and sprinkle with cinnamon. Jamaicans dip slices in batter and deep-fry them.

Nutrients for ½ cup cooked, sliced plantain
(3 ounces or 77 g).

Calories: 89
Exchange: 1 starch/bread

g	mg
carbohydrate: 24	potassium: 358
protein: negligible	sodium: 4
fat: negligible	cholesterol: 0
fiber: NA	

Soursop (Guanabana)

A large fruit with bumpy skin, the soursop adds a tart flavor to punches and mixed beverages.

Nutrients for 3.5 ounces (100 g).

Calories: 66
Exchanges: 1½ fruit

g	mg
carbohydrate: 17	potassium: 278
protein: 1	sodium: 14
fat: negligible	cholesterol: 0
fiber: 1	

Tamarind

For an incomparably tart and delicious touch, use tamarind in sauces, curries, and beverages or just to nibble.

Nutrients for 12 fruits (5 ounces or 24 g after cleaning).

Calories: 60
Exchange: 1 fruit

g	mg
carbohydrate: 12	potassium: 156
protein: negligible	sodium: 12
fat: negligible	cholesterol: 0
fiber: 1	

Red Raspberries

Exquisite fruits for beauty and flavor, raspberries seem at home among tropical fruits even though they are native to temperate Europe and Asia. Eat raspberries fresh, drop in cereals, use as garnish, or float on leaves in a punch bowl.

Nutrients for 1 cup (4.5 ounces or 123 g).

Calories: 61
Exchange: 1 fruit

g	mg
carbohydrate: 14	potassium: 187
protein: 1	sodium: 0
fat: negligible	cholesterol: 0
fiber: 4	

Strawberries

Bright and refreshing strawberries are also fruits of the temperate climes. They team excitingly with tropical fruits. Strawberries cultivated today were developed from American species. Serve strawberries plain, with yogurt, granola, or cereals, combined with other fruits, between layers of custard, in shakes. . . .

Nutrients for 1 cup (5 ounces or 149 g).

Calories: 45
Exchange: between ¾ and 1 fruit

g	mg
carbohydrate: 10	potassium: 247
protein: negligible	sodium: 2
fat: negligible	cholesterol: 0
fiber: negligible	

Berry/Fruit Sauce

You have ravishing strawberries, peaches, or raspberries on hand? Then, mash them, lightly flavor, and enjoy! Here are three options.

For 2 servings

PEACH SAUCE

1 ripe medium peach	Pinch fresh ginger, grated
1 teaspoon lime or lemon juice	(optional)
Noncaloric sweetener	Pinch ground cinnamon
(optional)	(optional)

1. Wash fruit. Peel over a bowl to catch the juices.
2. Mash fruit in a bowl with a fork or in a blender. Season to your taste. Divide into 2 portions. Serve over pudding, cake, or other dessert.

Nutrients for 1 serving.

Calories: 30

Exchange: ½ fruit

g	mg
carbohydrate: 8	potassium: 136
protein: negligible	sodium: 0
fat: 0	cholesterol: 0
fiber: 1	

STRAWBERRY SAUCE

Use recipe for Peach Sauce except substitute ¾ cup strawberries for the peach. Divide into 2 portions.

Nutrients for 1 serving.

Calories: 24

Exchange: ½ fruit

g	mg
carbohydrate: 4	potassium: 98
protein: negligible	sodium: negligible
fat: negligible	cholesterol: 0
fiber: 1	

BLACK RASPBERRY SAUCE

Use recipe for Peach Sauce except substitute 1 cup black raspberries for the peach. Divide into 2 portions.

Nutrients for 1 serving.

Calories: 32
Exchange: ½ fruit

g	mg
carbohydrate: 8	potassium: 99
protein: negligible	sodium: 0
fat: negligible	cholesterol: 0
fiber: 4.5	

Party Whipped Topping

Beat the calories with this recipe from Murray V. F. Jones of the New Zealand Diabetes Association.

For 4 servings

½ cup nonfat dry milk   **Noncaloric sweetener**
1 tablespoon lemon juice

1. Chill your bowl and beater before beginning.
2. Mix the dry milk and ½ cup ice water in the chilled bowl. Beat with an electric mixer until soft peaks form.
3. Add the lemon juice and sweetener to please your taste. Continue beating until stiff peaks form. Divide into 4 portions. Serve chilled.

Nutrients for 1 serving.

Calories: 32
Exchange: ½ skim milk

g	mg
carbohydrate: 5	potassium: 152
protein: 3	sodium: 48.5
fat: negligible	cholesterol: 2
fiber: 0	

BEVERAGES

Water is the king of food.
KANURI PROVERB

Fresh Tomato Juice

When tomatoes are plentiful in gardens and markets, treat yourself and guests to homemade tomato juice.

For 4 cups

6 ripe and juicy tomatoes
Salt and freshly ground pepper
(optional)

Large pinch dried oregano or
fresh thyme
4 small lemon wedges

Wash, blanch, peel, and chop the tomatoes. Put through a food mill or sieve directly into a bowl. Add enough ice water to make 4 cups. Season lightly with salt and pepper (if you are using them) and herb. Taste, and enhance the seasonings. Serve cold with a squeeze of lemon juice.

**Nutrients for 1 cup with
1 teaspoon lemon juice.**

Calories: 26
Exchange: 1 vegetable

g	mg
carbohydrate: 6	potassium: 280
protein: 1	sodium: 38
fat: negligible	cholesterol: 0
fiber: 1	

Watermelon Ice Drink

Juicy watermelon refreshes more than most fruits—and with the smallest number of calories.

For 2 servings

2½ cups watermelon
½ cup crushed ice

Rose geranium leaves for
garnish (optional)

1. Seed, and coarsely chop the watermelon in a bowl, and save all the juices. Drop into a blender with the crushed ice. Blend until crushed.
2. Pour into 2 tall glasses. Garnish with rose geranium leaves, if you wish, and serve immediately with long straw-spoons.

Nutrients for 1 serving.

Calories: 64
Exchange: 1 fruit

g	mg
carbohydrate: 14	potassium: 232
protein: 1	sodium: 4
fat: negligible	cholesterol: 0
fiber: 2	

Mint Tea

Fragrant and relaxing, mint tea is a favorite after-dinner beverage in many Middle Eastern countries. You can use mint of any variety from your garden or market.

For 1 cup

1 tablespoon fresh mint leaves
  or ½ teaspoon dried mint

Noncaloric sweetener
  (optional)

1. In a small saucepan, bring a cup of water to a boil with the fresh mint leaves, chopped, or the dried mint crumbled in your palms directly into the water. Boil for ½ minute or longer until the water becomes bright yellow. Cover pan, and steep for a minute or so.
2. Strain mint tea into a cup. Serve hot, plain or sweetened.

Nutrients for 1 cup.

No calories. Use freely.

Cardamom Tea

Crushed cardamom seeds can transform an ordinary cup of tea into a very fragrant and relaxing one. Cardamom tea is very pleasant following Indian or Afghan dishes. (To make anise tea, substitute 1 teaspoon aniseed for the cardamom.)

For 4 servings

8 cardamom seeds
4 cups freshly brewed boiling
   hot tea

Noncaloric sweetener
   (optional)

1. In a mortar, lightly crush the cardamom seeds. Divide among 4 teacups or place in a warm teapot.
2. Pour the hot tea over the seeds. Serve immediately, preferably without sweetener.

Nurtrients for 1 cup.

No calories. Use freely.

Russian Tea

Delicious any day of the year but especially in winter, this aromatic beverage should be served in glasses, Russian style, to warm your fingers.

For 10 servings

2 medium oranges	4 whole cloves
2 medium lemons	1 cup strong tea infusion
3 cups unsweetened pineapple juice	Noncaloric sweetener
½ cinnamon stick	Orange slices for garnish (optional)

1. Wash, and dry the oranges and lemons. Cut in half, and squeeze. Reserve the juices in a pitcher.

2. Combine the orange and lemon rinds with the pineapple juice in a saucepan. Add the cinnamon stick and cloves. Simmer for 5 minutes. Remove the rinds, squeezing all the juice into the pan. Pour into a pitcher. Cool, and store in the refrigerator.

3. When you are ready to serve, pour juices from pitcher into a large saucepan. Add the tea infusion and 5 cups water. Bring to a boil. Remove cinnamon stick and cloves. Sweeten to please your taste. Pour into cups or glasses. Garnish with ½ orange slice, if you like. Serve hot.

Nutrients for 1 cup.

Calories: 56

Exchange: 1 fruit

g	mg
carbohydrate: 14	potassium: 157
protein: negligible	sodium: 2
fat: negligible	cholesterol: 0
fiber: negligible	

Yogurt-Berry Shake

Choose your favorite berries, and treat a friend.

For 2 servings

1 cup frozen or fresh
strawberries, raspberries,
blackberries, or blueberries

1 cup plain low-fat yogurt

If you are using frozen berries, thaw slightly. Reserve a few tablespoons berries to add later. Combine yogurt and berries in a blender. Whirl quickly, and pour into 2 tall glasses. Rinse the blender with ice water, and add to the glasses, filling them to the top. Stir in the reserved berries, half for each glass. Mix with a tall spoon. Serve immediately with long straw-spoons.

Nutrients for 1 serving.

Calories: 98
Exchanges: ½ fruit; ½ low-fat milk

g	mg
carbohydrate: 15	potassium: 375.5
protein: 6	sodium: 81
fat: 2	cholesterol: 7
fiber: negligible	

Masala Lassi

Masala Lassi is a refreshing and nutritious beverage for a quick snack, as enjoyed in India.

For 1 serving

1 cup plain low-fat yogurt   **⅛–¼ teaspoon Garam Masala (page 2)**

1. In a blender, mix the yogurt, as much Garam Masala as you like, and 3 or 4 ice cubes or ¼ cup ice water. Blend until cubes are crushed.

2. Pour into a tall glass. Rinse out the blender bowl with a little ice water, and add to the glass. Enjoy through a straw.

Nutrients for 1 serving.

Calories: 108

Exchange: 1 low-fat milk

g	mg
carbohydrate: 12	potassium: 398
protein: 9	sodium: 119
fat: 3	cholesterol: 10
fiber: 0	

Wassail

Here's an international version of the traditional English holiday wassail—quick and easy to mix for a large party.

For 14 servings

3 cups apple cider
1 cup unsweetened pineapple juice
1½ cups orange juice
½ cup grapefruit juice
½ cup lemon juice
2 sticks cinnamon

1½ teaspoons allspice
½ teaspoon cloves
2 ounces dry white wine (optional)
Noncaloric sweetener
1 medium orange for garnish
14 cloves

1. In a large saucepan, combine the cider, juices, and cinnamon sticks. Tie the allspice and cloves in a cheesecloth, and drop into the juice. Bring to a boil, reduce heat, and simmer for 5 minutes. Remove the spice bag and cinnamon sticks.

2. Add the wine (if you are using it) and bring to the boiling point. Taste the wassail, and sweeten to please your taste.

3. With a very sharp knife, slice the orange crosswise into 7 slices. Cut each in half. Stud each half slice with a clove.

4. Ladle ½ cup wassail into each punch cup. Float 1 orange slice in each cup. Serve hot.

Nutrients for ½ cup with wine.

Calories: 59
Exchange: 1 fruit

g	mg
carbohydrate: 14	potassium: 183
protein: negligible	sodium: 4
fat: negligible	cholesterol: 0
fiber: negligible	

EXCHANGE LISTS FOR
MEAL PLANNING

The exchange lists are the basis of a meal planning system designed by a committee of the American Diabetes Association and The American Dietetic Association. While designed primarily for people with diabetes and others who must follow special diets, the exchange lists are based on principles of good nutrition that apply to everyone. Copyright © 1989 American Diabetes Association, The American Dietetic Association.

STARCH/BREAD LIST

Each item in this list contains approximately 15 grams of carbohydrate, 3 grams of protein, a trace of fat, and 80 calories. Whole grain products average about 2 grams of fiber per exchange. Some foods are higher in fiber. Those foods that contain 3 or more grams of fiber per exchange are identified with the fiber symbol ✳.

You can choose your starch exchanges from any of the items on this list. If you want to eat a starch food that is not on this list, the general rule is that:

- ½ cup of cereal, grain, or pasta is one exchange.
- 1 ounce of a bread product is one exchange.

Your dietitian can help you be more exact.

Cereals/Grains/Pasta

✳Bran cereals, concentrated (such as Bran Buds®, All Bran®)	⅓ cup
✳Bran cereals, flaked	½ cup
Bulgur (cooked)	½ cup
Cooked cereals	½ cup
Cornmeal (dry)	2½ Tbsp.
Grape-Nuts®	3 Tbsp.
Grits (cooked)	½ cup
Other ready-to-eat unsweetened cereals	¾ cup
Pasta (cooked)	½ cup
Puffed cereal	1½ cups
Rice, white or brown (cooked)	⅓ cup
Shredded Wheat	½ cup
✳Wheat germ	3 Tbsp.

Dried Beans/Peas/Lentils

✳Beans and peas (cooked) (such as kidney, white, split, blackeye)	⅓ cup
✳Baked beans	¼ cup
✳Lentils (cooked)	⅓ cup

Starchy Vegetables

✳Corn	½ cup
✳Corn on cob, 6 in. long	1
✳Lima beans	½ cup
✳Peas, green (canned or frozen)	½ cup
✳Plantain	½ cup
Potato, baked	1 small (3 oz.)
Potato, mashed	½ cup
Squash, winter (acorn, butternut)	1 cup
Yam, sweet potato, plain	⅓ cup

Bread

Bagel	½ (1 oz.)
Bread sticks, crisp, 4 in. × ½ in.	2 (⅔ oz.)
Croutons, low fat	1 cup

✳ 3 grams or more of fiber per serving.

Bread (continued)

English muffin	½
Frankfurter or hamburger bun	½ (1 oz.)
Pita, 6 in. across	½
Plain roll, small	1 (1 oz.)
Raisin, unfrosted	1 slice (1 oz.)
Rye, pumpernickel	1 slice (1 oz.)
Tortilla, 6 in. across	1
White (including French, Italian)	1 slice (1 oz.)
Whole wheat	1 slice (1 oz.)

Crackers/Snacks

Animal crackers	8
Graham crackers, 2½ in. square	3
Matzoth	¾ oz.
Melba toast	5 slices
Oyster crackers	24
Popcorn (popped, no fat added)	3 cups
Pretzels	¾ oz.
✳Rye crisp, 2 in. × 3½ in.	4
Saltine-type crackers	6
✳Whole wheat crackers, no fat added (crisp breads, such as Finn®, Kavli®, Wasa®)	2–4 slices (¾ oz.)

Starch Foods Prepared with Fat

(Count as 1 starch/bread exchange, plus 1 fat exchange.)

Biscuit, 2½ in. across	1
Chow mein noodles	½ cup
Corn bread, 2 in. cube	1 (2 oz.)
Cracker, round butter type	6
French fried potatoes, 2 in. to 3½ in. long	10 (1½ oz.)
Muffin, plain, small	1
Pancake, 4 in. across	2
Stuffing, bread (prepared)	¼ cup
Taco shell, 6 in. across	2
Waffle, 4½ in. square	1

✳ 3 grams or more of fiber per serving.

✳ Whole wheat crackers, fat added
    (such as Triscuit®)   4–6 (1 oz.)

MEAT LIST

Each serving of meat and substitutes on this list contains about 7 grams of protein. The amount of fat and number of calories varies, depending on what kind of meat or substitute you choose. The list is divided into three parts based on the amount of fat and calories: lean meat, medium-fat meat, and high-fat meat. One ounce (one meat exchange) of each of these includes:

	Carbohydrate (grams)	Protein (grams)	Fat (grams)	Calories
Lean	0	7	3	55
Medium-Fat	0	7	5	75
High-Fat	0	7	8	100

You are encouraged to use more lean and medium-fat meat, poultry, and fish in your meal plan. This will help decrease your fat intake, which may help decrease your risk for heart disease. The items from the high-fat group are high in saturated fat, cholesterol, and calories. You should limit your choices from the high-fat group to three times per week. Meat and substitutes do not contribute any fiber to your meal plan. Meats and meat substitutes that have 400 milligrams or more of sodium per exchange are indicated with a ✛ symbol.

Tips

1. Bake, roast, broil, grill, or boil these foods rather than frying them with added fat.
2. Use a nonstick pan spray or a nonstick pan to brown or fry these foods.
3. Trim off visible fat before and after cooking.
4. Do not add flour, bread crumbs, coating mixes, or fat to these foods when preparing them.
5. Weigh meat after removing bones and fat, and after cooking. Three ounces of cooked meat is about equal to four ounces of raw meat. Some examples of meat portions are:

2 ounces meat (2 meat exchanges) =
   1 small chicken leg or thigh
   ½ cup cottage cheese or tuna

3 ounces meat (3 meat exchanges) =
   1 medium pork chop
   1 small hamburger
   ½ of a whole chicken breast
   1 unbreaded fish fillet
   cooked meat, about the size of a deck of cards

6. Restaurants usually serve prime cuts of meat, which are high in fat and calories.

Lean Meat and Meat Substitutes

(One exchange is equal to any one of the following items.)

Beef	USDA Select or Choice grades of lean beef, such as round, sirloin, and flank steak; tenderloin; and chipped beef ✛	1 oz.
Pork	Lean pork, such as fresh ham; canned, cured or boiled ham ✛; Canadian bacon ✛; tenderloin	1 oz.
Veal	All cuts are lean except for veal cutlets (ground or cubed); examples of lean veal are chops and roasts	1 oz.
Poultry	Chicken, turkey, Cornish hen (without skin)	1 oz.
Fish	All fresh and frozen fish	1 oz.
	Crab, lobster, scallops, shrimp, clams (fresh or canned in water ✛)	2 oz.
	Oysters	6 medium
	Tuna (canned in water)	¼ cup
	Herring (uncreamed or smoked)	1 oz.
	Sardines (canned)	2 medium
Wild	Venison, rabbit, squirrel	1 oz.
Game	Pheasant, duck, goose (without skin)	1 oz.
Cheese	Any cottage cheese	¼ cup
	Grated parmesan	2 Tbsp.
	Diet cheeses ✛ (with less than 55 calories per oz.)	1 oz.

✛ 400 milligrams or more of sodium per exchange.

Other	95 percent fat-free luncheon meat ✣	1 oz.
	Egg whites	3 whites
	Egg substitutes with less than 55 calories per ½ cup	½ cup

Medium-Fat Meat and Substitutes

(One exchange is equal to any one of the following items.)

Beef	Most beef products fall into this category; examples are all ground beef, roast (rib, chuck, rump), steak (cubed, Porterhouse, T-bone), and meatloaf	1 oz.
Pork	Most pork products fall into this category; examples are chops, loin roast, Boston butt, and cutlets	1 oz.
Lamb	Most lamb products fall into this category; examples are chops, leg, and roast	1 oz.
Veal	Cutlet (ground or cubed, unbreaded)	1 oz.
Poultry	Chicken (with skin), domestic duck or goose (well drained of fat), ground turkey	1 oz.
Fish	Tuna (canned in oil and drained)	¼ cup
	Salmon (canned)	¼ cup
Cheese	Skim or part-skim milk cheeses, such as:	
	Ricotta	¼ cup
	Mozzarella	1 oz.
	Diet cheeses ✣ (with 56–80 calories per ounce)	1 oz.
Other	86 percent fat-free luncheon meat	1 oz.
	Egg (high in cholesterol, limit to 3 per week)	1
	Egg substitutes with 56–80 calories per ¼ cup	¼ cup
	Tofu (2½ in. × 2¾ in. × 1 in.)	4 oz.
	Liver, heart, kidney, sweetbreads (high in cholesterol)	1 oz.

✣ 400 milligrams or more of sodium per exchange.

High-Fat Meat and Substitutes

Remember, these items are high in saturated fat, cholesterol, and calories, and should be used only three (3) times per week.
(One exchange is equal to any one of the following items.)

Beef	Most USDA Prime cuts of beef, such as ribs, corned beef	1 oz.
Pork	Spareribs, ground pork, pork sausage ✛ (patty or link)	1 oz.
Lamb	Patties (ground lamb)	1 oz.
Fish	Any fried fish product	1 oz.
Cheese	All regular cheeses, such as American ✛, Blue ✛, Cheddar, Monterey Jack, Swiss	1 oz.
Other	Luncheon meat ✛, such as bologna, salami, pimiento loaf	1 oz.
	Sausage ✛, such as Polish, Italian smoked	1 oz.
	Knockwurst ✛	1 oz.
	Bratwurst	1 oz.
	Frankfurter ✛ (turkey or chicken)	1 frank (10/lb.)
	Peanut butter (contains unsaturated fat)	1 Tbsp.

Count as one high-fat meat plus one fat exchange:

	Frankfurter ✛ (beef, pork, or combination)	1 frank (10/lb.)

VEGETABLE LIST

Each vegetable serving on this list contains about 5 grams of carbohydrate, 2 grams of protein, and 25 calories. Vegetables contain 2 to 3 grams of dietary fiber. Vegetables that contain 400 milligrams of sodium per exchange are identified with a ✛ symbol.

Vegetables are a good source of vitamins and minerals. Fresh and frozen vegetables have more vitamins and less added salt. Rinsing canned vegetables will remove much of the salt.

Unless otherwise noted, the serving size for vegetables (one vegetable exchange) is:

• ½ cup of cooked vegetables or vegetable juice
• 1 cup of raw vegetables

✛ 400 milligrams or more of sodium per exchange.

Vegetable List (continued)

Artichoke (½ medium)

Asparagus

Beans (green, wax,
Italian)

Bean sprouts

Beets

Broccoli

Brussels sprouts

Cabbage, cooked

Carrots

Cauliflower

Eggplant

Greens (collard, mustard,
turnip)

Kohlrabi

Leeks

Mushrooms, cooked

Okra

Onions

Pea pods

Peppers (green)

Rutabaga

Sauerkraut ✛

Spinach, cooked

Summer squash
(crookneck)

Tomato (one large)

Tomato/vegetable
juice ✛

Turnips

Water chestnuts

Zucchini, cooked

Starchy vegetables such as corn, peas, and potatoes are found on the Starch/Bread List.

For free vegetables, see Free Food List on pages 325–26.

FRUIT LIST

Each item on this list contains about 15 grams of carbohydrate and 60 calories. Fresh, frozen, and dried fruits have about 2 grams of fiber per exchange. Fruits that have 3 or more grams of fiber per exchange have a ✳ symbol. Fruit juices contain very little dietary fiber.

   The carbohydrate and calorie contents for a fruit exchange are based on the usual serving of the most commonly eaten fruits. Use fresh fruits or fruits frozen or canned without sugar added. Whole fruit is more filling than fruit juice and may be a better choice for those who are trying to lose weight. Unless otherwise noted, the serving size for one fruit exchange is:

- ½ cup of fresh fruit or fruit juice
- ¼ cup of dried fruit

✛ 400 milligrams or more of sodium per serving.

Fresh, Frozen, and Unsweetened Canned Fruit

Apple (raw, 2 in. across)	1 apple
Applesauce (unsweetened)	½ cup
Apricots (medium, raw)	4 apricots
Apricots (canned)	½ cup or 4 halves
Banana (9 in. long)	½ banana
*Blackberries (raw)	¾ cup
*Blueberries (raw)	¾ cup
Cantaloupe (5 in. across)	⅓ melon
(cubes)	1 cup
Cherries (large, raw)	12 cherries
Cherries (canned)	½ cup
Figs (raw, 2 in. across)	2 figs
Fruit cocktail (canned)	½ cup
Grapefruit (medium)	½ grapefruit
Grapefruit (segments)	¾ cup
Grapes (small)	15 grapes
Honeydew melon (medium)	⅛ melon
(cubes)	1 cup
Kiwi (large)	1 kiwi
Mandarin oranges	¾ cup
Mango (small)	½ mango
*Nectarine (2½ in. across)	1 nectarine
Orange (2½ in. across)	1 orange
Papaya	1 cup
Peach (2¾ in. across)	1 peach or ¾ cup
Peaches (canned)	½ cup or 2 halves
Pear	½ large or 1 small
Pears (canned)	½ cup or 2 halves
Persimmon (medium, native)	2 persimmons
Pineapple (raw)	¾ cup
Pineapple (canned)	⅓ cup
Plum (raw, 2 in. across)	2 plums
*Pomegranate	½ pomegranate

* 3 grams or more of fiber per serving.

Fresh, Frozen, and Unsweetened Canned Fruit (continued)

*Raspberries (raw)	1 cup
*Strawberries (raw, whole)	1¼ cups
Tangerine (2½ in. across)	2 tangerines
Watermelon (cubes)	1¼ cups

Dried Fruit

*Apples	4 rings
*Apricots	7 halves
Dates	2½ medium
*Figs	1½
*Prunes	3 medium
Raisins	2 Tbsp.

Fruit Juice

Apple juice/cider	½ cup
Cranberry juice cocktail	⅓ cup
Grapefruit juice	½ cup
Grape juice	⅓ cup
Orange juice	½ cup
Pineapple juice	½ cup
Prune juice	⅓ cup

MILK LIST

Each serving of milk or milk products on this list contains about 12 grams of carbohydrate and 8 grams of protein. The amount of fat in milk is measured in percent of butterfat. The calories vary, depending on what kind of milk you choose. The list is divided into three parts based on the amount of fat and calories: skim/very lowfat milk, lowfat milk, and whole milk. One serving (one milk exchange) of each of these includes:

	Carbohydrate (grams)	Protein (grams)	Fat (grams)	Calories
Skim/very lowfat	12	8	trace	90
Lowfat	12	8	5	120
Whole	12	8	8	150

* 3 grams or more of fiber per serving.

Milk is the body's main source of calcium, the mineral needed for growth and repair of bones. Yogurt is also a good source of calcium. Yogurt and many dry or powdered milk products have different amounts of fat. If you have questions about a particular item, read the label to find out the fat and calorie contents.

Milk is good to drink, but it can also be added to cereal and to other foods. Many tasty dishes such as sugar-free pudding are made with milk (see the Combination Food List on pages 326–27). Add life to plain yogurt by adding one of your fruit servings to it.

Skim/Very Lowfat Milk

Skim milk	1 cup
½ percent milk	1 cup
1 percent milk	1 cup
Lowfat buttermilk	1 cup
Evaporated skim milk	½ cup
Dry nonfat milk	⅓ cup
Plain nonfat yogurt	8 oz.

Lowfat Milk

2 percent milk	1 cup fluid
Plain lowfat yogurt (with added nonfat milk solids)	8 oz.

Whole Milk

The whole milk group has much more fat per serving than the skim and lowfat groups. Whole milk has more than 3¼ percent butterfat. Try to limit your choices from the whole milk group as much as possible.

Whole milk	1 cup
Evaporated whole milk	½ cup
Whole plain yogurt	8 oz.

FAT LIST

Each serving on the fat list contains about 5 grams of fat and 45 calories.

The foods on the fat list contain mostly fat, although some items may also contain a small amount of protein. All fats are high in calories and should be carefully measured. Everyone should modify fat intake by eating unsaturated fats instead of saturated fats. The sodium content of these foods varies widely. Check the label for sodium information.

Unsaturated Fats

Avocado	⅛ medium
Margarine	1 tsp.
☆Margarine, diet	1 Tbsp.
Mayonnaise	1 tsp.
☆Mayonnaise, reduced-calorie	1 Tbsp.
Nuts and seeds:	
Almonds, dry roasted	6 whole
Cashews, dry roasted	1 Tbsp.
Peanuts	20 small or 10 large
Pecans	2 whole
Walnuts	2 whole
Other nuts	1 Tbsp.
Seeds, pine nuts, sunflower (without shells)	1 Tbsp.
Pumpkin seeds	2 tsp.
Oil (corn, cottonseed, safflower, soybean, sunflower, olive, peanut)	1 tsp.
☆Olives	10 small or 5 large
Salad dressing, mayonnaise-type	2 tsp.
Salad dressing, mayonnaise-type, reduced-calorie	1 Tbsp.
☆Salad dressing (oil varieties)	1 Tbsp.
✣Salad dressing, reduced-calorie	2 Tbsp.

(Two tablespoons of low-calorie salad dressing is a free food.)

Saturated Fats

Butter	1 tsp.
☆Bacon	1 slice
Chitterlings	½ oz.
Coconut, shredded	2 Tbsp.
Coffee whitener, liquid	2 Tbsp.
Coffee whitener, powder	4 tsp.
Cream (light, coffee, table)	2 Tbsp.
Cream, sour	2 Tbsp.
Cream (heavy, whipping)	1 Tbsp.

☆ If more than one or two servings are eaten, these foods have 400 milligrams or more of sodium.
✣ 400 milligrams or more of sodium per serving.

Saturated Fats (continued)

Cream cheese	1 Tbsp.
☆Salt pork	¼ oz.

FREE FOOD LIST

A free food is any food or drink that contains less than 20 calories per serving. You can eat as much as you want of those items that have no serving size specified. You may eat two or three servings per day of those items that have a specific serving size. Be sure to spread them out through the day.

Drinks

Bouillon ✣ or broth
   without fat
Bouillon, low-sodium
Carbonated drinks,
   sugar-free
Carbonated water
Club soda
Cocoa powder,
   unsweetened (1 Tbsp.)
Coffee/tea
Drink mixes, sugar-free
Tonic water, sugar-free

Nonstick pan spray

Fruit

Cranberries,
   unsweetened (½ cup)
Rhubarb, unsweetened
   (½ cup)

Vegetables
(raw, 1 cup)
Cabbage
Celery
Chinese cabbage ✱
Cucumber
Green onion

Vegetables (continued)
Hot peppers
Mushrooms
Radishes
Zucchini ✱

Salad Greens
Endive
Escarole
Lettuce
Romaine
Spinach

Sweet substitutes
Candy, hard, sugar-free
Gelatin, sugar-free
Gum, sugar-free
Jam/jelly, sugar-free
   (less than 20 cal./2 tsp.)
Pancake syrup, sugar-
   free (1–2 Tbsp.)
Sugar substitutes
   (saccharin, aspartame)
Whipped topping
   (2 Tbsp.)

Condiments
Catsup (1 Tbsp.)
Horseradish

☆ If more than one or two servings are eaten, these foods have 400
   milligrams or more of sodium.
✣ 400 milligrams or more of sodium per serving.
✱ 3 grams or more of fiber per serving.

Mustard	Salad dressing, low-
Pickles ✛, dill,	calorie (2 Tbsp.)
unsweetened	Taco sauce (3 Tbsp.)
	Vinegar

Seasonings can be very helpful in making food taste better. Be careful of how much sodium you use. Read the label, and choose those seasonings that do not contain sodium or salt.

Basil (fresh)	Lemon juice
Celery seeds	Lemon pepper
Chili powder	Lime
Chives	Lime juice
Cinnamon	Mint
Curry	Onion powder
Dill	Oregano
Flavoring extracts	Paprika
(vanilla, almond,	Pepper
walnut, peppermint,	Pimiento
butter, lemon, etc.)	Soy sauce ✛
Garlic	Soy sauce ✛, low sodium
Garlic powder	("lite")
Herbs	Spices
Hot-pepper sauce	Wine, used in cooking
Lemon	(¼ cup)
	Worcestershire sauce

COMBINATION FOOD LIST

Much of the food we eat is mixed together in various combinations. These combination foods do not fit into only one exchange list. It can be quite hard to tell what is in a certain casserole dish or baked food item. This is a list of average values for some typical combination foods. This list will help you fit these foods into your meal plan. Ask your dietitian for information about any other foods you'd like to eat. The *American Diabetes Association/American Dietetic Association Family Cookbooks* and the *American Diabetes Association Holiday Cookbook* have many recipes and further information about many foods, including combination foods. Check your library or local bookstore.

✛ 400 milligrams or more of sodium per serving.

Food	Amount	Exchanges
Casseroles, homemade	1 cup (8 oz.)	2 starch, 2 medium-fat meat, 1 fat
Cheese pizza ✛, thin crust	¼ of 15 oz. or ¼ of 10 in.	2 starch, 1 medium-fat meat, 1 fat
Chili with beans ✹, ✛ (commercial)	1 cup (8 oz.)	2 starch, 2 medium-fat meat, 2 fat
Chow mein ✛ (without noodles or rice)	2 cups (16 oz.)	1 starch, 2 vegetable, 2 lean meat
Macaroni and cheese ✛	1 cup (8 oz.)	2 starch, 1 medium-fat meat, 2 fat
Soup		
Bean ✹, ✛	1 cup (8 oz.)	1 starch, 1 vegetable, 1 lean meat
Chunky, all varieties ✛	10¾ oz. can	1 starch, 1 vegetable, 1 medium-fat meat
Cream ✛ (made with water)	1 cup (8 oz.)	1 starch, 1 fat
Vegetable ✛ or broth ✛	1 cup (8 oz.)	1 starch
Spaghetti and meatballs ✛ (canned)	1 cup (8 oz.)	2 starch, 1 medium-fat meat, 1 fat
Sugar-free pudding (made with skim milk)	½ cup	1 starch
If beans are used as a meat substitute Dried beans ✹, peas ✹, lentils ✹	1 cup (cooked)	2 starch, 1 lean meat

✛ 400 milligrams or more of sodium per serving; ✹ 3 grams or more of fiber per serving.

RESOURCES

The American Diabetes Association and The American Dietetic Association. *Exchange Lists for Meal Planning.* 1986.

Coyle, L. Patrick. *The World Encyclopedia of Food.* Facts on File, 1982.

de Candolle, Alphonse. *The Origin of Cultivated Plants.* Hafner Publishing Co., 1959.

Food and Agriculture Organization of the United Nations, Nutrition Division. *Food Composition Table for Use in Africa.* 1968.

Gopalan, C., et al. *Nutritive Value of Indian Foods.* National Institute of Nutrition, Indian Council of Medical Research. Hyderabad, India, 1987.

Gurney, Selwyn. *Racial Proverbs.* 1938.

Harrison, S. G., et al. *The Oxford Book of Food Plants.* Oxford University Press, 1969.

Instituto de Nutrición de Centro América y Panamá. *Tabla de Composición de Alimentos para Uso en America Latina.* 1961.

Lowenberg, Miriam E., et al. *Food & People.* 3d ed. John Wiley & Sons, 1979.

Pasricha, S., et al. "Common Indian Snacks and Their Nutritive Value." *The Indian Journal of Nutr. Dietet.:* 24.8. 1987.

Sanjur, Diva. *Social and Cultural Perspectives in Nutrition.* Prentice-Hall, 1982.

U.S. Dept. of Agriculture. *Composition of Foods, Agriculture Handbook No. 8.* Sections 8–1 to 8–16. 1976–1986.

U.S. Dept. of Agriculture. *Nutritive Value of American Foods in Common Units, Handbook No. 456.* 1976–1986.

Ward, Artemas. *The Encyclopedia of Foods.* Peter Smith, 1923.

Williams, Sue Rodwell. *Nutrition and Diet Therapy.* 5th ed. Times Mirror/
Mosby College Publishing, 1985.

Zee, S. Y., and L. H. Hui. *Hong Kong Food Plants.* University of Hong
Kong, 1981.

INDEX

Acar Kuning (Indonesian Pickled Vegetable), 143
Afelia (Cypriot Coriander-Spiced Pork), 226
Afghan Dishes. *See also* Indian Dishes
  Baunjaun Bauranee (Eggplant with Chaka and Mint), 144
  Maushauwa (Soup), 93
  Naun (Bread), 262
  Teka Kebab, 221
  Yogurt Chaka, 28
African, Yard-Long Beans, 161
Ajies Rellenos con Carne (Baked Stuffed Peppers with Meat), 236
Alecha (Ethiopian Vegetable Stew), 78
Aljotta (Maltese Fish Soup), 85
Almonds, Toasted, 4
Amaranth ("Chinese Spinach"), 131
American (Central and South) Dishes. *See also name of individual country*
  Calabaza (Pumpkin), 129
  Chayote Salad, 139
  Sofrito, 8
American Diabetes Association and American Dietetic Association, exchange lists, 313–27
American Indian, Stewed Tomatoes, 134
American (USA), Wild Rice, 171

Appelpannekoeken (Dutch Apple Pancakes), 60
Appetizer, 36–53
  Bagna Cauda, 38
  Caponatina, Italian, 43
  Celery, Marinated, Hellenic Style, 41
  Eggs, Curried, 50
  Eggs, Pickled Beet, 51
  Guacamole, 39
  Hummus with Tahini, 53
  Mushrooms, Spanish Broiled (Pinchos), 42
  Mussels, French Style (Moules), 48
  Octopus, Marinated, 46
  Onion-Lime, Indian Style, 36
  Onion, Persian, 37
  Quesadilla, Especial, 52
  Ratatouille, 44
  Shrimp Tapas, 45
  Tofu, Spicy, 49
  Tzatziki, 40
Apple(s)
  Pancakes, Dutch, 60
  Persian, Stuffed, 246
  Rings, Dutch, 145
Applesauce, Easy Old-World, 287
Argentinean Dishes
  Carbonada, 258
  Empanada, 256

Argentinean Dishes *(cont.)*
  Humita (Corn Cakes), 160
  Locro (Vegetable-Beef Casserole),
    240
Armenian Dishes
  Patijan Karni Yarek (Stuffed
    Eggplant), 237
Ärter (Swedish Peas), 151
Artichokes, Tuna-Stuffed (Qaqqocc
    Mimli), 196
Ashe Reshte (Persian Meatball-Noodle
    Soup), 96
Asian, Taro, 158
Asparagus
  and Almonds, Chinese Style, 141
  with Tomato, 117
Avgolemono, Soupa (Egg-Lemon
    Soup), 88
Avocado Salad, Brazilian (Abacate),
    108

Bagna Cauda, Italian Dipping Sauce,
    38
Bakmi Goreng (Indonesian Noodle-
    Meat-Vegetable Dish), 235
Balkans, Baked Quince, 283
Balsam Pear or Bitter Gourd, 138
Banana
  Dessert from India, 286
  in Wine Sauce, 285
Bangladesh Style Dishes
  Chicken Korma, 227
  Fish Dopeyaja, 205
  Lentils, Boiled, 183
  Porota (Bread), 264
  Vegetable Niramish, 164
Basil Soup, Monegasque, 72
Baunjaun Bauranee (Afghan Eggplant
    with Chaka and Mint), 144
Bean Curd (Tofu), 25
Bean Curd and Vegetables, Tibetan,
    137
Beans
  Broad, Malta Style (Bigilla), 175
  Cannellini, and Sausages, Tuscan
    Style, 232
  Cranberry, 163
  Egyptian (Ful Madamis), 186
  Garbanzos Salteados, 187
  Green, Yard-Long, 161

Beans *(cont.)*
  Haricot Soleas, Cypriot, 185
  and Pasta, Italian Style, 180
  Soy, Cooked and Roasted, 179
Beef
  Cocido, Mexican Style, 234
  -Corn-Vegetable Casserole,
    Argentinean (Locro), 240
  exchange list, 317–19
  Hungarian Goulash, 243
  Meat and Dipping Sauce, Japanese
    Style, 217
  Polish Meat Rolls, 218
  Roast, Maltese Style, 216
  Shish Kebab, Indonesian, 220
  Stock, White, 99
  -Tomato Sauce/Gravy, 20
  -Vegetable Carbonada, 258
Beet Eggs, Pickled, 51
Bermuda Style Dishes
  Hopping John, 190
  Mussel Stew, 87
  Pawpaw Montespan, 242
Berner Linsensuppe (Lentil Soup,
    Bern Style), 79
Berry/Fruit Sauce, 300
Berry-Yogurt Shake, 309
Beurre Blanc, Mock, 6
Beverage, 304–11
  Cardamom Tea, 307
  free food exchange, 325
  Masala Lassi, 310
  Mint Tea, 306
  Russian Tea, 308
  Tomato Juice, Fresh, 304
  Wassail, 311
  Watermelon Ice Drink, 305
  Yogurt-Berry Shake, 309
Bigilla (Broad Beans, Malta Style),
    175
Birchermuesli, 56
Bitter Gourd or Balsam Pear, 138
Blinde Vinken (Blind Finches or Veal
    Birds), 214
Borscht, Vegetable, 76
Brazilian Dishes
  Quibebe (Pumpkin Stew), 162
  Salada de Abacate (Avocado), 108
  Salada de Palmito e Batatas (Palm
    Heart and Potato), 113

Bread(s) and Muffins, 260–72
  Afghan (Naun), 262
  Chapati, 271
  Cheese Muffins, New Zealand Style,
    260
  exchange list, 314–15
  of India, 270
  Papadum, 268
  Pita, 271
  Porota, 264
  Wheat-Bran, English, 266
  Whole Wheat Dosa, 261
Breadfruit, 296
Breakfast and Brunch Dishes, 56–60.
    See also Lunch
  Birchermuesli, 56
  Dutch Apple Pancakes, 60
  Mediterranean Vegetable-Egg Dish,
    58
  Spanish Omelet, 59
Broad Beans, Malta Style (Bigilla), 175
Broth, Scotch, 91
Buckwheat, Cracked (Kasha), 176
Bulgur, 173

Cabbage Red, Dutch, 126
Calabaza (West Indian Pumpkin), 129
  Pumpkin Stew, Brazilian (Quibebe),
    162
Calamari in Wine Sauce, 206
Cannellini Beans and Sausages,
    Tuscan Style, 232
Caponatina, Italian, 43
Carambola (Star Fruit), 294
Carbonada, 258
Cardamom Tea, 307
Caribbean, Sofrito, 8
Carrot(s)
  Celery and Apple Salad, 109
  Halwa, Easy, 281
  Lyonnaise, 135
  Salad, 103
Cauliflower, Marinated, Spanish, 130
Celery, Marinated, Hellenic Style, 41
Cereals exchange list, 314
Chapati, Indian Bread, 271
Chayote Salad, 139
Cheese
  exchange list, 317–19
  and Fruit, Open Sandwich, 61

Cheese *(cont.)*
  Gâteau, Fresh, 278
  Kefir (Polish, Homemade), 33
  Muffins, New Zealand Style, 260
  Panir (Indian, Homemade), 31
  Quesadilla, Especial, 52
Chestnut(s), 155. *See also* Water
    Chestnuts
  Puree, 156
Chick-Peas, Spanish Sautéed
    (Garbanzos Salteados), 187
Chicken
  Couscous, Tunisian, 244
  exchange list, 317–18
  Korma, 227
  Lemony, 228
  Luau, Hawaiian, 229
  Noodle Casserole with, 239
  Soup, Classic, 89
  Stock, White, 98
Chinese Dishes
  Almonds, Toasted, 4
  Asparagus and Almonds, 141
  Balsam Pear, 138
  Egg Roll, 248
  Kale, 127
  Lotus Rhizome Salad, 112
  Sautéed Shrimp, 194
  Shrimp Toast, 63
  Soy Dressing, 123
  "Spinach" (Amaranth), 131
  Sprout Salad, 107
  Tofu, 25
    Spicy, 49
  Water Chestnuts, 157
Chutney, Mint, 22
Cocido, Mexican Style, 234
Coconut Water, Milk, and Cream, 30
Combination dishes food exchange list,
    327
Condiment. *See also* Relish, Sauce,
    Seasoning
  Almonds, Toasted, 4
  Coconut Water, Milk, and Cream, 30
  Crème Fraîche, 24
  Cucumber Raita, 119
  free food exchange list, 326
  Ghee, Indian, 7
  Kefir (Polish Cheese), 33
  Panir (Homemade Cheese of India), 31

Condiment *(cont.)*
  Pesto Genovese, 23
  Sofrito, 8
  Tofu (Soybean or Bean Curd), 25
  Yogurt Chaka, Afghan, 28
  Yogurt, Uncle Bill's Homemade, 26
Corn Cakes, Argentinean (Humita), 160
Corn-Vegetable-Beef Casserole, Argentinean (Locro), 240
Cornmeal Polenta, 177
Cottage Cheese–flecked Hamburgers, 65
Couscous, Chicken, Tunisian, 244
Crab
  Enchiladas, 202
  and Okra, Haitian, 201
Crackers exchange list, 315
Cranberry Beans, 163
Crema Ghiacciata alla Vaniglia (Frozen Vanilla Cream), 279
Crème Fraîche, 24
Cucumber(s)
  Raita, 119
  Salad, Russian, 118
  Steamed, English, 136
Curry(ied)
  Dal, 184
  Eggs, 50
  Fish (Dopeyaja), 205
  Okra, Bombay Style, 128
  Potato, 152
Cypriot Dishes. *See also* Greek Dishes
  Afelia (Coriander-Spiced Pork), 226
  Haricot Beans Soleas, 185
  Kota Lemonato (Lemony Chicken), 228
  Strapatsada (Omelet), 58
  Vegetable Salad, Boiled, 114

Dal
  Curried, 184
  Snack, Spiced, 192
Dessert, 274–287. *See also* Fruit(s)
  Applesauce, Easy Old-World, 287
  Banana from India, 286
  Banana in Wine Sauce, 285
  Carrot Halwa, Easy, 281
  Cheese Gâteau, Fresh, 278

Dessert *(cont.)*
  Frozen Vanilla Cream, 279
  Fruit Delight, Persian, 282
  Kheer (Milk, Indian), 277
  Orange, Moroccan, 284
  Pavlova, Mock, 276
  Pikelets, New Zealand, 280
  Quince, Baked Balkan Style, 283
  Whipped Topping, Party, 301
  Yogurt and Fruit, 274
  Yogurt, Tibetan (Deysel), 275
Deysel (Tibetan Yogurt Dessert), 275
Dim Sum, Shrimp Toast, Chinese, 63
Dolmeh Sib (Persian Stuffed Apples), 246
Dressing. *See* Salad Dressing
Dried beans exchange list, 314
Drink. *See* Beverage
  free food exchange, 325
Dutch Style Dishes
  Appelpannekoeken (Apple Pancakes), 60
  Apple Rings, 145
  Blinde Vinken (Veal Birds), 214
  Red Cabbage, 126

Eastern European, Kasha, 176
Egg(s)
  Curried, 50
  egg/egg substitutes, exchange list, 318
  -Lemon Soup (Avgolemono), 88
  Pickled Beet, 51
  Roll, Chinese, 248
  Tortilla (Spanish Omelet), 59
  -Vegetable Dish, Mediterranean (Strapatsada), 58
Eggplant
  Caponatina, Italian, 43
  with Chaka and Mint, Afghan, 144
  Kima, 148
  Moussaka for Vegetable Lovers, 146
  Soup, Indonesian, 82
  Stuffed, Armenian, 237
Egyptian, Ful Madamis (Beans), 186
Empanada, Argentinean, 256
Endive Salad, German, 106
English Style Dishes
  Steamed Cucumber, 136

English Style Dishes *(cont.)*
  Wassail, 311
  Wheat-Bran Bread, 266
Escabeche (Jamaican Tangy Fish), 210
Ethiopian, Alecha (Vegetable Stew), 78
European Dishes (including Eastern
    and Northern European)
  Kasha, 176
  Mesclun, 102
  Potato Knishes, 154
  Potato Kugel, 153
  Rutabaga, Mashed, 140
Exchange list meal planning system,
    xv–xvi, 313–27
  cheese, 317–19
  combination dishes, 326–27
  condiments, 326
  drinks, 325
  egg/egg substitutes, 318
  fat (saturated and unsaturated), 323–
    25
  fish, 317–19
  free food, 325–26
  fruit, 320–22, 325
  meat/meat substitutes, 316–19
    beef, 317–19
    lamb, 318–19
    luncheon meat, 318–19
    pork, 317–19
      sausage, 319
    poultry, 317–18
      chicken, 317–18
      turkey, 317
    organ meats, 318
    veal, 317–19
    wild game, 317
  milk, 322–23
  peanut butter, 319
  seasonings, 326
  shellfish, 317
  starch/bread, 313–16
    bread, 314–15
    cereals, 314
    crackers, 315
    dried beans, 314
    grains, 314
    lentils, 314
    pasta, 314
    peas, 314
    prepared with fat, 315–16

Exchange list meal planning
    system *(cont.)*
  snacks, 315
  tofu, 318
  vegetables, 319–20, 325
    starchy, 314

Faki (Hellenic Lentil Soup), 80
Fat (saturated and unsaturated)
    exchange list, 323–25
Filipino, Pansit Bihon or Lug-Lug
    (Dried Rice Thread), 178
Filo (Phyllo), 251
Fish, 196–211. *See also* Shellfish
  Calamari in Wine Sauce, 206
  Dopeyaja (Curried), 205
  exchange list, 317–19
  Fillets, Marinated, 200
  Sardines, Grilled Portuguese, 199
  Seaman's Kebabs, 197
  Sole, Mountain of Gold, 207
  Soup, Maltese (Aljotta), 85
  Stock, White, 100
  Stockfish in Wine Sauce, Monaco
    Style, 204
  Sushi, 211
  Tangy Jamaican (Escabeche), 210
  and Vegetables, Steamed, 198
Food exchange list. *See* Exchange list
    meal planning system
Free food exchange list, 325–26. *See
    also* Exchange list meal
    planning system
French Dishes
  Beurre Blanc, Mock, 6
  Carrots Lyonnaise, 135
  Crème Fraîche, 24
  Lemon Dressing, 121
  Mirepoix, 10
  Moules (Mussels), 48
  Onion Soup, 74
  Ratatouille, 44
  Salade Niçoise, 111
  Vinaigrette, 120
    Spicier, 120
Fruhlingssuppe (Spring Soup), 75
Fruit(s), 288–301. *See also* Dessert
  /Berry Sauce, 300
  Breadfuit, 296
  Carambola (Star Fruit), 294

Fruit(s) *(cont.)*
  and Cheese Open Sandwich, 61
  Delight, Persian, 282
  exchange list, 320–22, 325
  Kiwi, 290
  Lichi (Lychee), 289
  Longan, 294
  Mamey, 293
  Mango, 291
  Papaya, 296
  Persimmon, American and
    Japanese, 292
  Plantain, 297
  Pomegranate, 288
  Raspberries, Red, 299
  Sapodilla (Naseberry), 295
  Sapote (Persimmon), 295
  Soup, Cool Tropical, 81
  Soursop (Guanabana), 298
  Strawberries, 299
  Tamarind, 298
  and Whole Wheat (Kolyva), 166
  and Yogurt Dessert, 274
Ful Madamis (Egyptian Beans), 186

Game Stew, German Style, 230
Garam Masala, 2
Garbanzos Salteados (Chick-Peas,
  Spanish, Sautéed), 187
Gâteau, Fresh Cheese, 278
Gazpacho (Andalusian Vegetable
  Dish), 142
German Style (East and West) Dishes
  Carrot, Celery, and Apple Salad, 109
  Endive Salad, 106
  Fruhlingssuppe (Spring Soup), 75
  Gâteau, Fresh Cheese, 278
  Hamburgers, Cottage Cheese–
    flecked, 65
  Kartoffelsalat (Potato Salad), 116
  Noodle Casserole with Chicken, 239
  Pumpkin, Spicy Stewed, 159
  Seemannsspiechen (Seaman's
    Kebabs), 197
  Venison or Game Stew, 230
Ghee, Indian, 7
Goulash, Hungarian, 243
Gourd. *See also* Chayote Salad
  Bitter or Balsam Pear, 138
  Snake, 150

Grains. *See also name of grain*
  exchange list, 314
Gravy, Beef-Tomato, 20
Greek Dishes. *See also* Cypriot Dishes
  Avgolemono Soupa, 88
  Celery, Marinated, 41
  Eggplant Kima, 148
  Faki (Lentil Soup), 80
  Filo (Phyllo), 251
  Horiatiki Salata, 104
  Kolyva (Whole Wheat and Fruits), 166
  Souvlaki apo Arni, 219
  Spanakopitakia, 252
Gremolata (Italian Seasoning), 9
Guacamole, 39

Haitian Crab and Okra, 201
Hamburgers, Cottage Cheese–flecked,
  65
Haricot Beans, Soleas, Cypriot, 185
Harissa (Tunisian Hot Sauce), 16
Hawaiian Chicken Luau, 229
Hellenic. *See* Greek Dishes
Hero Sandwich, Italian, 68
Hopping John, 190
Horiatiki Salata (Hellenic Village
  Salad), 104
Hot Pepper Sauce, 12
  Indonesian (Sambal), 15
Hot Sauce, Tunisian (Harissa), 16
Humita (Argentinean Fresh Corn
  Cakes), 160
Hummus with Tahini, 53
Hungarian Goulash, 243

Indian Dishes. *See also* Afghan Dishes
  Banana Dessert, 286
  Breads, 270
  Cardamom Tea, 307
  Chapati, 272
  Cucumber Raita, 119
  Curried Dal, 184
  Curried Eggs, 50
  Dal Snack, Spiced, 192
  Garam Masala, 2
  Ghee, 7
  Halwa, Easy Carrot, 281
  Kadhi (Yogurt Relish), 29
  Kheer, 277
  Masala Lassi, 310

Indian Dishes (cont.)
  Mint Chutney, 22
  Okra Curry, Bombay Style, 128
  Onion-Lime Appetizer, 36
  Panir (Homemade Cheese), 31
  Papadum, 268
  Potato Curry, 152
  Snake Gourd, 150
  Vadas, 188
  Vegetable Kichuri, 182
  Vegetable Pilau, 172
  Vegetable Samosa, 254
  Whole Wheat Dosa, 261
Indonesian Dishes
  Acar Kuning (Pickled Vegetable), 143
  Bakmi Goreng (Noodle-Meat-
      Vegetables), 235
  Nasi Kuning (Yellow Coconut Rice),
      168
  Onion Flakes, Fried, 5
  Peanut Sauce, 18
  Sambal, 15
  Sambal Bajak (Relish), 21
  Sate Manis (Shish Kebab), 220
  Sayur Lodeh (Eggplant Soup), 82
International Dishes
  Amaranth, 131
  Applesauce, Easy Old-World, 287
  Banana in Wine Sauce, 285
  Berry/Fruit Sauce, 300
  Breadfruit, 296
  Carambola (Star Fruit), 294
  Cheese and Fruit Open Sandwich,
      61
  Fruit (Dessert), 287–300
  Fruit Soup, Cool Tropical, 81
  Hot Pepper Sauce, 12
  Italian Hero Sandwich, 68
  Kiwi Fruit, 290
  Lichi, 289
  Longan (Fruit), 294
  Mamey (Fruit), 293
  Mango, 291
  Papaya, 296
  Passion Fruit (Granadilla), 293
  Peanuts, Fresh, 189
  Persimmon
    American, 292
    Japanese, 292
  Pita, 271

International Dishes (cont.)
  Plantain, 297
  Pomegranate, 288
  Pumpkin Seed, 181
  Raspberries, Red, 299
  Rice, Steamed, 169
  Sapodilla (Naseberry), 295
  Sapote, 295
  Soursop (Guanabana), 298
  Soybeans (Cooked and Roasted),
      179
  Stock, White
    Beef, 99
    Chicken, 98
    Fish, 100
  Strawberries, 299
  Sweet-Sour Mustard Greens, 133
  Tamarind, 298
  Tomato Juice, Fresh, 304
  Vinegar, Spiced, 13
  Watermelon Ice Drink, 305
  Yogurt-Berry Shake, 309
  Yogurt Dressing, 122
  Yogurt and Fruit Dessert, 274
Israeli Dishes
  Carrot Salad, 103
  Chicken Soup, Classic, 89
  Knaidlach, 90
Italian Dishes
  Bagna Cauda, 38
  Caponatina, 43
  Crema Ghiacciata alla Vaniglia
      (Frozen Vanilla Cream), 279
  Fish and Vegetable, Steamed,
      198
  Gremolata, 9
  Hero Sandwich, 68
  Pasta e Fagioli, 180
  Pesto Genovese, 23
  Pizza Margherita, 64
  Polenta, 177
  Sausages and Cannellini Beans,
      Tuscan Style, 232

Jamaican, Escabeche, 210
Japanese Style Dishes
  Meat and Dipping Sauce, 217
  Soup, 77
  Spinach with Tofu, 115
  Sushi, 211

Kadhi (Yogurt Relish), 29
Kale
  Chinese, 127
  and Red Peppers, Kenya Style, 132
Kartoffelsalat (Potato Salad, German
  Style), 116
Kasha (Cracked Buckwheat), 176
Kefir (Homemade Cheese, Polish), 33
Kenyan Dishes
  Kale and Red Peppers, 132
  Stew, 92
Kheer, Indian Milk Dessert, 277
Kibbe bi Saniyeh (Moroccan Baked
  Specialty), 222
Kichuri, Vegetable, 182
Kiwi Fruit, 290
Knaidlach, 90
Knishes, Potato, 154
Kolyva (Whole Wheat and Fruits), 166
Korean, Sesame Salt, 3
Kota Lemonato (Lemony Chicken),
  228
Kugel, Potato, 153

Lamb
  exchange list, 318–19
  Kebabs, Afghan, 221
  Kibbe bi Saniyeh, Moroccan, 222
  Pita, Sephardic, 223
  Souvlaki, Hellenic, 219
Lebanese, Tabbouleh, 110
Lemon Panir, 32
Lemon Salad Dressing, 121
Lentil(s)
  Boiled, à la Bangladesh, 183
  exchange list, 314
  Soup, Bern Style, 79
  Soup, Hellenic Style (Faki), 80
  Vadas, 188
Lichi (Lychee), 289
Lime Panir, 31
Locro (Argentinean Corn-Vegetable-
  Beef Casserole and Piquant
  Sauce), 240
Longan (Fruit), 294
Lotus Rhizome Salad, 112
Lug-Lug or Pansit Bihon (Filipino
  Dried Rice Thread), 178
Lunch, 61–70. See also Breakfast and
  Brunch Dishes

Lunch (cont.)
  Cheese and Fruit Open Sandwich, 61
  Cottage Cheese–flecked
    Hamburgers, 65
  Hero Sandwich, Italian, 68
  Open-Faced Sandwich, Tunisian, 67
  Pan Bagnat (Sandwiches), 62
  Pita Sandwich Medley, 66
  Pizza Margherita, 64
  Shrimp Toast, Chinese, 63
  Tacos, Mexican, 69
  Tacos, Vegetarian, 70
Luncheon meat exchange list, 318–19

Maltese Style Dishes
  Aljotta (Fish Soup), 85
  Baked Rice, 174
  Bigilla (Broad Beans), 175
  Qaqqocc Mimli (Tuna-Stuffed
    Artichokes), 196
  Roast Beef, 216
Mamey (Fruit), 293
Mango, 291
Marinade, Wine à la Maria Nicole, 11
Marinated Dishes
  Cauliflower, Spanish, 130
  Celery, Hellenic Style, 41
  Fish Fillets, 200
  Octopus, 46
Masala Lassi (Beverage), 310
Maushauwa (Afghan Soup), 93
Meal planning system, exchange list,
  xv-xvi, 313–27
Meat
  and Dipping Sauce, Japanese Style,
    217
  -Noodle-Vegetable Dish, Indonesian,
    235
  Rolls, Polish (Zrazy), 218
Meatball-Noodle Soup, Persian (Ashe
  Reshte), 96
Mediterranean Style Dishes. See also
  name of individual country
  Beef-Tomato Sauce/Gravy, 20
  Calamari in Wine Sauce, Spicy, 206
  Chestnuts, 155
    Puree, 156
  Cranberry Beans, 163
  Marinade, Wine, 11
  Marinated Fish Fillets, 200

Mediterranean Style Dishes *(cont.)*
  Marinated Octopus, 46
  Tomato Sauce, Homemade, 19
Mesclun (Salad), 102
Mexican Style Dishes
  Cocido, 234
  Crab Enchiladas, 202
  Guacamole, 39
  Quesadilla Especial, 52
  Salsa Picante, 17
  Tacos, 69
  Vegetarian Tacos, 70
Middle East Dishes. *See also name of*
    individual country
  Bulgur, 173
  Hummus with Tahini, 53
  Mint Tea, 306
  Moussaka for Vegetable Lovers,
    146
  Pita Sandwich Medley, 66
  Tzatziki (Herbed Yogurt), 41
  Yogurt, 26
Milk exchange list, 322–23
Mint
  Chutney, 22
  Tea, 306
Mirepoix, French, 10
Mock Beurre Blanc, 6
Mock Pavlova, 276
Monaco Style Dishes
  Basil Soup, 72
  Pan Bagnat, 62
  Stockfish in Wine Sauce, 204
Monegasque Basil Soup, 72
Moroccan Style Dishes
  Kibbe bi Saniyeh, 222
  Orange Dessert, 284
Moules (Mussels, French Style), 48
Moussaka for Vegetable Lovers, 146
Muffins. *See also* Scones
  Cheese, New Zealand Style, 260
Mushrooms, Spanish Broiled
    (Pinchos), 42
Mussel Stew, Bermuda, 87
Mussels, French Style (Moules), 48
Mustard Greens, Sweet-Sour, 133

Nasi Kuning (Yellow Coconut Rice,
    Indonesian), 168
Naun (Afghan Bread), 262

New Zealand Style Dishes
  Cheese Muffins, 260
  Mock Pavlova, 276
  Pikelets, 280
  Whipped Topping, Party, 301
Niçoise Salade, 111
Noodle
  Casserole with Chicken, 239
  -Meat-Vegetable Dish, Indonesian, 235
  -Meatball Soup, Persian, 96
Northern European. *See* European
    Dishes
Norwegian, Spinatsuppe (Spinach
    Soup), 73
Nuoc Mam Sauce, Vietnamese, 14
Nutrition, principles of, xiv-xv
Nuts exchange list, 324

Oat Scones, Scottish, 265
Octopus, Marinated, 46
Oil exchange list, 324
Okra
  and Crab, Haitian, 201
  Curry, Bombay Style, 128
Onion
  Appetizer, Persian, 37
  Flakes, Fried, 5
  -Lime Appetizer, Indian Style, 36
  Soup, French, 74
Orange Dessert, Moroccan, 284
Organ meats exchange list, 318

Paella, 208
Palm Heart and Potato Salad, 113
Paludeh (Persian Fruit Delight), 282
Pan Bagnat (Sandwiches, Monaco
    Style), 62
Panamanian, Sanchocho Panameno, 86
Pancakes, Apple, 60
Panir (Homemade Cheese of India), 31
  Lemon, 31
  Lime, 31
Pansit Bihon or Lug-Lug (Filipino
    Dried Rice Thread), 178
Papadum, Indian Bread, 268
Papaya, 296
    Bermuda Pawpaw Montespan, 242
Passion Fruit (Granadilla), 293
Pasta e Fagioli (Pasta and Beans,
    Italian Style), 180

Pasta exchange list, 314
Patlijan Karni Yarek (Armenian
    Stuffed Eggplant), 237
Pavlova, Mock, 276
Peanut butter exchange list, 319
Peanut Sauce, Indonesian, 18
Peanuts, Fresh, 189
Pear. *See* Balsam Pear
Peas
    Black-Eye, Hopping John, 190
    exchange list, 314
    Swedish (Ärter), 151
Pennsylvania Dutch, Pickled Beet
    Eggs, 51
Peppers
    Red, and Kale, Kenya Style, 132
    Stuffed with Meat, Baked, 236
Persian Style Dishes
    Ashe Reshte (Meatball-Noodle
        Soup), 96
    Dolmeh Sib (Stuffed Apples), 246
    Onion Appetizer, 37
    Paludeh (Fruit), 282
    Salade Sabzi, 105
    Spice Blend, 34
Persimmon
    American, 292
    Japanese, 292
Pesto Genovese, 23
Phyllo (Filo), 251
Pickled Beet Eggs, 51
Pikelets, New Zealand, 280
Pilau, Vegetable, 172
Pinchos (Spanish Broiled Mushrooms),
    42
Pita Bread, 271
Pita Sandwich Medley, 66
Pizza Margherita, 64
Plantain (Fruit), 297
Polenta, 177
Polish Style Dishes
    Kefir (Homemade Cheese), 33
    Zrazy (Meat Rolls), 218
Pomegranate, 288
Pork
    Coriander-Spiced, Cypriot, 226
    exchange list, 317–19
    in Wine, Zurich Style, 225
Porota (Paratha), 264
Portuguese Sardines, Grilled, 199

Potato
    Curry, 152
    Knishes, 154
    Kugel, 153
    and Palm Heart Salad, 113
    Salad, German Style, 116
Poultry exchange list, 317–18
Pumpkin (or Calabaza)
    Seed, 181
    Spicy Stewed, 159
    Stew, Brazilian, 162
    West Indian, 129

Qaqqocc Mimli (Tuna-Stuffed
    Artichokes), 196
Quesadilla, Especial, 52
Quibebe (Brazilian Pumpkin Stew),
    162
Quince, Baked Balkan Style, 283

Raita, Cucumber, 119
Raspberries, Red, 299
Ratatouille, French, 44
Red Cabbage, Dutch, 126
Red Peppers and Kale, Kenya Style,
    132
Relish. *See also* Condiment
    Mint Chutney, 22
    Sambal Bajak with Nuts
        (Indonesian), 21
    Yogurt (Kadhi), 29
Rice
    Indonesian, Yellow Coconut, 168
    Maltese, Baked, 174
    Paella, 208
    Spanish, 170
    Steamed, 169
    Thread, Filipino Dried, 178
    Vegetable Pilau, 172
    Wild, 171
Russian Style Dishes
    Balkan Baked Quince, 283
    Cucumber Salad, 118
    Tea, 308
    Vegetable Borscht, 76
Rutabaga, Mashed, 140

Sabzi Salade (Persian), 105
Salad, 102–19
    Asparagus with Tomato, 117

Salad *(cont.)*
  Avocado, Brazilian, 108
  Carrot, 103
  Carrot, Celery and Apple, 109
  Chayote, 139
  Cucumber, Raita, 119
  Cucumber, Russian, 118
  Endive, German, 106
  Gazpacho, 142
  Hellenic Village, 104
  Lotus Rhizome, 112
  Mesclun, 102
  Niçoise, 111
  Palm Heart and Potato, Brazilian,
    113
  Persian, 105
  Potato, German Style, 116
  Spinach with Tofu, Japanese Style,
    115
  Sprout, Chinese, 107
  Tabbouleh, 110
  Vegetable, Boiled, 114
Salad Dressing
  exchange list, 324
  Lemon, 121
  Soy, 123
  Vinaigrette, 120
    Spicier, 120
  Yogurt, 122
Salsa Picante, Mexican, 17
Sambal (Hot Pepper Sauce), 15
Sambal Bajak (Indonesian Relish with
    Nuts), 21
Samosa, Vegetable, 254
Sanchocho Panameno (Spicy
    Panamanian Stew), 86
Sandwich(es)
  Hero, Italian, 68
  Open, Cheese and Fruit, 61
  Open-Faced, Tunisian, 67
  Pan Bagnat, Monaco Style, 62
  Pita Medley, 66
Sapodilla (Naseberry), 295
Sapote (Fruit), 295
Sardines, Grilled Portuguese, 199
Sate Manis (Indonesian Shish Kebab),
    220
Saturated fats exchange list, 324–25
Sauce
  Beef-Tomato, 20

Sauce *(cont.)*
  Berry/Fruit, 300
  Beurre Blanc, Mock, 6
  Harissa (Tunisian, Hot), 16
  Hot Pepper, 12
  Italian Dipping, Bagna Cauda, 38
  Nuoc Mam, Vietnamese, 14
  Peanut, Indonesian, 18
  Picante, Mexican Salsa, 17
  Sambal, Indonesian (Hot Pepper), 15
  Tomato, Homemade, 19
Sausage exchange list, 319
Sausages and Cannellini Beans,
    Tuscan Style, 232
Sayur Lodeh (Indonesian Eggplant
    Soup), 82
Scones, Oat, Scottish, 265
Scotch Broth, 91
Scottish Oat Scones, 265
Seafood. *See* Shellfish
Seaman's Kebabs, 197
Seasoning(s). *See also* Condiment
  Crème Fraîche, 24
  free food exchange list, 326
  Gremolata, Italian, 9
  Indian Garam Masala, 2
  Mirepoix, French, 10
  Onion Flakes, Fried, 5
  Sesame Salt, Korean, 3
  Spice Blend, Persian, 34
  Spiced Vinegar, 13
Seemannsspiesschen (Seaman's
    Kebabs), 197
Sephardic Lamb Pita, 223
Sesame Salt, Korean, 3
Shellfish, 196–211. *See also name of*
    shellfish; Fish
  exchange list, 317
  Paella, 208
  Seaman's Kebabs, 197
  Sushi, 211
Shish Kebab, Indonesian, 220
Shrimp
  Chinese, Sautéed, 195
  Sour, Soup, 84
  Tapas, 45
  Toast, Chinese, 63
Slatit Blanquit (Tunisian Open-Faced
    Sandwich), 67
Snacks exchange list, 315

Snake Gourd, 150
Sofrito, Caribbean, 8
Sole, Mountain of Gold, 207
Soup, 72–100. *See also* Stew
 Afghan, 93
 Avgolemono (Egg-Lemon), 88
 Basil, Monegasque, 72
 Chicken, Classic, 89
 Eggplant, Indonesian, 82
 Fish, Maltese, 85
 Fruit, Cool Tropical, 81
 Japanese, 77
 Knaidlach for, 90
 Lentil, Bern Style, 79
 Lentil, Hellenic, 80
 Meatball-Noodle, Persian, 96
 Onion, French, 74
 Scotch Broth, 91
 Shrimp, Sour, 84
 Spinach, Norwegian, 73
 Spring, 75
 Stock, 98–100. *See also* Stock
 Vegetable Borscht, 76
 Yogurt, Turkish, 83
Soursop (Guanabana), 298
South American. *See* American
 (Central and South) Dishes
Souvlaki apo Arni (Hellenic Lamb),
 219
Soy Salad Dressing, 123
Soybean Curd (Tofu), 25
Soybeans, Cooked and Roasted, 179
Spanakopitakia (Spinach Triangles),
 252
Spanish Style Dishes
 Cauliflower, Marinated, 130
 Garbanzos Salteados, 187
 Gazpacho, 142
 Paella, 208
 Pinchos (Broiled Mushrooms), 42
 Rice, 170
 Shrimp Tapas, 45
 Tortilla (Omelet), 59
Spice Blend, Persian, 34
Spiced Vinegar, 13
Spinach
 "Chinese" (Amaranth), 131
 Soup, Norwegian, 73
 with Tofu, Japanese Style, 115
 Triangles (Spanakopitakia), 252

Spinatsuppe (Norwegian Spinach
 Soup), 73
Spring Soup, 75
Sprout Salad, Chinese, 107
Squid, Calamari in Wine Sauce, 206
Star Fruit (Carambola), 294
Starch/bread exchange list, 313–16
Starch foods prepared with fat,
 exchange list, 315–16
Starchy vegetable exchange list, 314
Stew, 78, 86–87, 92. *See also* Soup
 Calabaza or Pumpkin, Brazilian, 162
 Kenya, 92
 Mussel, Bermuda, 87
 Spicy Panamanian, 86
 Vegetable, Ethiopian, 78
 Venison or Game, German Style, 230
Stock, 98–100. *See also* Soup
 Beef, White, 99
 Chicken, White, 98
 Fish, White, 100
Stockfish in Wine Sauce, Monaco
 Style, 204
Strapatsada (Mediterranean Vegetable-
 Egg Dish), 58
Strawberries, 299
Sushi, 211
Swedish Ärter (Peas), 151
Sweet-Sour Mustard Greens, 133
Swiss Style Dishes
 Birchermuesli, 56
 Lentil Soup, 79
 Pork in Wine, 225
 Tripes à la Vaudoise, 231

Tabbouleh Salad, 110
Tacos
 Mexican, 69
 Vegetarian, 70
Tamarind (Fruit), 298
Tapas, Shrimp, 45
Taro, 158
Tea
 Cardamom, 307
 Mint, 306
 Russian, 308
Teka Kebab (Afghan Broiled Kebabs),
 221
Thai, Tom Yum Goong (Shrimp Soup),
 84

Tibetan Style Dishes
  Vegetable and Bean Curd, 137
  Yogurt Dessert (Deysel), 275
Tofu (Soybean or Bean Curd), 25
  exchange list, 318
  Spicy, 49
Tom Yum Goong (Sour Shrimp Soup), 84
Tomato(es)
  -Beef Sauce/Gravy, 20
  Juice, Fresh, 304
  Sauce, Homemade, 19
  Stewed, American Indian Style, 134
Tortilla (Spanish Omelet), 59
Tripes à la Vaudoise (Swiss Style), 231
Tropical
  Coconut Water, Milk, and Cream, 30
  Fruit Soup, Cool, 81
Tsel Dofu (Tibetan Vegetable and
    Bean Curd), 137
Tuna-Stuffed Artichokes, Maltese, 196
Tunisian Style Dishes
  Chicken Couscous, 244
  Harissa, 16
  Open-Faced Sandwiches, 67
Turkey exchange list, 317
Turkish Yogurt Soup, 83
Tzatziki (Herbed Yogurt), 40

United States. See American (USA)
Unsaturated fats exchange list, 324
Uruguayan Style Dishes
  Ajies Rellenos con Carne (Stuffed
      Peppers), 236
  Asparagus with Tomato, 117
  Lenguado "Monte de Oro" (Sole), 207

Vadas, 188
Vanilla Cream, Frozen, 279
Veal
  Birds (Blinde Vinken), 214
  exchange list, 317–19
Vegetable(s), 126–64. See also name of
    vegetable
  and Almonds, Chinese Style, 141
  and Bean Curd, Tibetan, 137
  -Beef Carbonada, 258
  Borscht, 76
  -Corn-Beef Casserole, Argentinean
      (Locro), 240
  -Egg Dish, Mediterranean
      (Strapatsada), 58

Vegetable(s) (cont.)
  exchange list, 319–20, 325
  and Fish, Steamed, 198
  Gazpacho Salad, 142
  Kichuri, 182
  Moussaka for Vegetable Lovers, 146
  Niramish, Bangladesh Style, 164
  -Noodle-Meat Dish, Indonesian, 235
  Pickled, Indonesian, 143
  Pilau, 172
  Ratatouille, French, 44
  Salad, Boiled, 114
  Samosa, 254
  Stew, Ethiopian (Alecha), 78
Vegetarian Tacos, 70
Venison Stew, German Style, 230
Vietnamese Style Dishes
  Cha Gio (Rolls), 249
  Nuoc Mam Sauce, 14
Vinaigrette, 120
  Spicier, 120
Vinegar, Spiced, 13

Wassail, 311
Water Chestnuts, Chinese, 157
Watermelon Ice Drink, 305
Wheat-Bran Bread, English, 266
Whipped Topping, Party, 301
Whole Wheat Dosa, 261
Whole Wheat and Fruits (Kolyva),
    166
Wild game exchange list, 317
Wild Rice, 171
Wine Marinade à la Maria Nicole, 11

Yard-Long Beans, 161
Yogurt
  -Berry Shake, 309
  Chaka, Afghan, 28
  Dessert, Tibetan, 275
  and Fruit Dessert, 274
  Herbed (Tzatziki), 40
  Relish (Kadhi), 29
  Salad Dressing, 122
  Soup, Turkish, 83
  Uncle Bill's Homemade, 26

Zrazy (Polish Meat Rolls), 218
Zurcher Geschnetzeltes (Pork in Wine,
    Zurich Style), 225

ABOUT THE AUTHOR

VILMA LIACOURAS CHANTILES hones her food and nutrition knowledge by researching, writing, and teaching International Foods and Cultural Understanding Through Foods at New York University, Department of Home Economics and Nutrition. She has interviewed people about their food habits and recipes in China, Japan, the Philippines, India, Brazil, Mexico, Israel, Greece and other European countries, and the United States. A frequent contributor to magazines and books, she is author of *The New York Ethnic Food Market Guide & Cookbook* and *The Food of Greece* and is food editor of *The Athenian* magazine, published in Athens. For this book, *Diabetic Cooking from Around the World,* she tested, adapted, and calculated nutrients for recipes from every continent. Many of the fascinating dishes were contributed by diabetes associations, nutritionists, and physicians specializing in diabetes worldwide.